De: TALES™

FÁBIO MOON
GABRIEL BÁ

STORIES FROM URBAN BRAZIL

DARK HORSE BOOKS™

DIANA SCHUTZ editor

KATIE MOODY assistant editor

AMY ARENDTS & LIA RIBACCHI design

DAN JACKSON digital production

MIKE RICHARDSON publisher

De:TALES ™

Published by
Dark Horse Books
A division of Dark Horse Comics, Inc.
10956 SE Main Street
Milwaukie, Oregon 97222

www.darkhorse.com
www.10paezinhos.com.br

First Edition: June 2006
ISBN-10: 1-59307-485-9
ISBN-13: 978-1-59307-485-2

10 9 8 7 6 5 4 3 2 1

Printed in Canada

CONTENTS

5 EL CAMINO ("THE PATH")

11 ESTRELA ("STAR")

21 OUTDATED

29 LATE FOR COFFEE

53 AS IF

55 REFLECTIONS I

60 REFLECTIONS II

64 ALL YOU NEED IS LOVE

67 QU'EST–CE QUE C'EST? ("WHAT IS IT?")

75 HAPPY BIRTHDAY, MY FRIEND!

91 SATURDAY

103 OUTRAS PALAVRAS ("OTHER WORDS")

REFLECTION

Imagine looking over to see . . . yourself standing beside you. Imagine further that you spoke to that other person—yourself, that is—and he or she spoke back, in a voice that was yours, in words you might have chosen. Or perhaps you needn't even speak at all, because surely you'd know exactly what each other was thinking, and no sooner would one of you start a sentence than the other would complete it. Imagine living with this person, who is you—or, at least, who could be you—all your life. Where do you end and where does he (or she) begin? Where do you draw the line? Or . . . do you?

Twins are one of nature's wonders. Science tells us that only one in every thirty-three births results in multiple babies. And only one quarter of those births brings twin *brothers* into the world. Unlike identical twins, fraternals develop from *two* different fertilized eggs sharing the mother's womb but not a matching genetic code. How rare is it, then, when fraternal twins *look* identical, even though (strictly) they're not? How curious it must be to see one's reflection in another person, one with whom you've shared almost every moment, including those critical first nine months. That's just . . . fascinating, if you think about it.

The International Comic-Con in San Diego brought Fábio Moon and Gabriel Bá into my world several years ago. They'd flown all the way from São Paulo, in their native Brazil. I couldn't tell them apart. Sometimes I still can't. They handed me a copy of their first U.S.-published work, an action-adventure tale they'd drawn in their early twenties, when they still believed in superheroes. I chose to politely ignore this story they did not write, despite its Xeric-winning status.

But the twins were—are—persistent. And . . . unforgettable. They came back the next year, and the year after that, until at some point I was forced to stop being polite—because I was genuinely excited by the quantum leap their artwork had taken since the previous year. And they were telling their *own* stories, real-life stories full of the passion and vibrancy of their Brazilian culture. Charming stories, of love and loss, of coming of age, of the questions of youth and life's search for answers.

The twins told one of these stories in *AutobioGraphix,* an anthology I edited in 2003. It was only then that I learned their family surname, *Moon* and *Bá* being reflections of their distinctive artistic spirit—inasmuch as Fábio and Gabriel are reflections of each other.

This apparent paradox of nature—this individualism within identity—is mirrored in these pages, as the twins draw their lines both together and apart. In one case (or should that be *two*?), they each tell the same story, one after the other. The differences are revealing, but the similarities are what is most striking, and the total effect is . . . fascinating, if you think about it.

We invite you to think about it.

Diana Schutz
March 2006

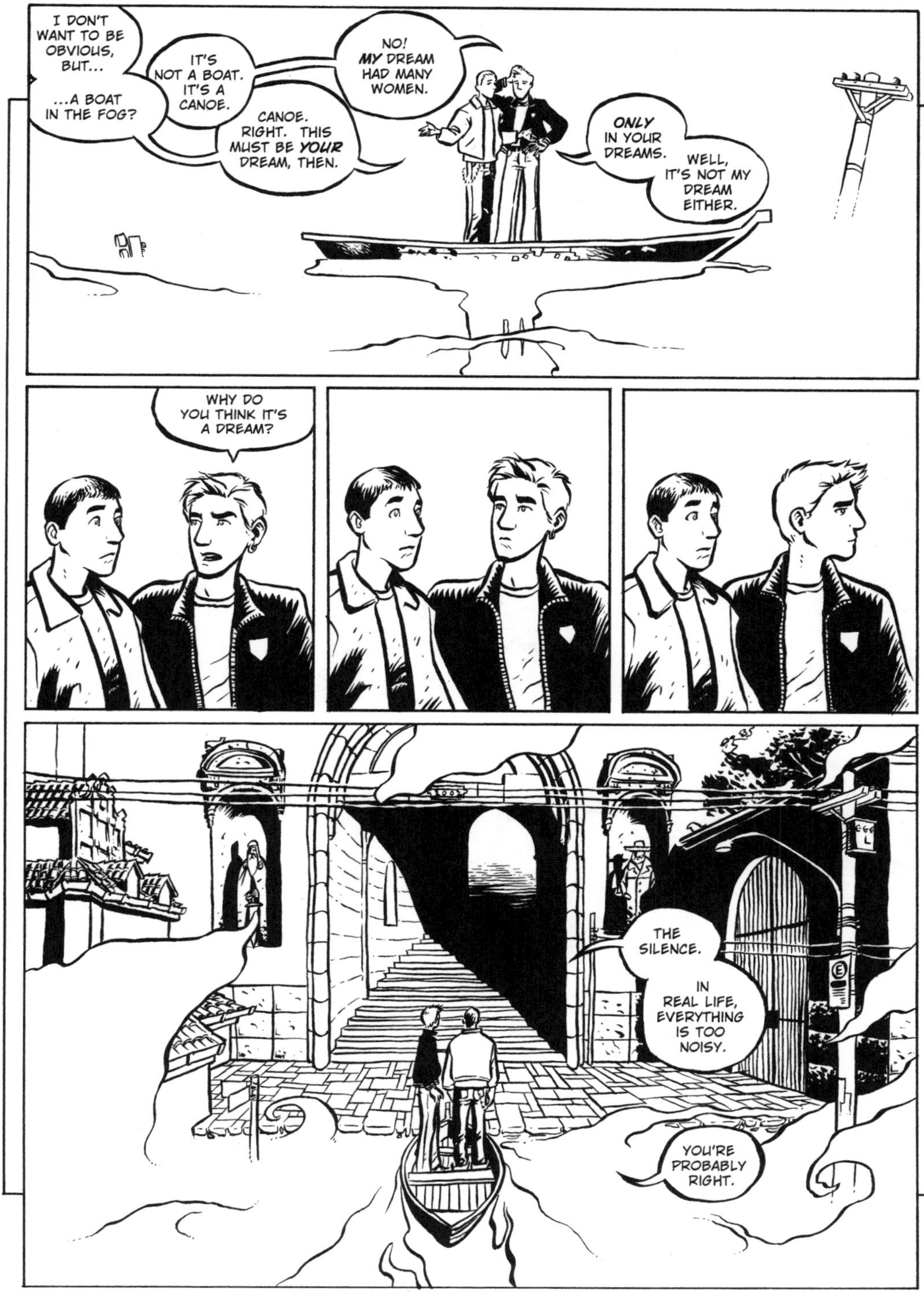
I DON'T WANT TO BE OBVIOUS, BUT...
...A BOAT IN THE FOG?
IT'S NOT A BOAT. IT'S A CANOE.
CANOE. RIGHT. THIS MUST BE YOUR DREAM, THEN.
NO! MY DREAM HAD MANY WOMEN.
ONLY IN YOUR DREAMS.
WELL, IT'S NOT MY DREAM EITHER.
WHY DO YOU THINK IT'S A DREAM?
THE SILENCE.
IN REAL LIFE, EVERYTHING IS TOO NOISY.
YOU'RE PROBABLY RIGHT.

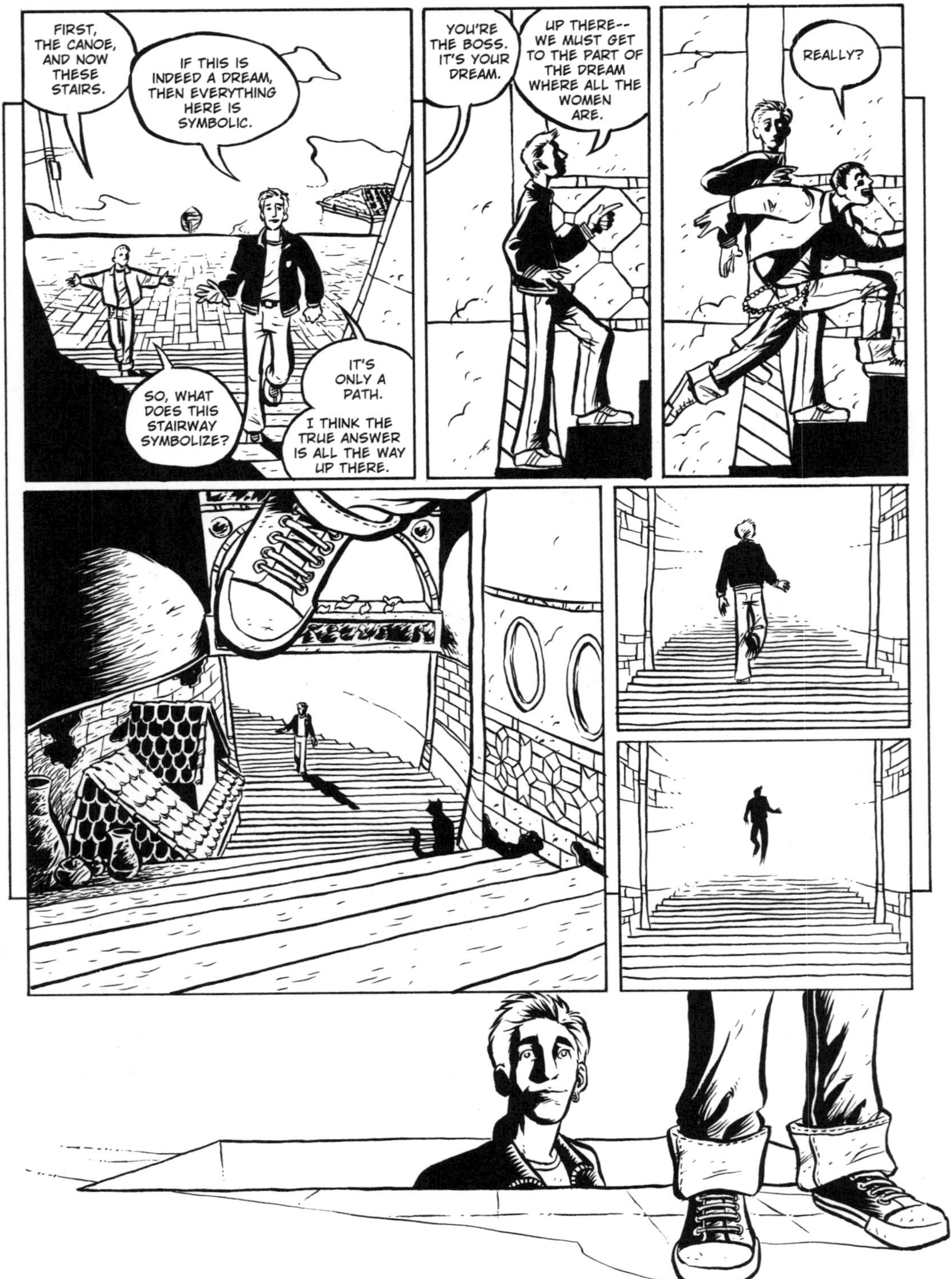

FIRST, THE CANOE, AND NOW THESE STAIRS.
IF THIS IS INDEED A DREAM, THEN EVERYTHING HERE IS SYMBOLIC.
SO, WHAT DOES THIS STAIRWAY SYMBOLIZE?
IT'S ONLY A PATH.
I THINK THE TRUE ANSWER IS ALL THE WAY UP THERE.
YOU'RE THE BOSS. IT'S YOUR DREAM.
UP THERE-- WE MUST GET TO THE PART OF THE DREAM WHERE ALL THE WOMEN ARE.
REALLY?

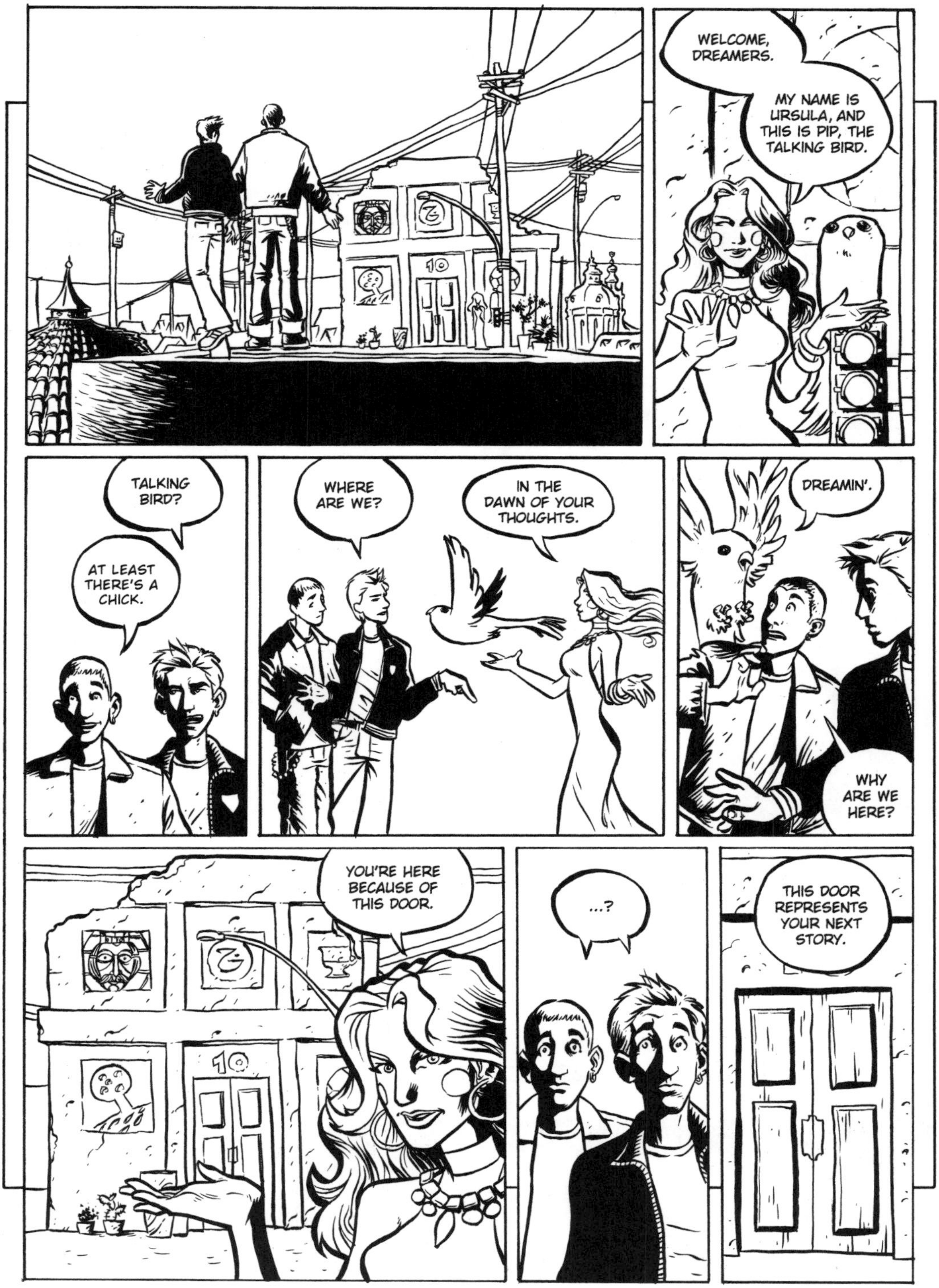
WELCOME, DREAMERS.
MY NAME IS URSULA, AND THIS IS PIP, THE TALKING BIRD.
TALKING BIRD?
AT LEAST THERE'S A CHICK.
WHERE ARE WE?
IN THE DAWN OF YOUR THOUGHTS.
DREAMIN'.
WHY ARE WE HERE?
YOU'RE HERE BECAUSE OF THIS DOOR.
...?
THIS DOOR REPRESENTS YOUR NEXT STORY.

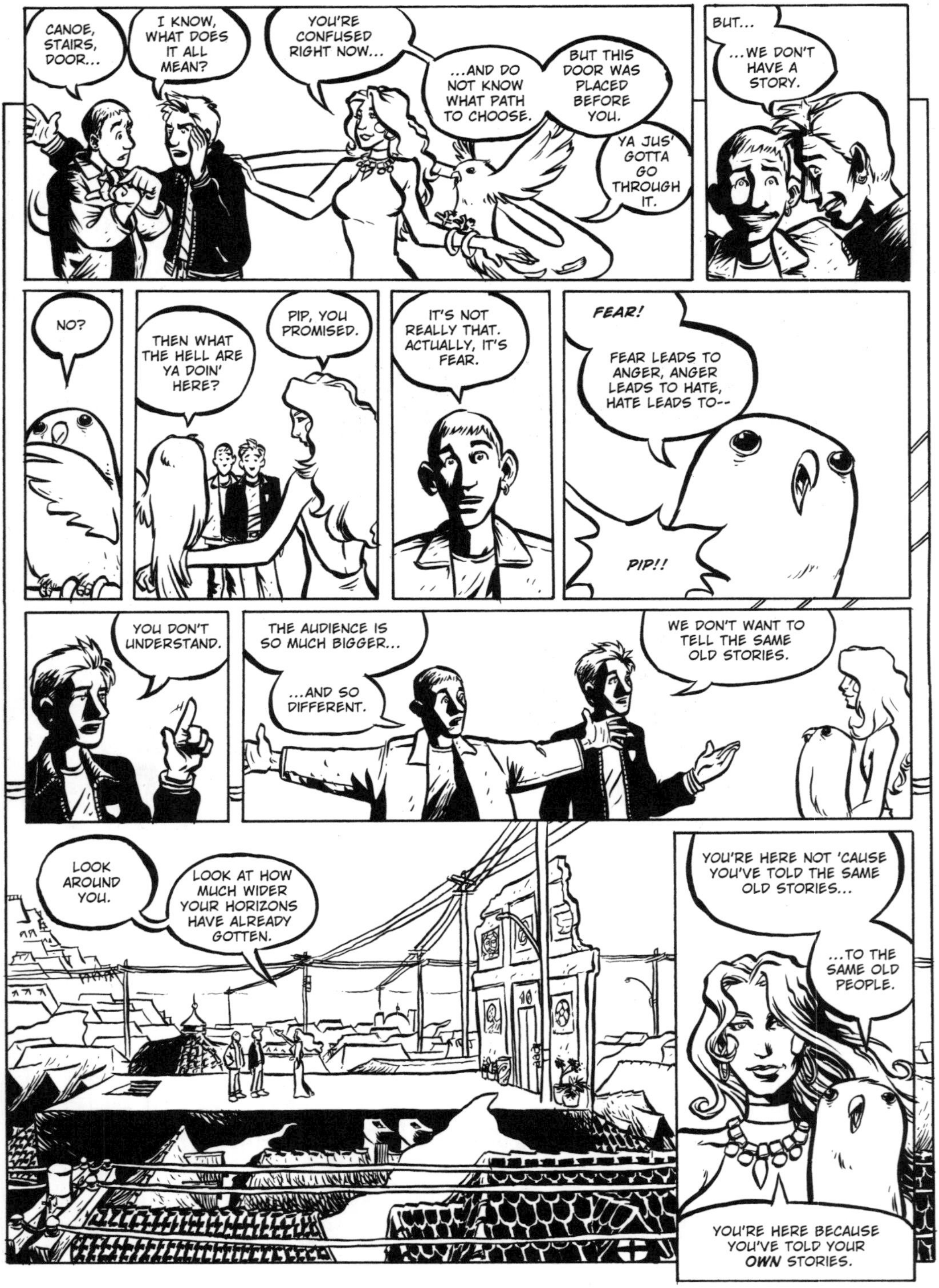
CANOE, STAIRS, DOOR...
I KNOW, WHAT DOES IT ALL MEAN?
YOU'RE CONFUSED RIGHT NOW...
...AND DO NOT KNOW WHAT PATH TO CHOOSE.
BUT THIS DOOR WAS PLACED BEFORE YOU.
YA JUS' GOTTA GO THROUGH IT.
BUT...
...WE DON'T HAVE A STORY.
NO?
THEN WHAT THE HELL ARE YA DOIN' HERE?
PIP, YOU PROMISED.
IT'S NOT REALLY THAT. ACTUALLY, IT'S FEAR.
FEAR!
FEAR LEADS TO ANGER, ANGER LEADS TO HATE, HATE LEADS TO--
PIP!!
YOU DON'T UNDERSTAND.
THE AUDIENCE IS SO MUCH BIGGER...
...AND SO DIFFERENT.
WE DON'T WANT TO TELL THE SAME OLD STORIES.
LOOK AROUND YOU.
LOOK AT HOW MUCH WIDER YOUR HORIZONS HAVE ALREADY GOTTEN.
YOU'RE HERE NOT 'CAUSE YOU'VE TOLD THE SAME OLD STORIES...
...TO THE SAME OLD PEOPLE.
YOU'RE HERE BECAUSE YOU'VE TOLD YOUR *OWN* STORIES.

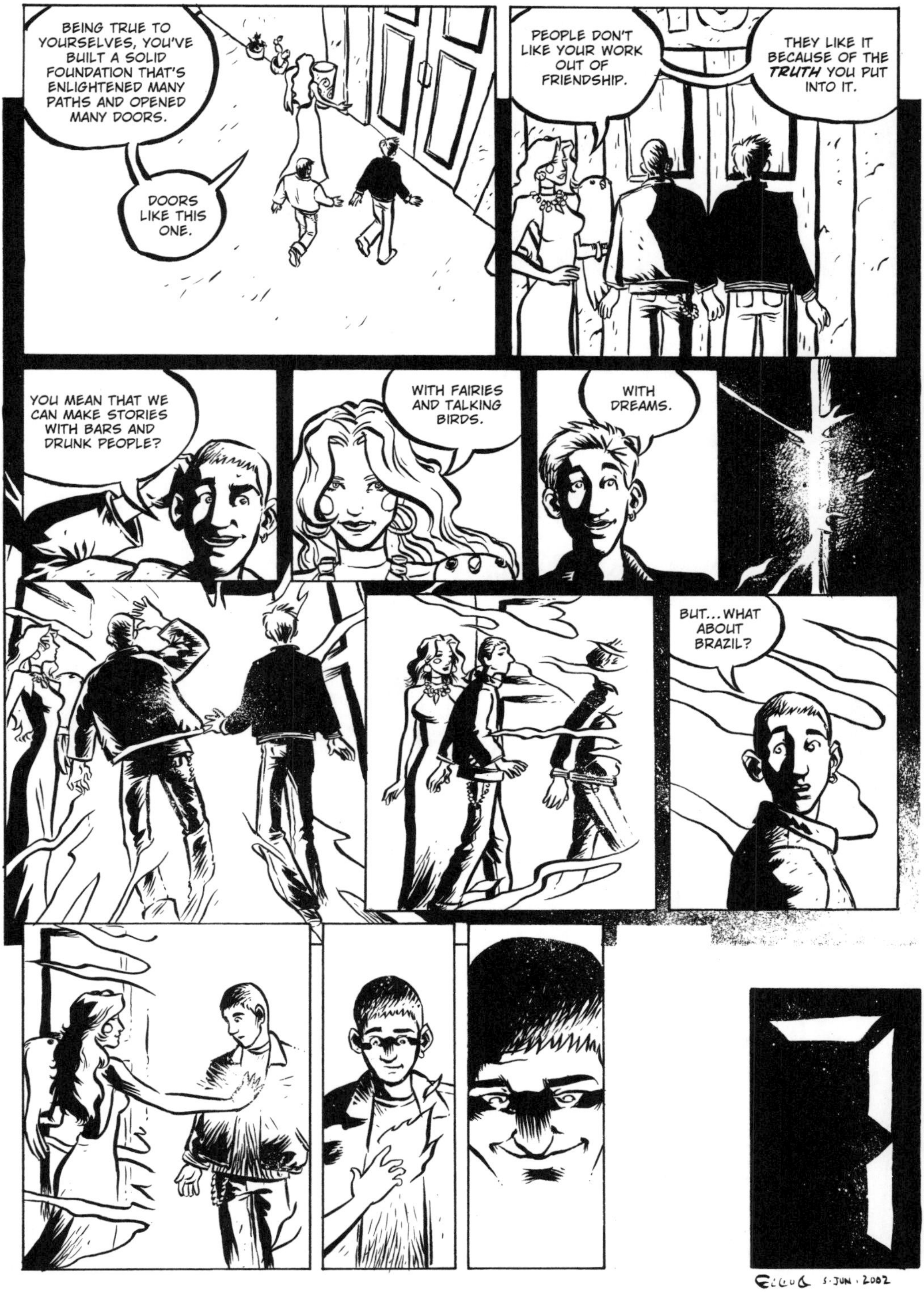
BEING TRUE TO YOURSELVES, YOU'VE BUILT A SOLID FOUNDATION THAT'S ENLIGHTENED MANY PATHS AND OPENED MANY DOORS.
DOORS LIKE THIS ONE.
PEOPLE DON'T LIKE YOUR WORK OUT OF FRIENDSHIP.
THEY LIKE IT BECAUSE OF THE *TRUTH* YOU PUT INTO IT.
YOU MEAN THAT WE CAN MAKE STORIES WITH BARS AND DRUNK PEOPLE?
WITH FAIRIES AND TALKING BIRDS.
WITH DREAMS.
BUT...WHAT ABOUT BRAZIL?
5 · JUN · 2002

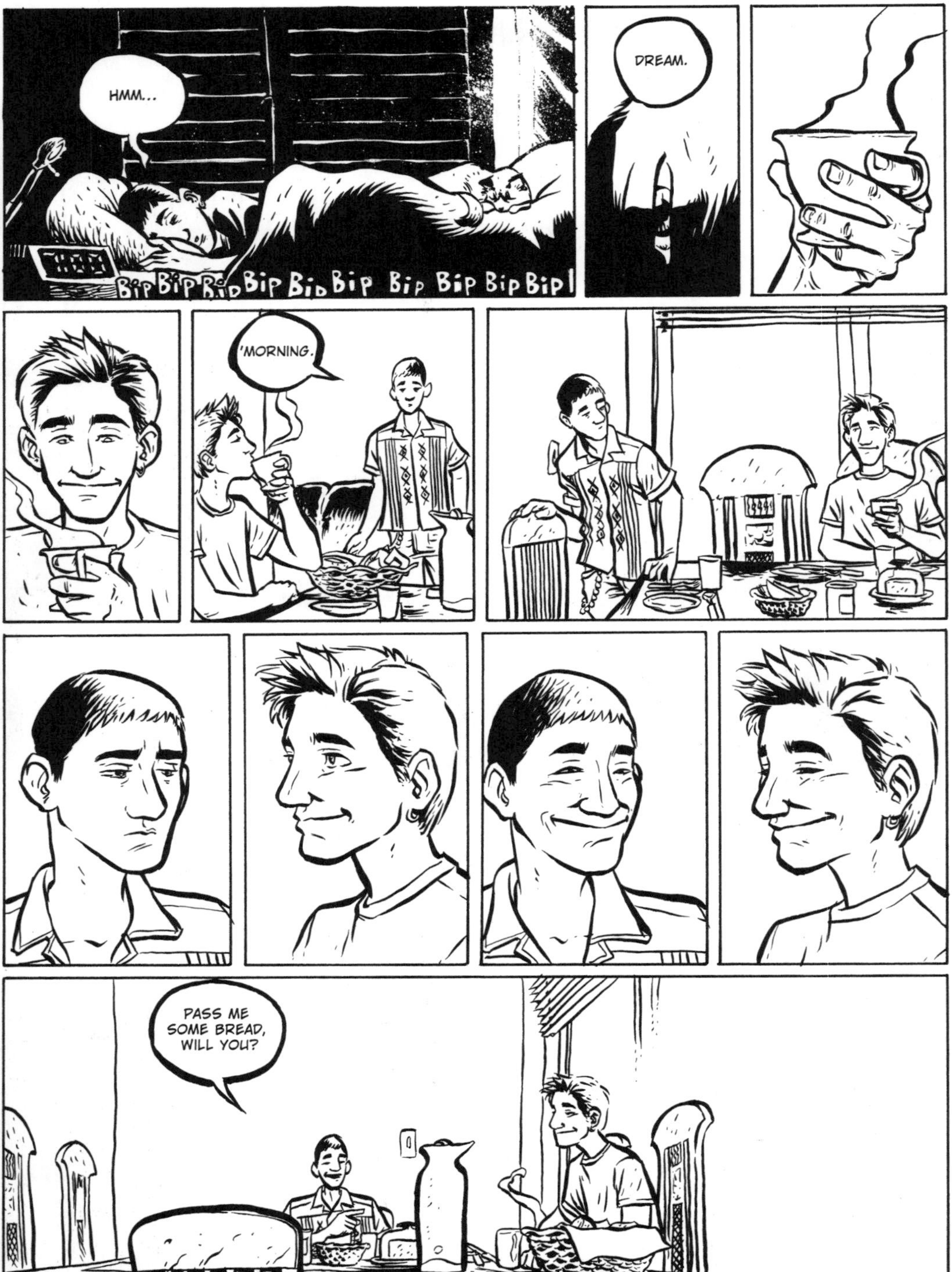
HMM...
BiP BiP BiP BiP BiP BiP BiP BiP BiP BiP!
DREAM.
'MORNING.
PASS ME SOME BREAD, WILL YOU?

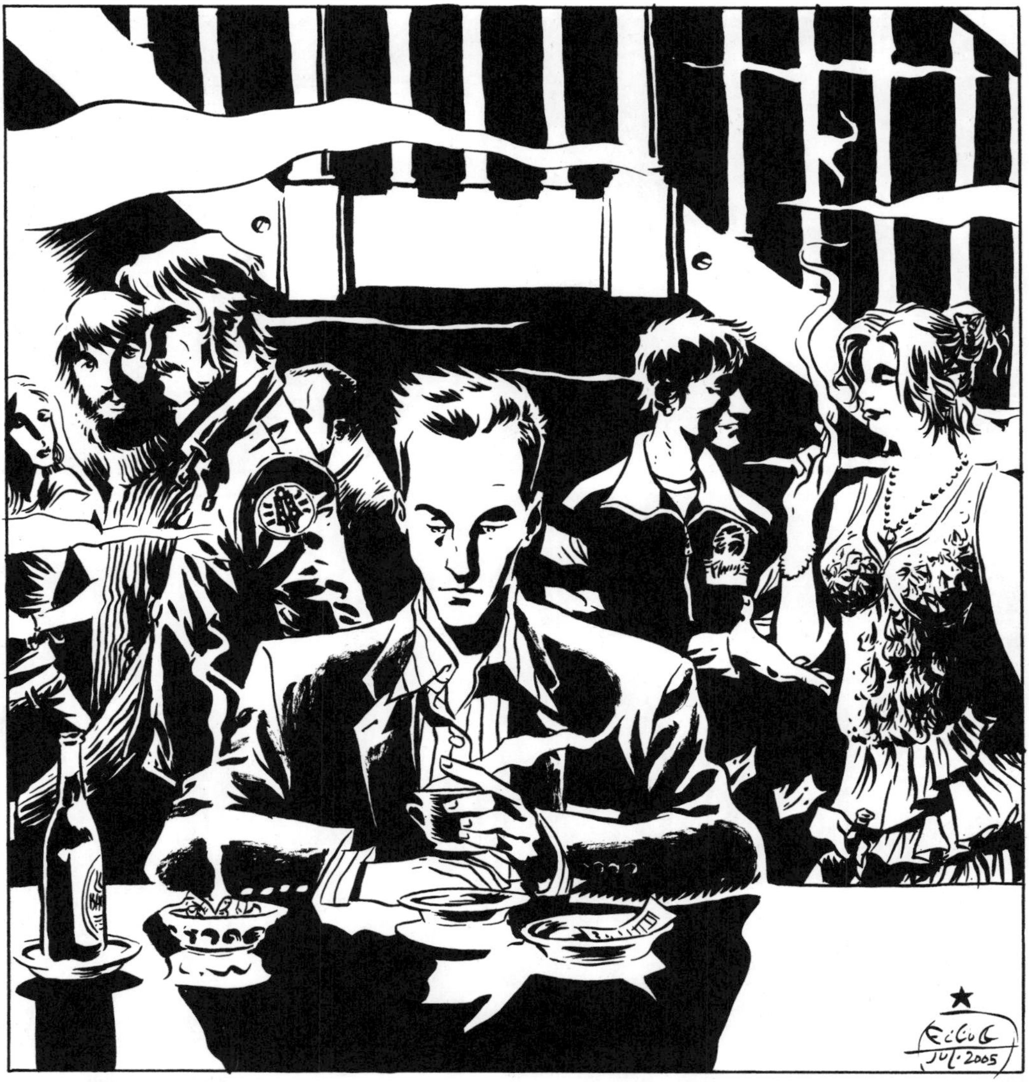

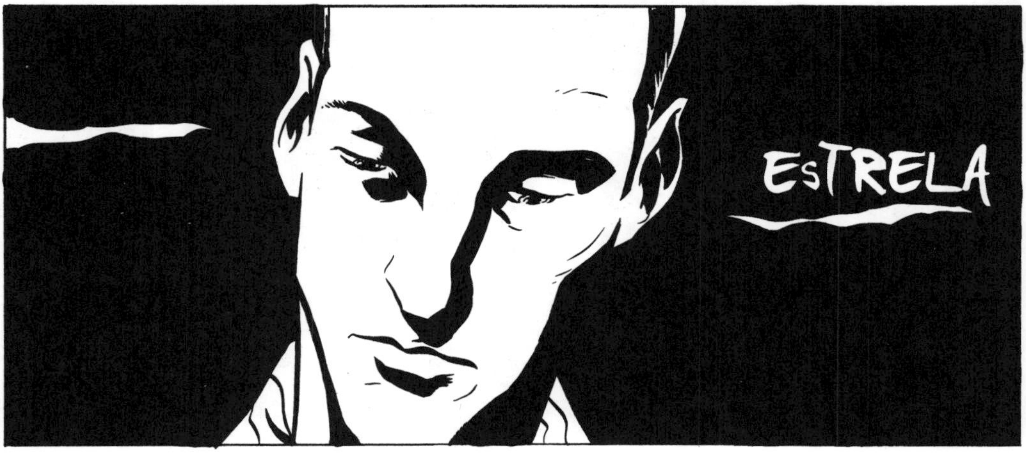
EsTRELA

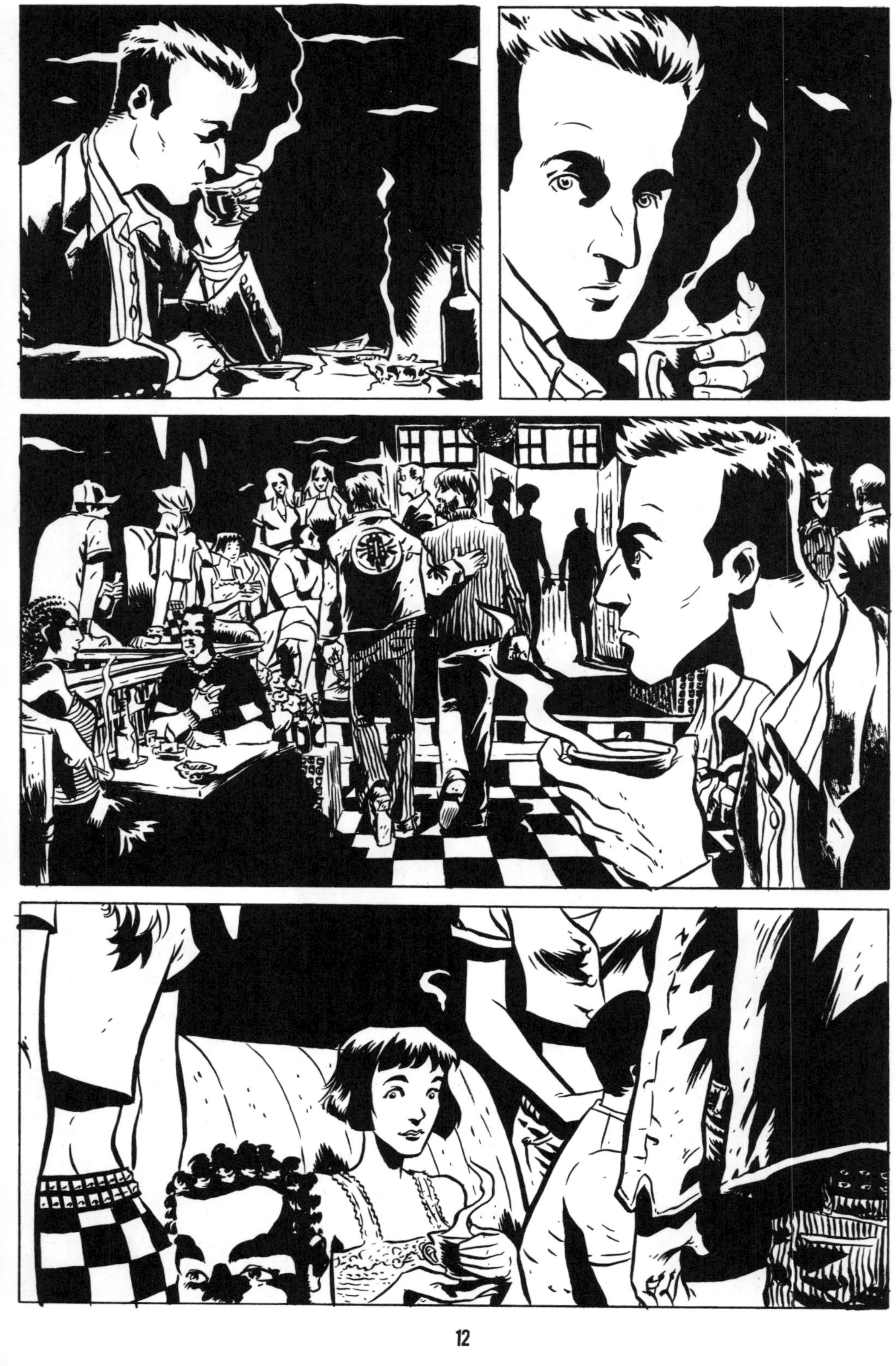

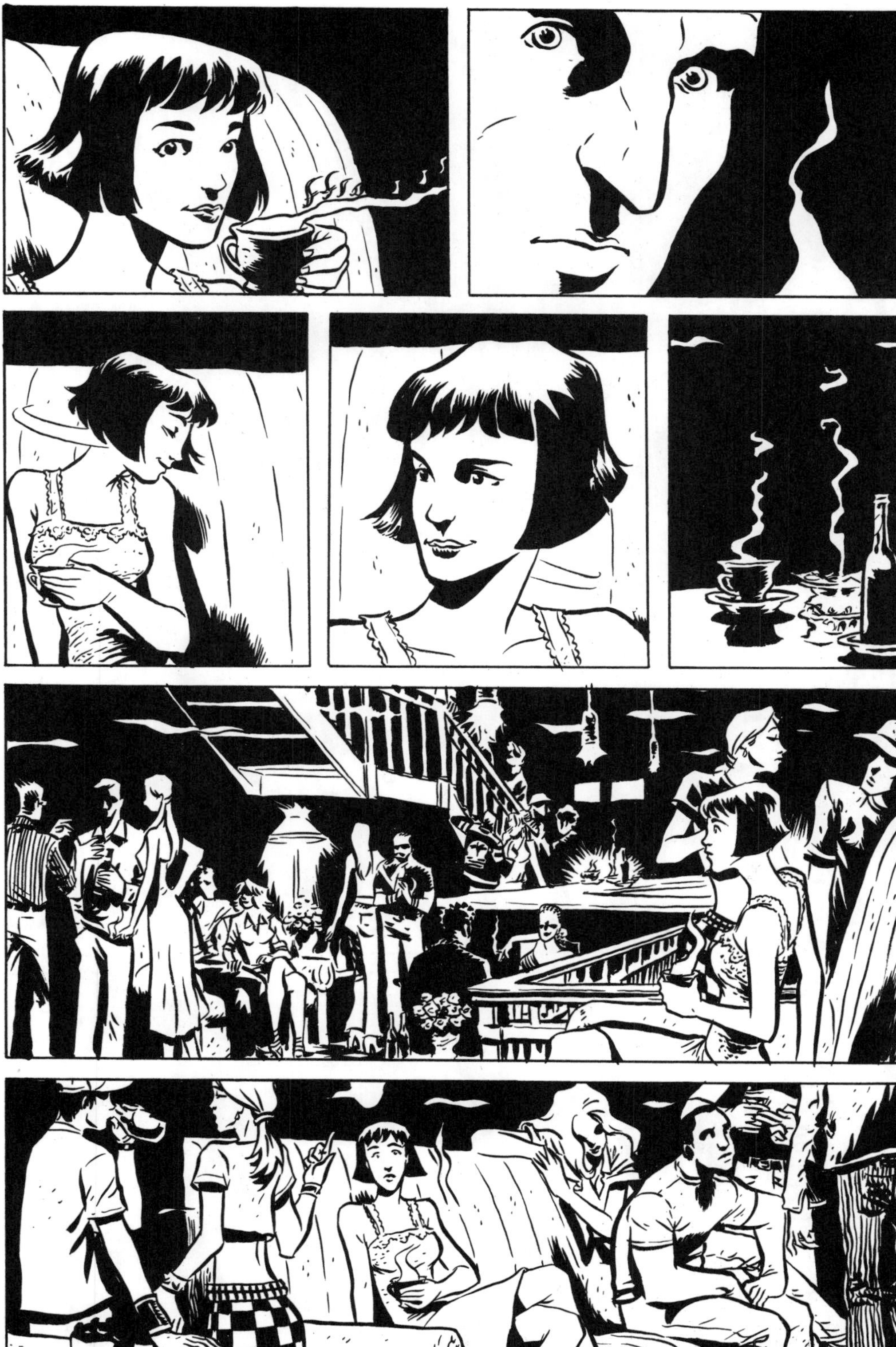

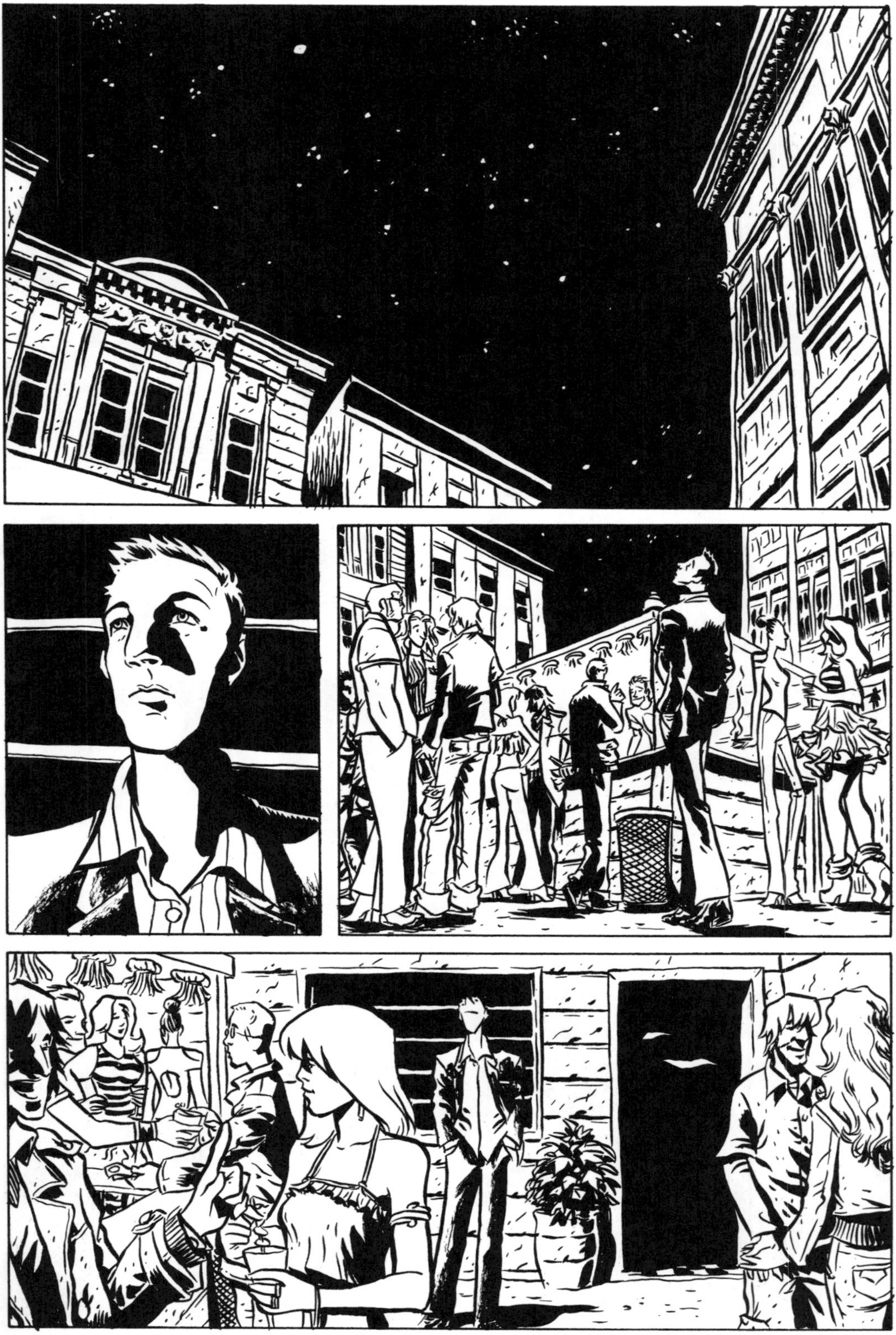

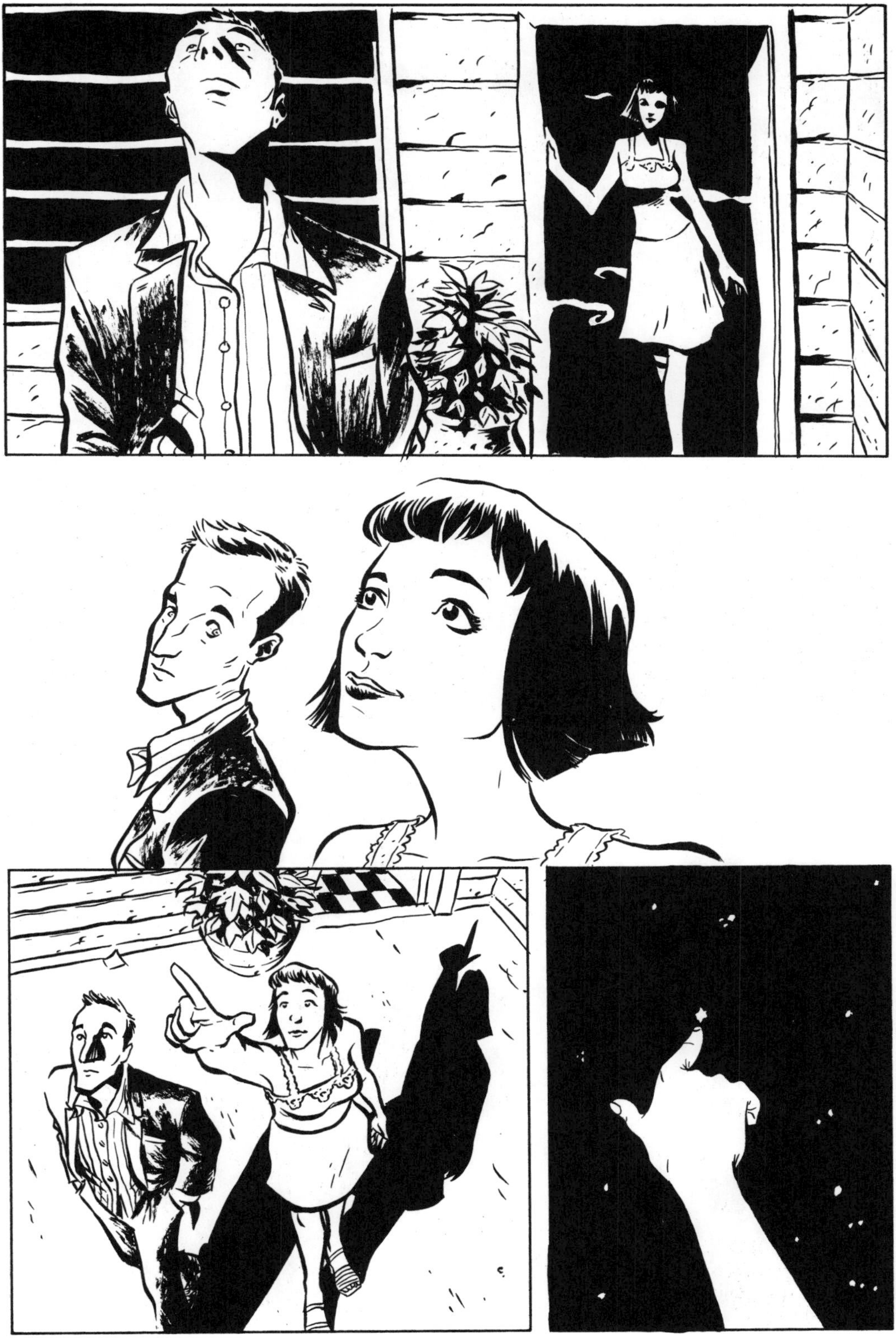

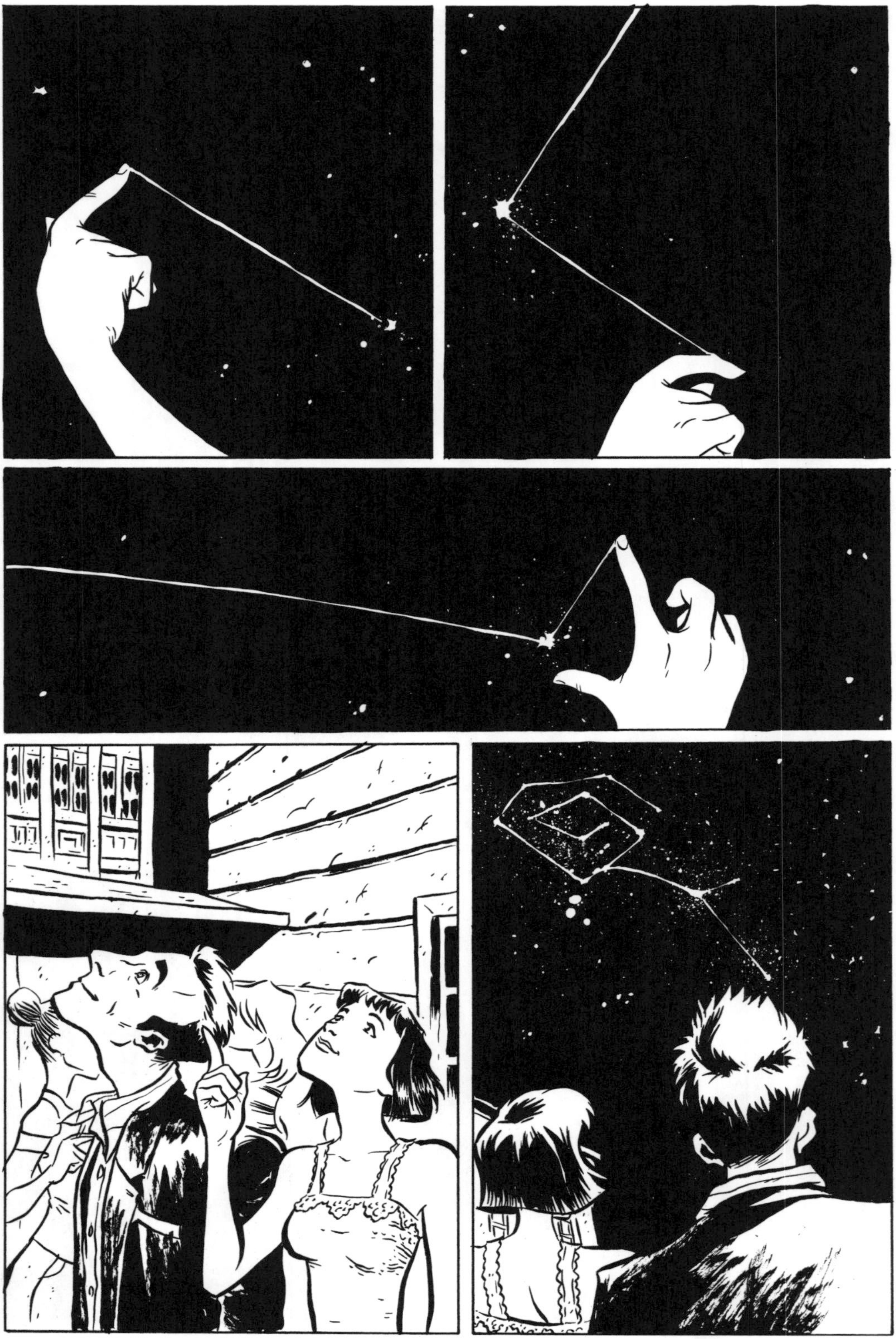

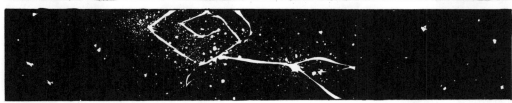

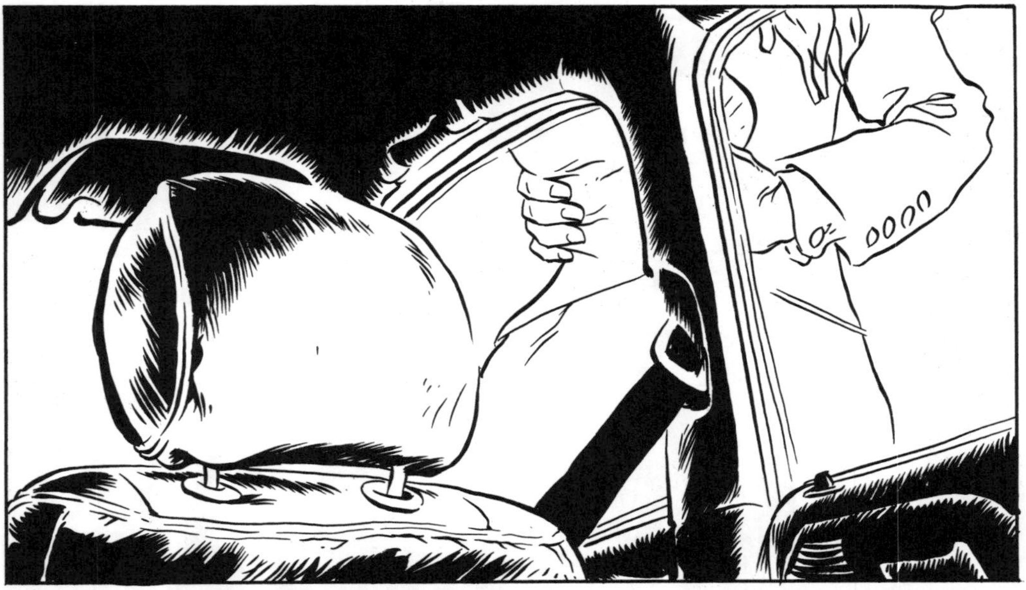

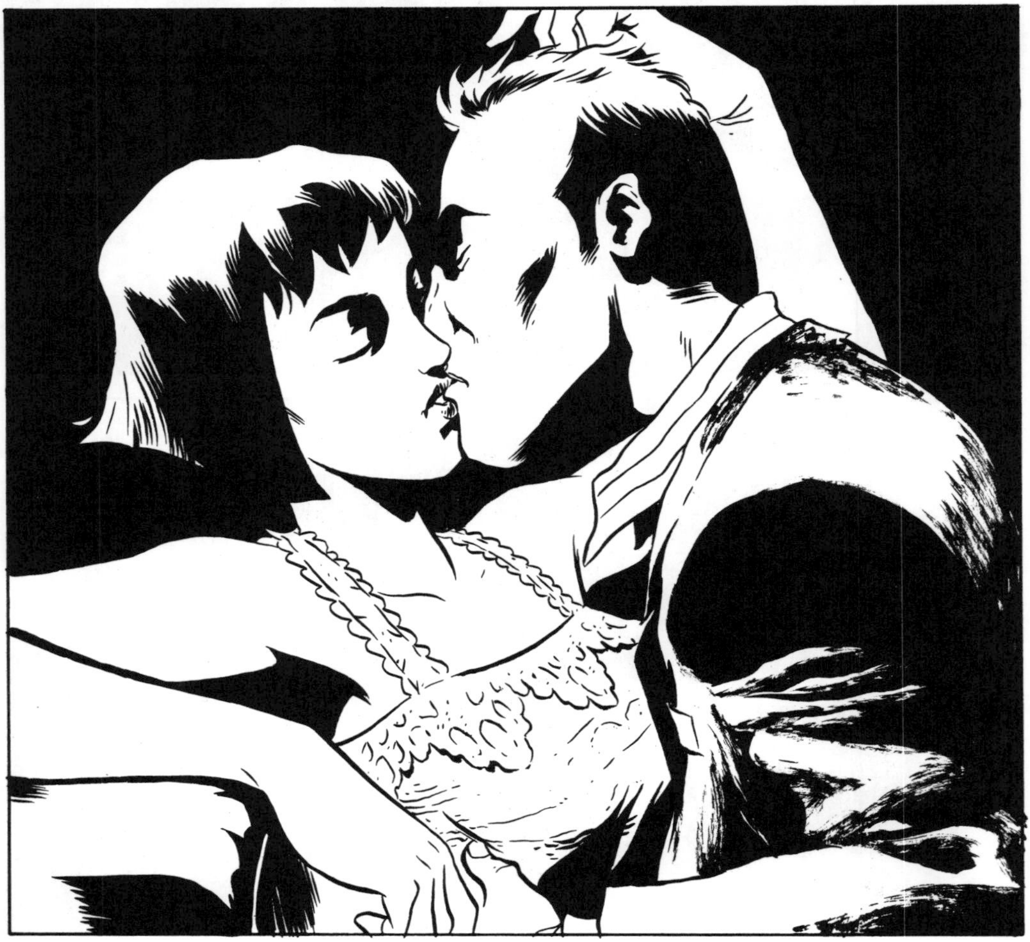

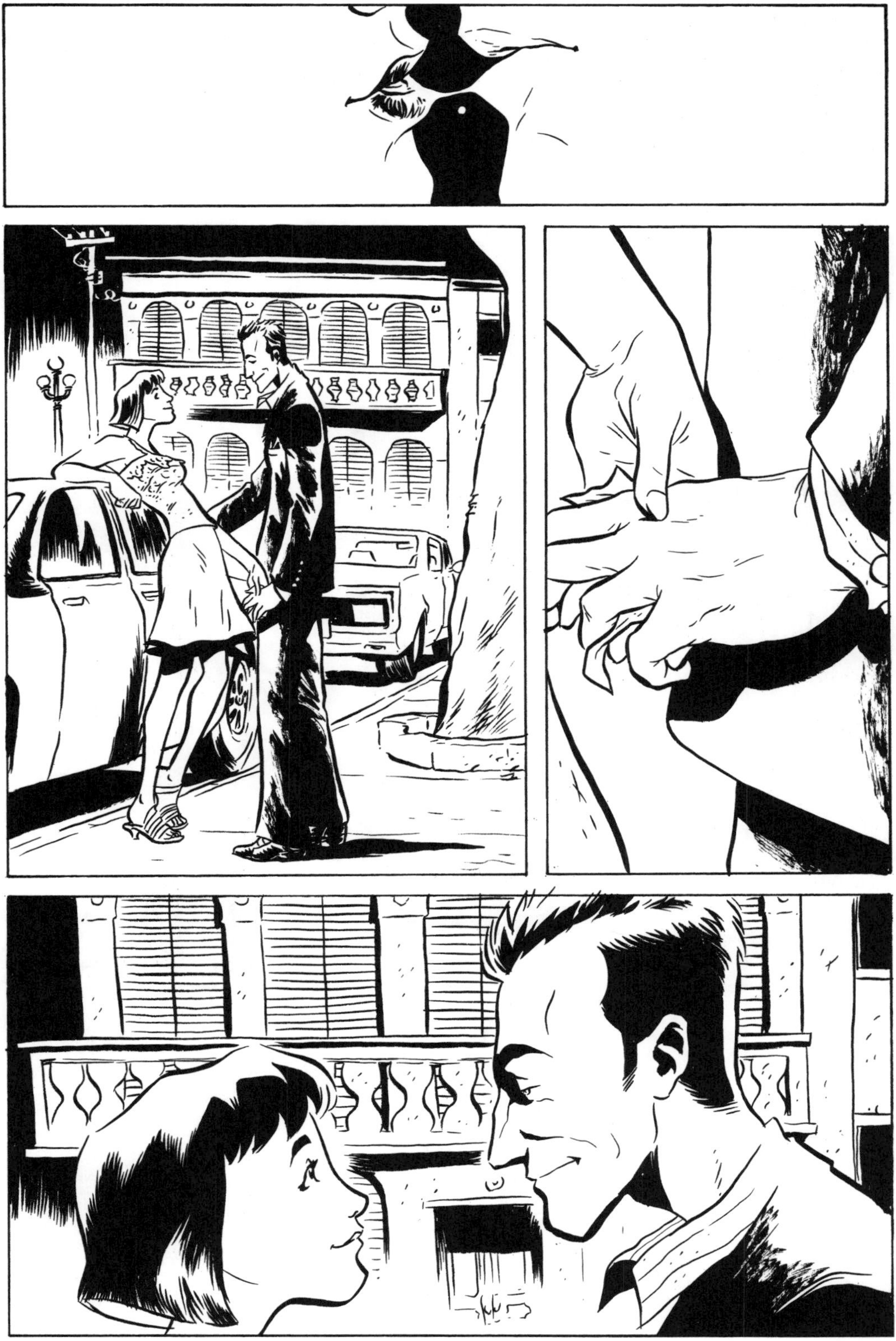

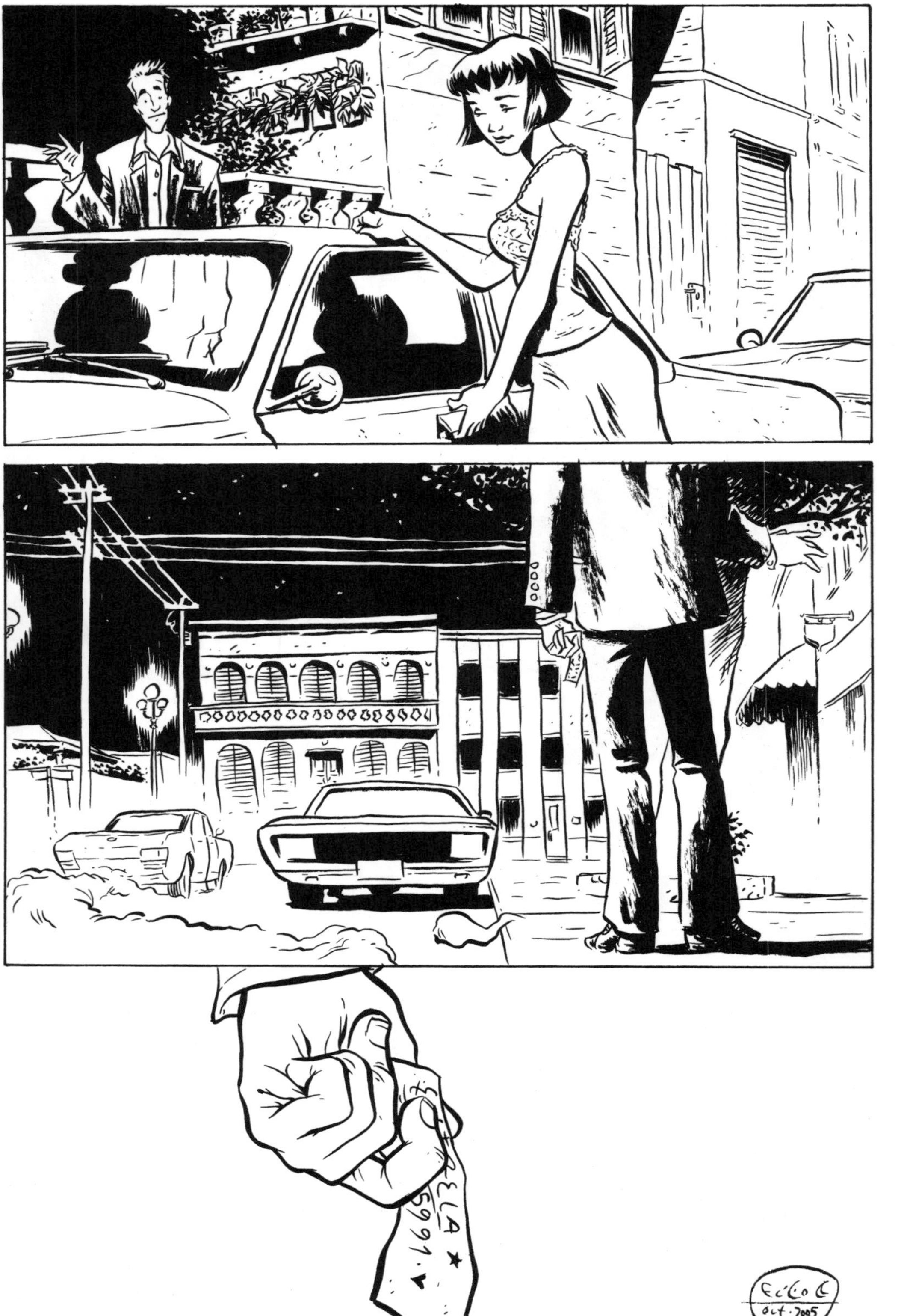
oct · 2005

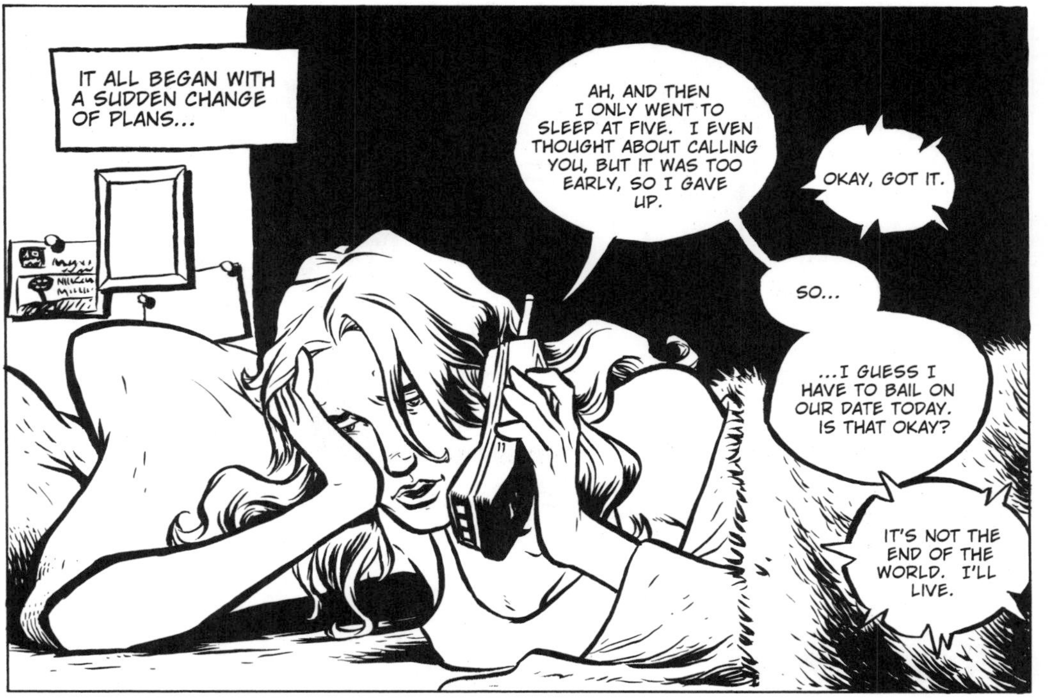
IT ALL BEGAN WITH A SUDDEN CHANGE OF PLANS...
AH, AND THEN I ONLY WENT TO SLEEP AT FIVE. I EVEN THOUGHT ABOUT CALLING YOU, BUT IT WAS TOO EARLY, SO I GAVE UP.
OKAY, GOT IT.
SO...
...I GUESS I HAVE TO BAIL ON OUR DATE TODAY. IS THAT OKAY?
IT'S NOT THE END OF THE WORLD. I'LL LIVE.

outdated.

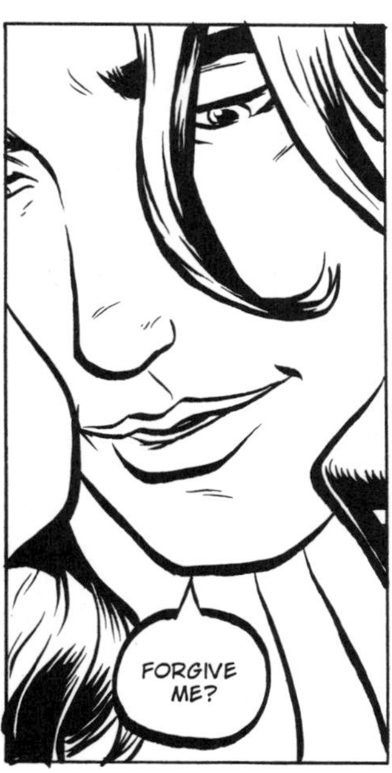
FORGIVE ME?

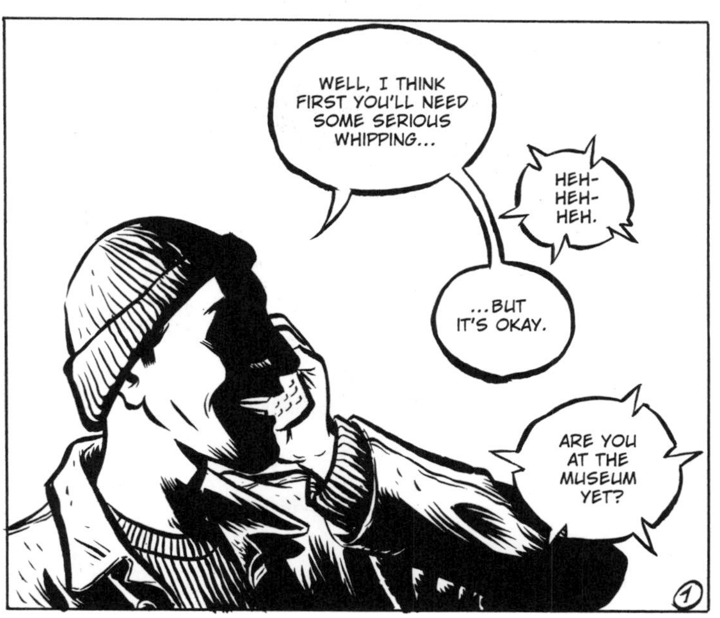
WELL, I THINK FIRST YOU'LL NEED SOME SERIOUS WHIPPING...
HEH-HEH-HEH.
...BUT IT'S OKAY.
ARE YOU AT THE MUSEUM YET?

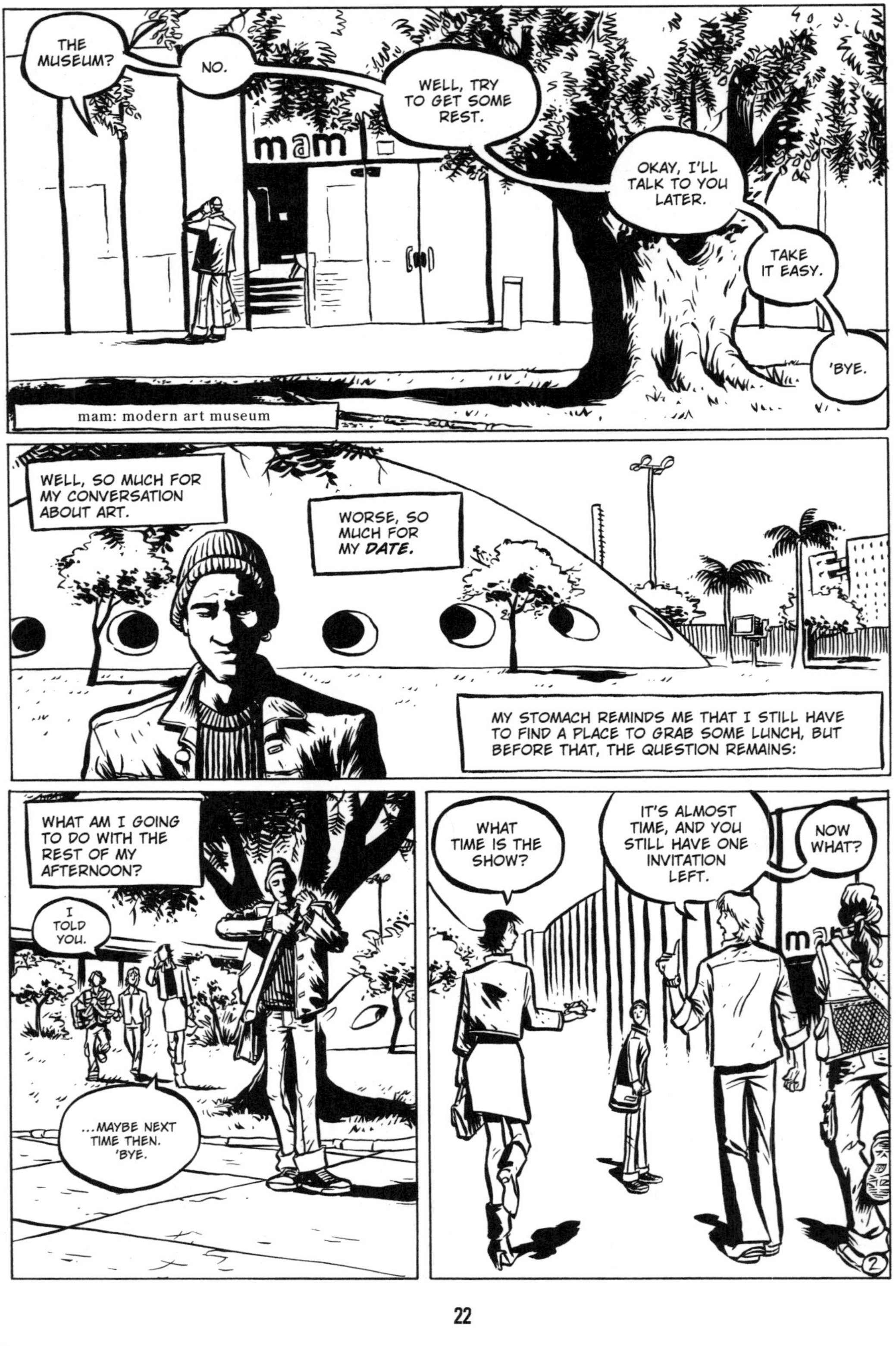
THE MUSEUM?
NO.
WELL, TRY TO GET SOME REST.
OKAY, I'LL TALK TO YOU LATER.
TAKE IT EASY.
'BYE.
mam
mam: modern art museum
WELL, SO MUCH FOR MY CONVERSATION ABOUT ART.
WORSE, SO MUCH FOR MY *DATE.*
MY STOMACH REMINDS ME THAT I STILL HAVE TO FIND A PLACE TO GRAB SOME LUNCH, BUT BEFORE THAT, THE QUESTION REMAINS:
WHAT AM I GOING TO DO WITH THE REST OF MY AFTERNOON?
I TOLD YOU.
...MAYBE NEXT TIME THEN. 'BYE.
WHAT TIME IS THE SHOW?
IT'S ALMOST TIME, AND YOU STILL HAVE ONE INVITATION LEFT.
NOW WHAT?

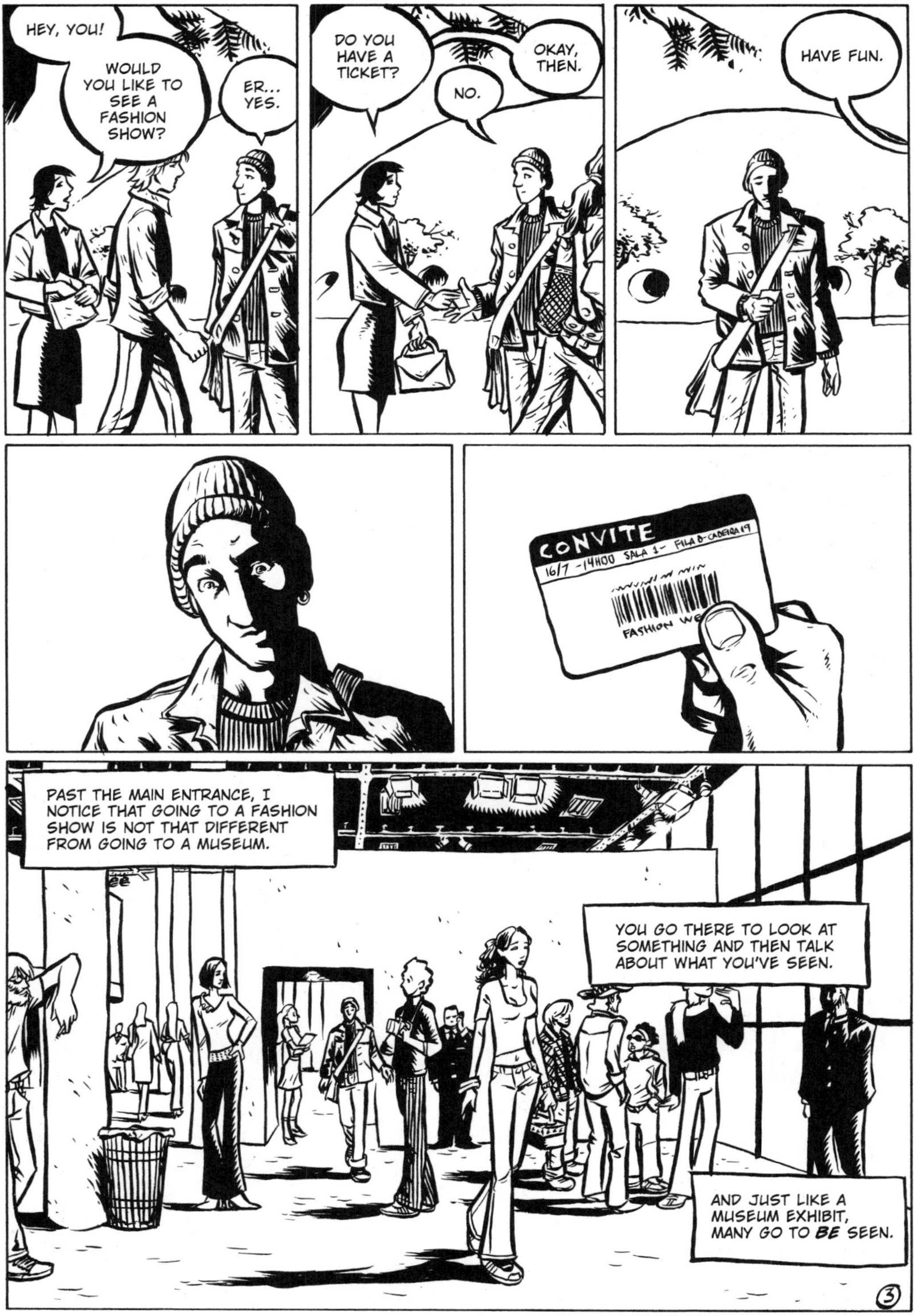
HEY, YOU!
WOULD YOU LIKE TO SEE A FASHION SHOW?
ER... YES.
DO YOU HAVE A TICKET?
NO.
OKAY, THEN.
HAVE FUN.
CONVITE
16/7 -14H00 SALA 1- FILA B-CADEIRA 19
FASHION WE
PAST THE MAIN ENTRANCE, I NOTICE THAT GOING TO A FASHION SHOW IS NOT THAT DIFFERENT FROM GOING TO A MUSEUM.
YOU GO THERE TO LOOK AT SOMETHING AND THEN TALK ABOUT WHAT YOU'VE SEEN.
AND JUST LIKE A MUSEUM EXHIBIT, MANY GO TO ***BE*** SEEN.
3

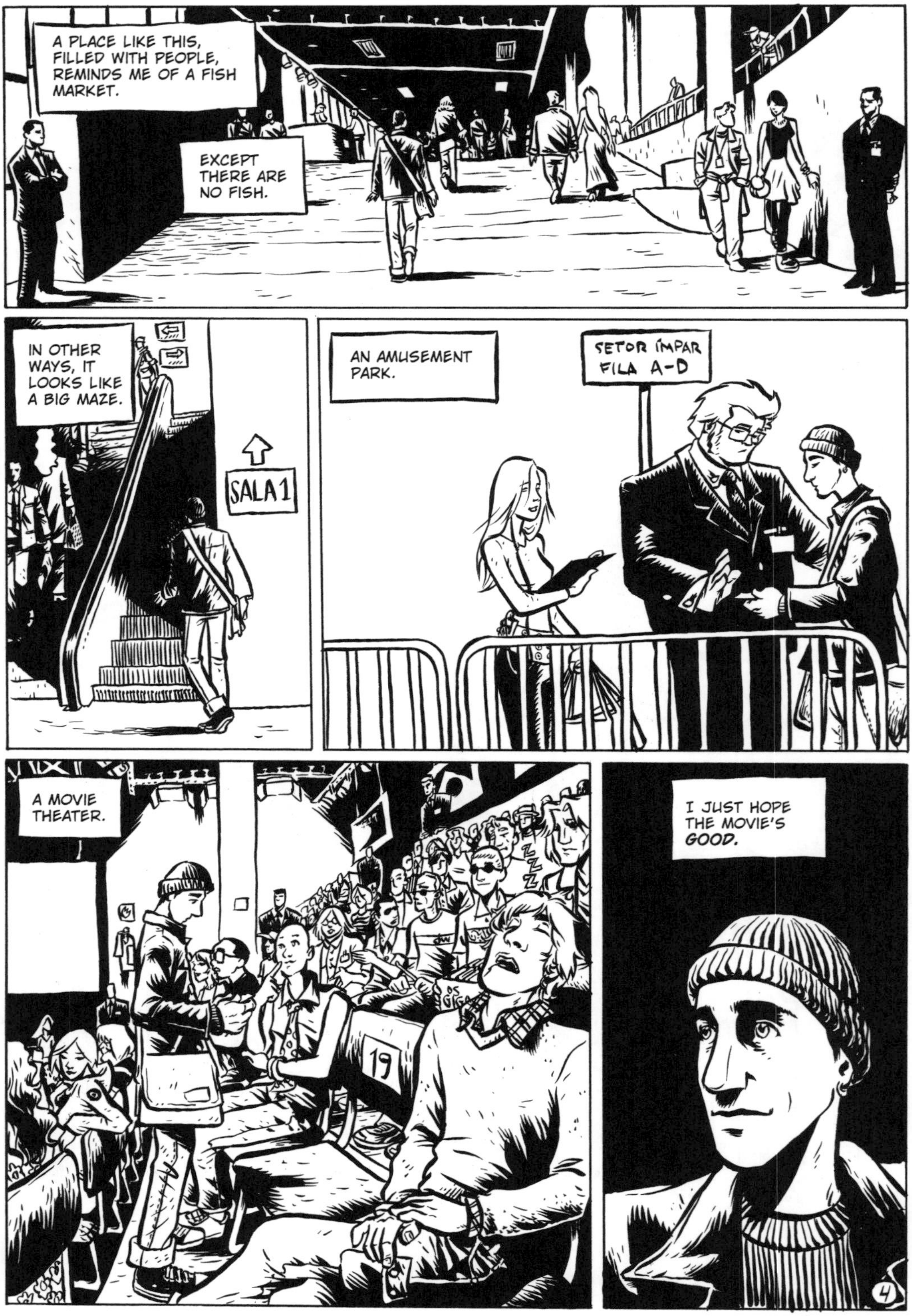
A PLACE LIKE THIS, FILLED WITH PEOPLE, REMINDS ME OF A FISH MARKET.
EXCEPT THERE ARE NO FISH.
IN OTHER WAYS, IT LOOKS LIKE A BIG MAZE.
SALA 1
AN AMUSEMENT PARK.
SETOR ÍMPAR FILA A-D
A MOVIE THEATER.
19
I JUST HOPE THE MOVIE'S ***GOOD.***

WHAT DEFINES A REALLY GOOD FASHION SHOW?

MAGIC!

ONE BY ONE, THE MODELS DAZZLE THE AUDIENCE AS THEY WALK BY, WITH THEIR EXOTIC HAIRDOS AND THEIR EXUBERANT DRESSES.

EACH ONE HAS A LUMINOSITY OF HER OWN...

...AND I REALIZE I CAN'T *HELP* BUT LOOK AT THEM.

EVERY POSE.

EVERY SMILE.

EVERY TOUCH.

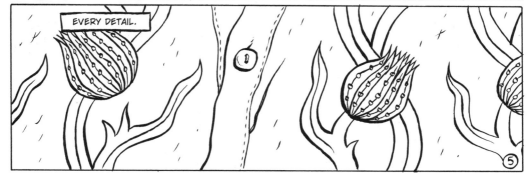

EVERY DETAIL.

⑤

25

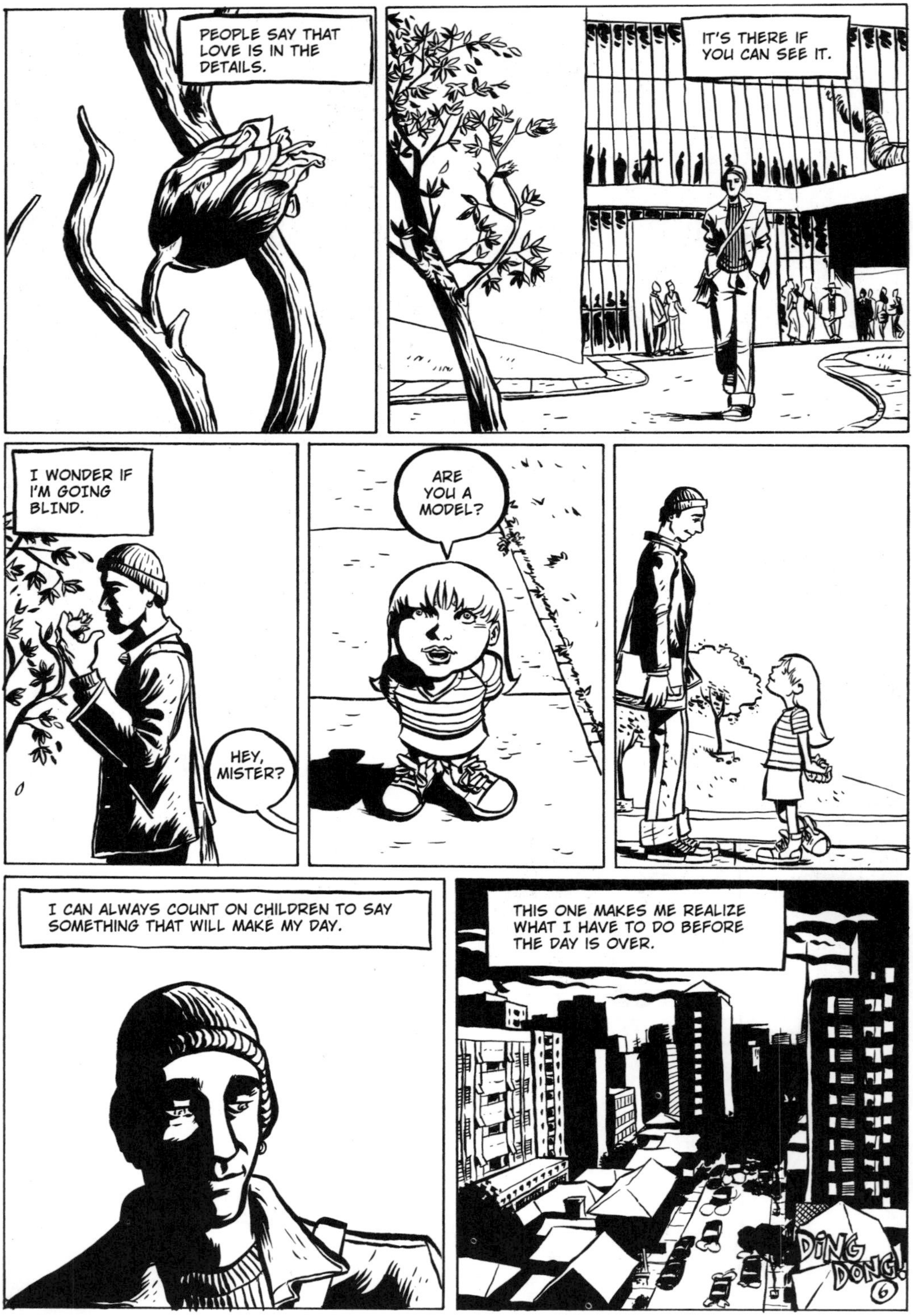
PEOPLE SAY THAT LOVE IS IN THE DETAILS.
IT'S THERE IF YOU CAN SEE IT.
I WONDER IF I'M GOING BLIND.
HEY, MISTER?
ARE YOU A MODEL?
I CAN ALWAYS COUNT ON CHILDREN TO SAY SOMETHING THAT WILL MAKE MY DAY.
THIS ONE MAKES ME REALIZE WHAT I HAVE TO DO BEFORE THE DAY IS OVER.
DING DONG!
6

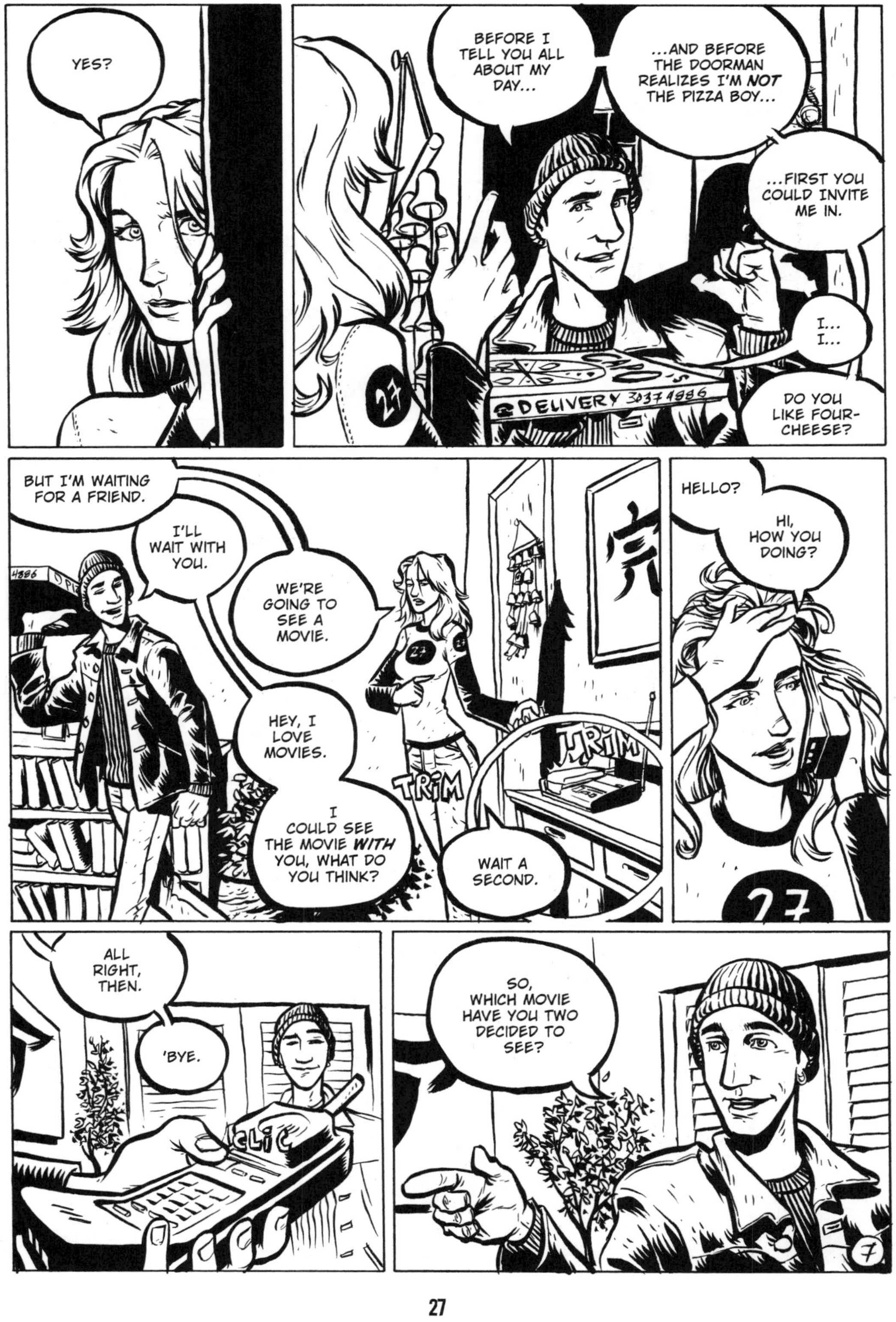
YES?
BEFORE I TELL YOU ALL ABOUT MY DAY...
...AND BEFORE THE DOORMAN REALIZES I'M ***NOT*** THE PIZZA BOY...
...FIRST YOU COULD INVITE ME IN.
DELIVERY 3037 4886
I... I...
DO YOU LIKE FOUR-CHEESE?
BUT I'M WAITING FOR A FRIEND.
I'LL WAIT WITH YOU.
WE'RE GOING TO SEE A MOVIE.
HEY, I LOVE MOVIES.
I COULD SEE THE MOVIE ***WITH*** YOU, WHAT DO YOU THINK?
TRIM
TRIM
WAIT A SECOND.
HELLO?
HI, HOW YOU DOING?
ALL RIGHT, THEN.
'BYE.
CLIC
SO, WHICH MOVIE HAVE YOU TWO DECIDED TO SEE?

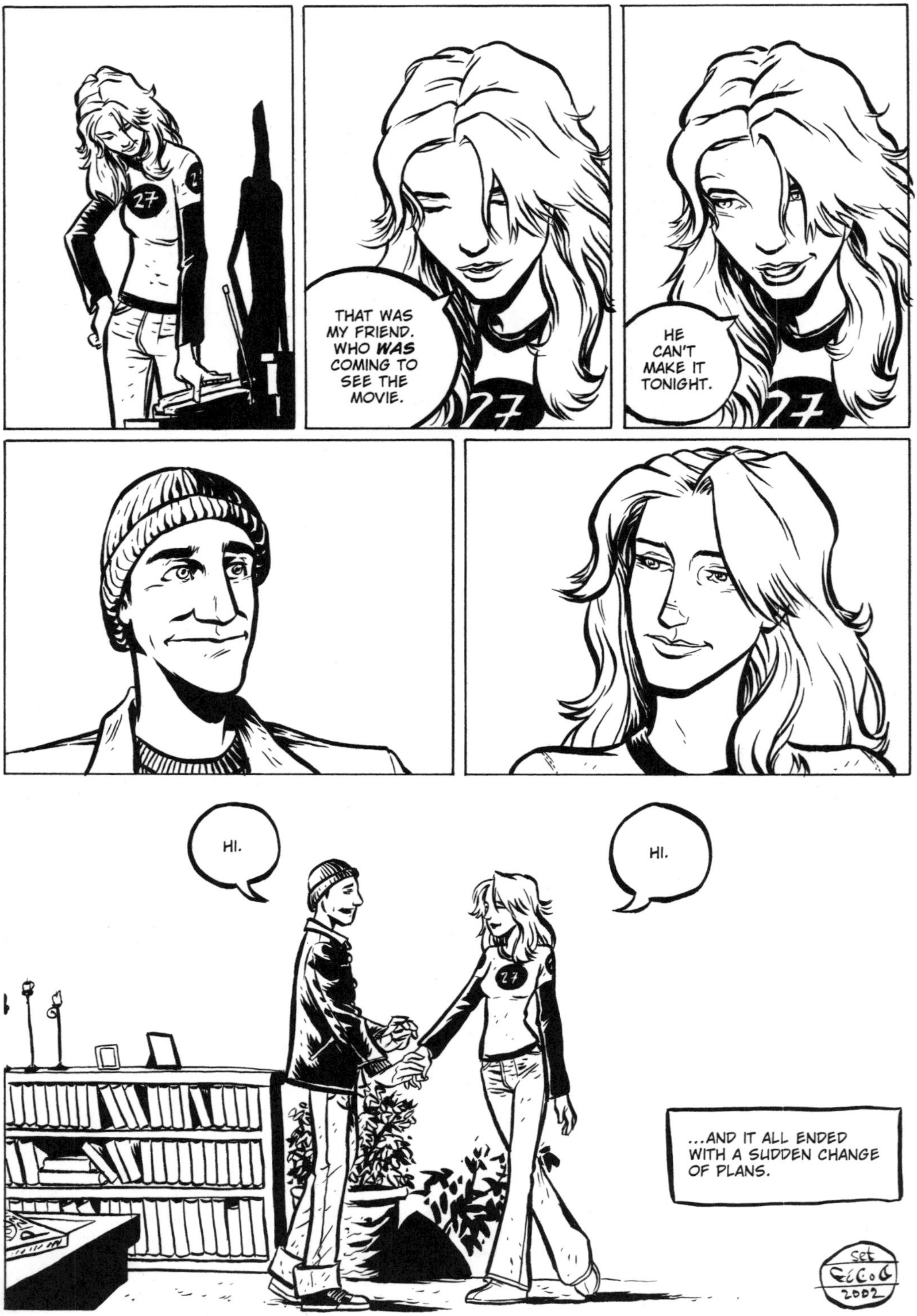
THAT WAS MY FRIEND. WHO **WAS** COMING TO SEE THE MOVIE.
HE CAN'T MAKE IT TONIGHT.
HI.
HI.
...AND IT ALL ENDED WITH A SUDDEN CHANGE OF PLANS.

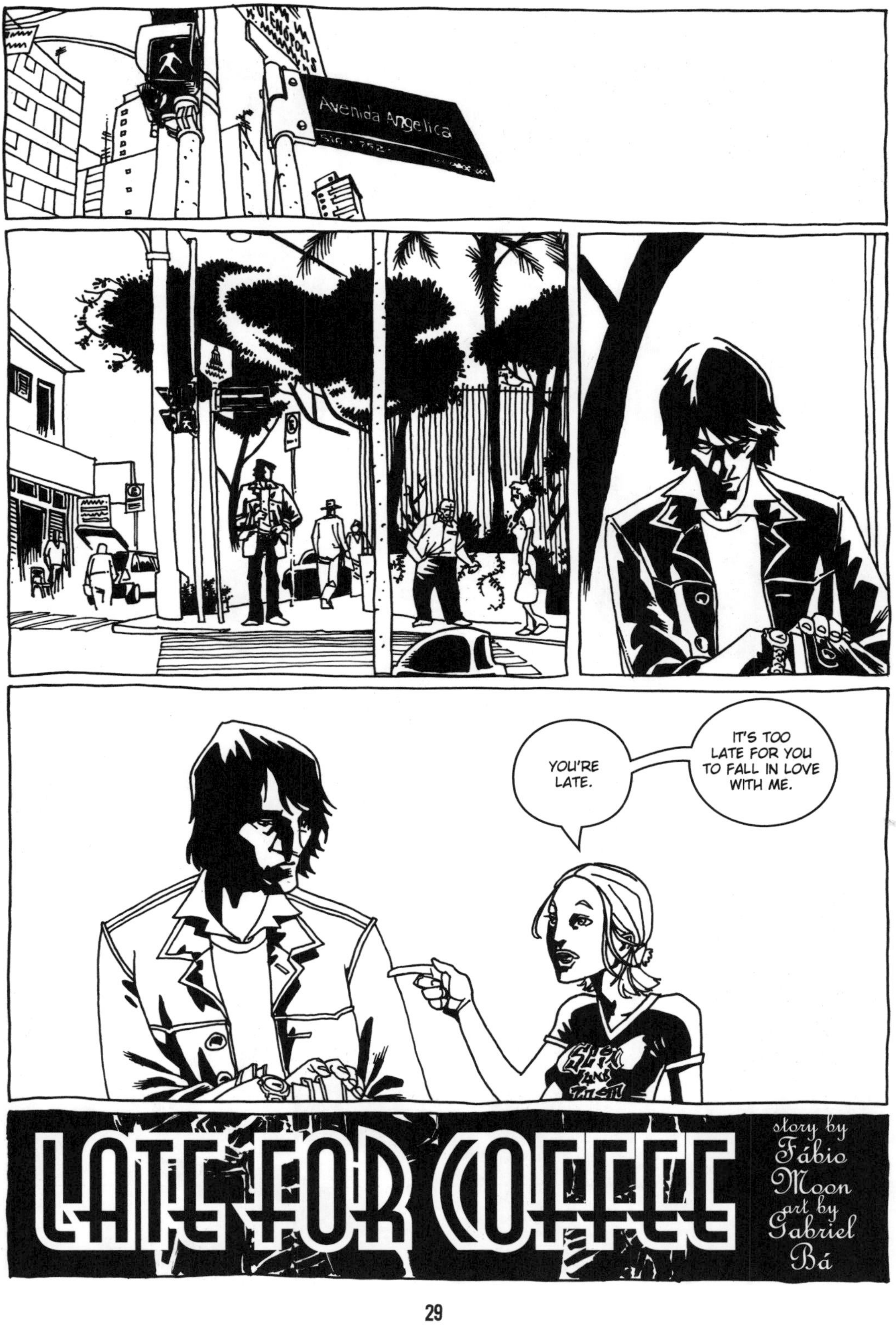
Avenida Angelica
YOU'RE LATE.
IT'S TOO LATE FOR YOU TO FALL IN LOVE WITH ME.

LATE FOR COFFEE

story by Fábio Moon
art by Gabriel Bá

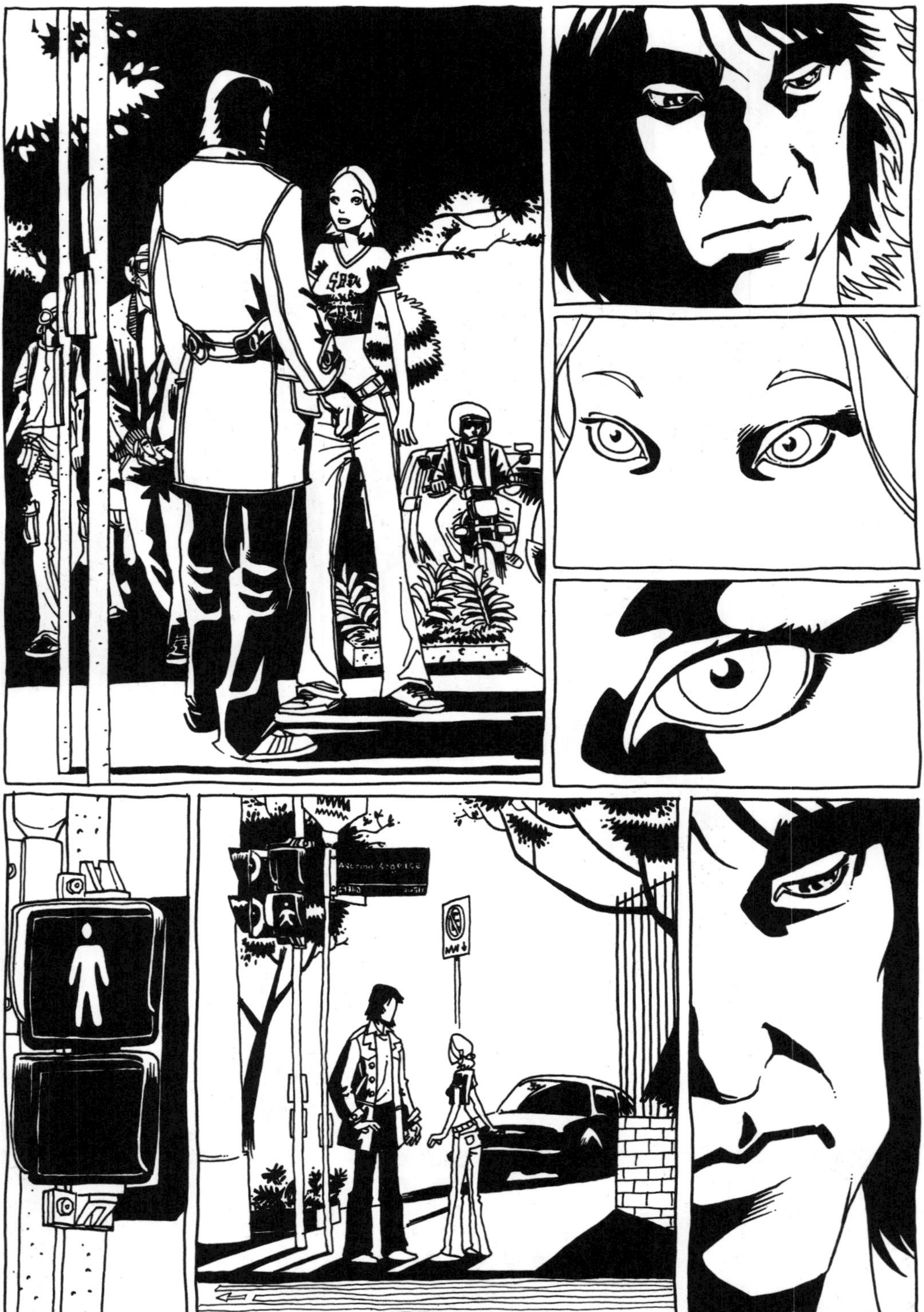

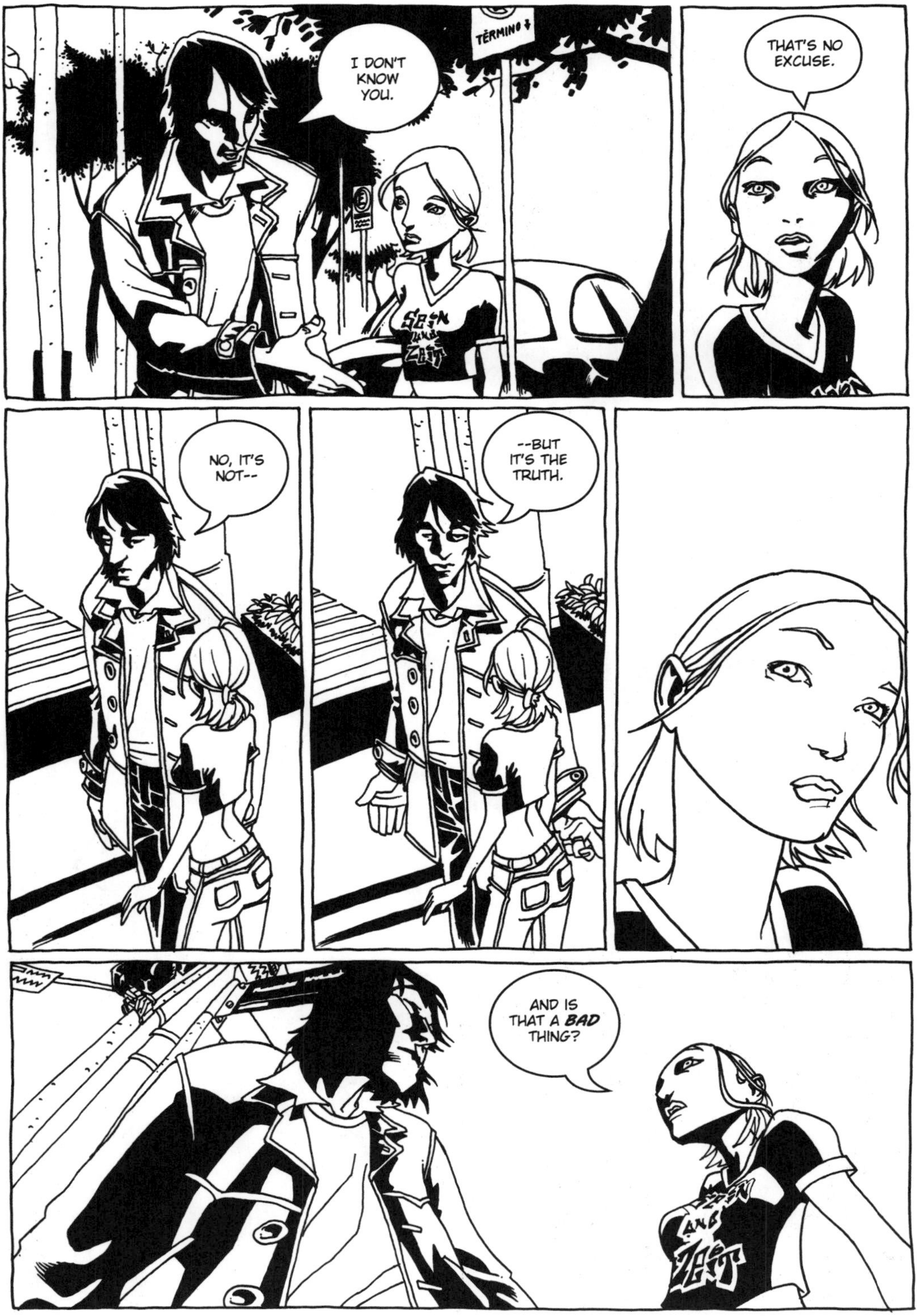
TÉRMINO
I DON'T KNOW YOU.
THAT'S NO EXCUSE.
NO, IT'S NOT--
--BUT IT'S THE TRUTH.
AND IS THAT A ***BAD*** THING?

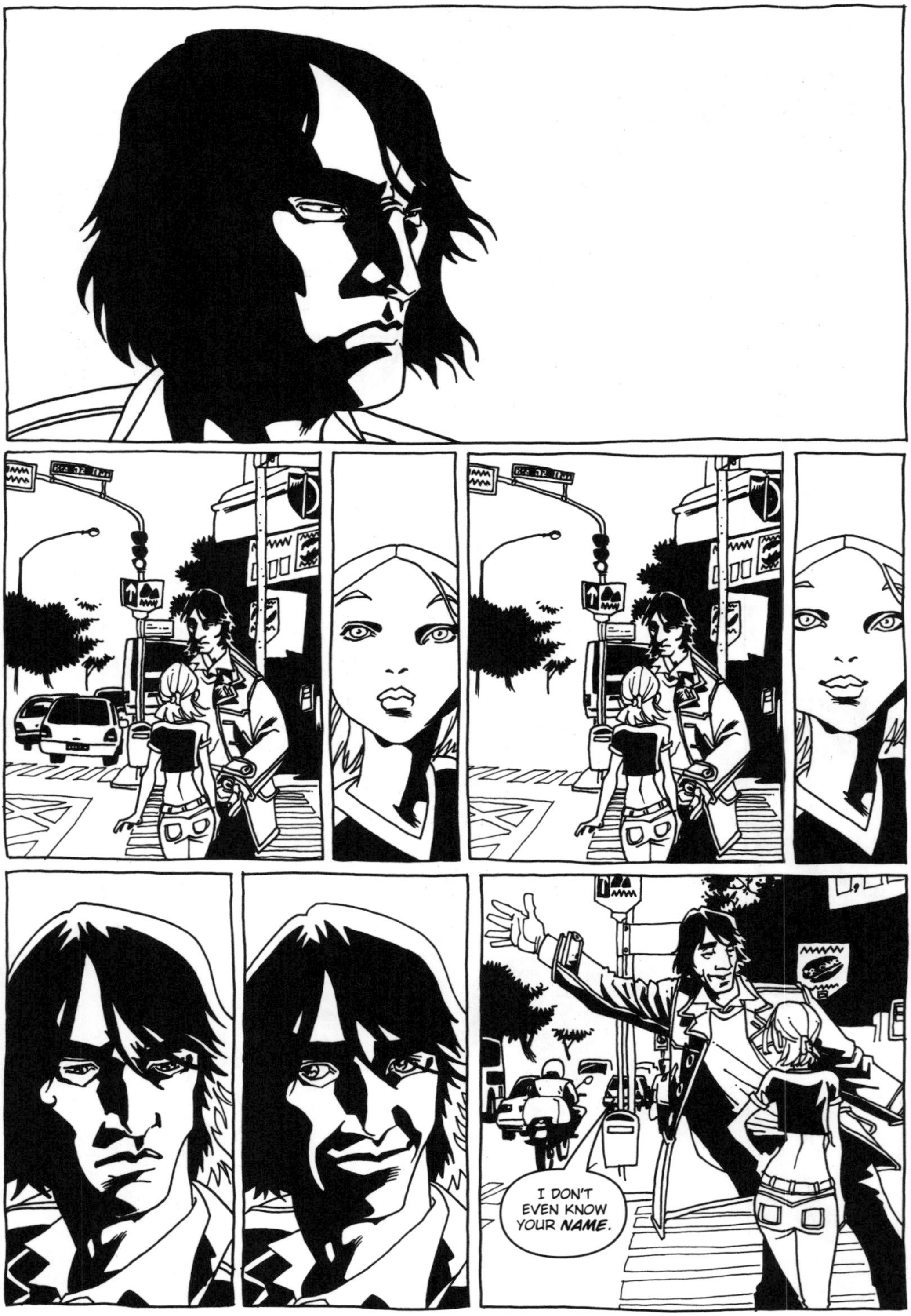
I DON'T EVEN KNOW YOUR NAME.

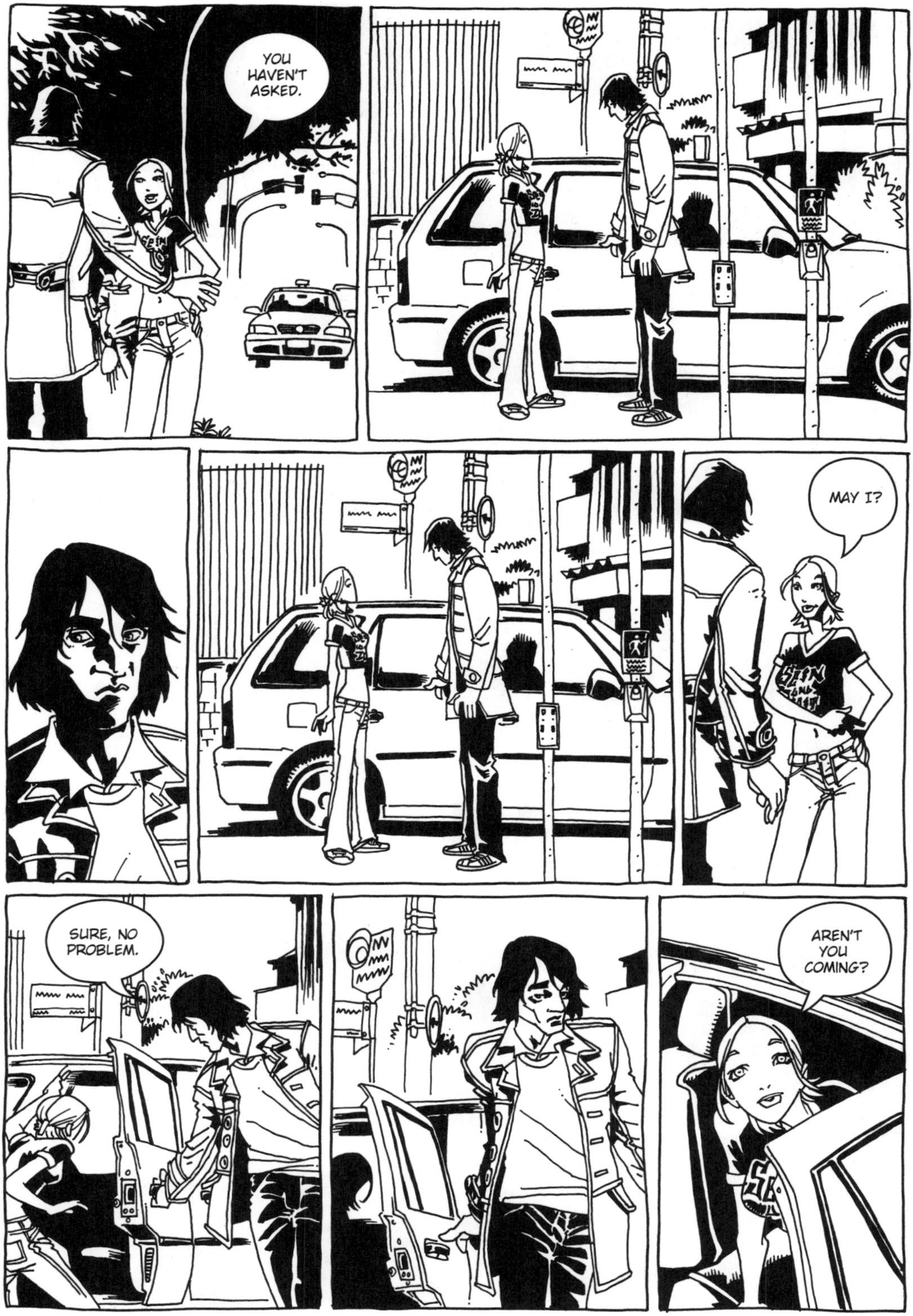
YOU HAVEN'T ASKED.
MAY I?
SURE, NO PROBLEM.
AREN'T YOU COMING?

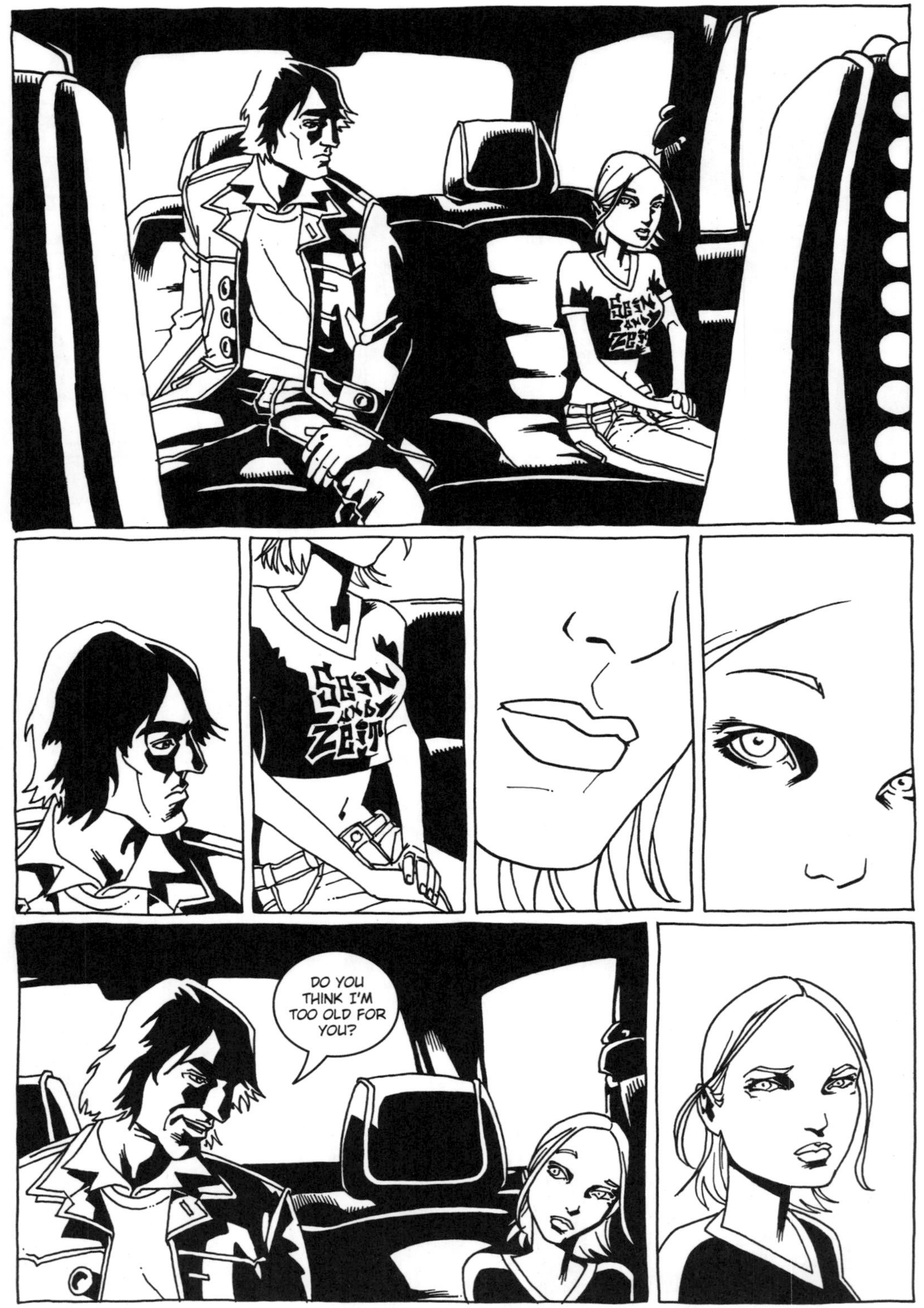
SEIN AND ZEIT
SEIN AND ZEIT
DO YOU THINK I'M TOO OLD FOR YOU?

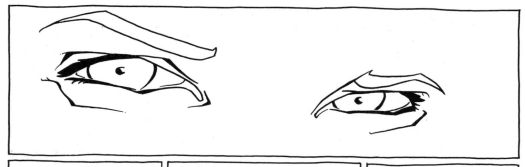

YOU'RE NOT BALD.

NO, I'M NOT.

THEN YOU'RE NOT OLD.

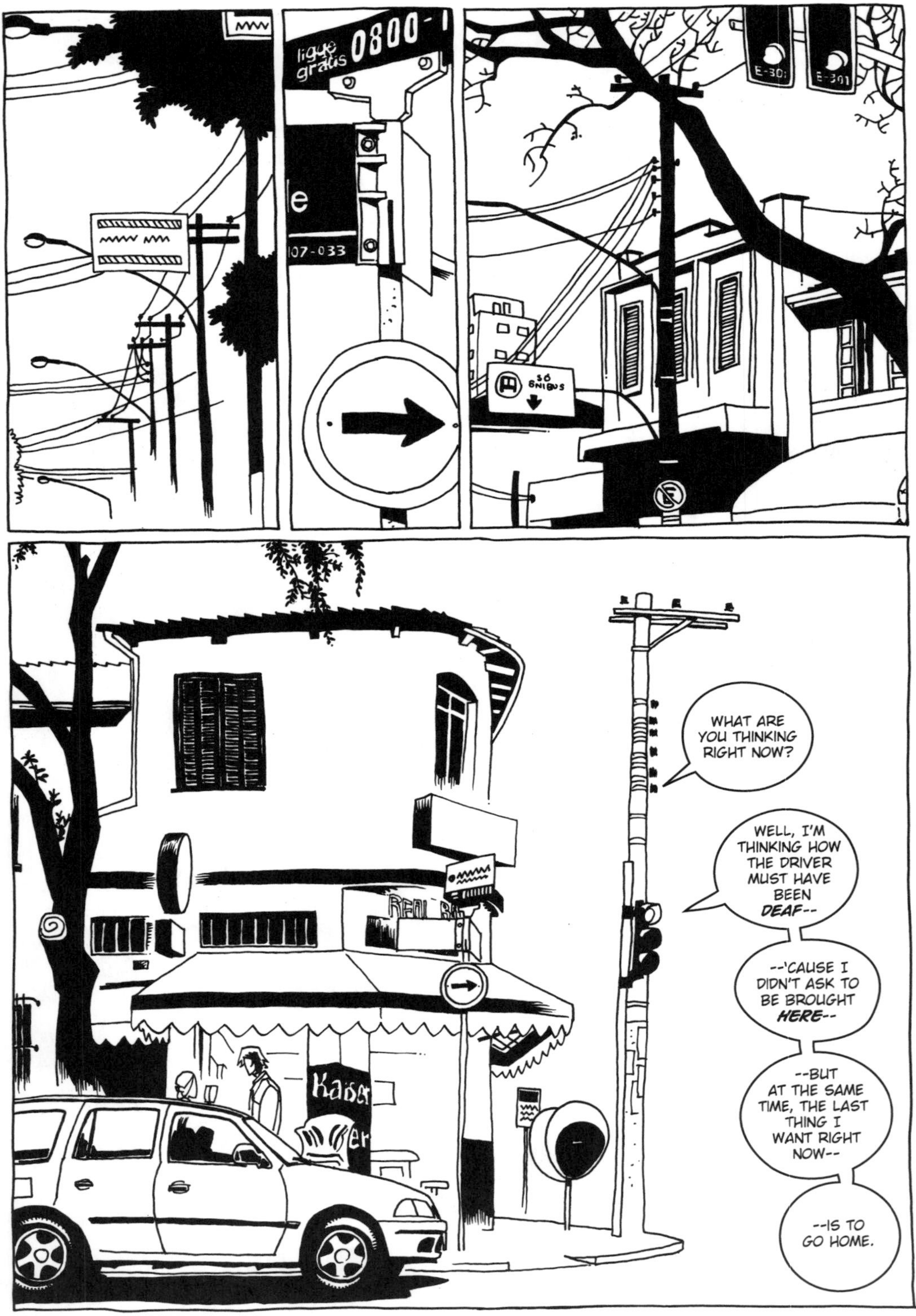

ligue grátis 0800-
107-033
E-301
E-301
SÓ ÔNIBUS
WHAT ARE YOU THINKING RIGHT NOW?
WELL, I'M THINKING HOW THE DRIVER MUST HAVE BEEN *DEAF*--
--'CAUSE I DIDN'T ASK TO BE BROUGHT *HERE*--
--BUT AT THE SAME TIME, THE LAST THING I WANT RIGHT NOW--
--IS TO GO HOME.

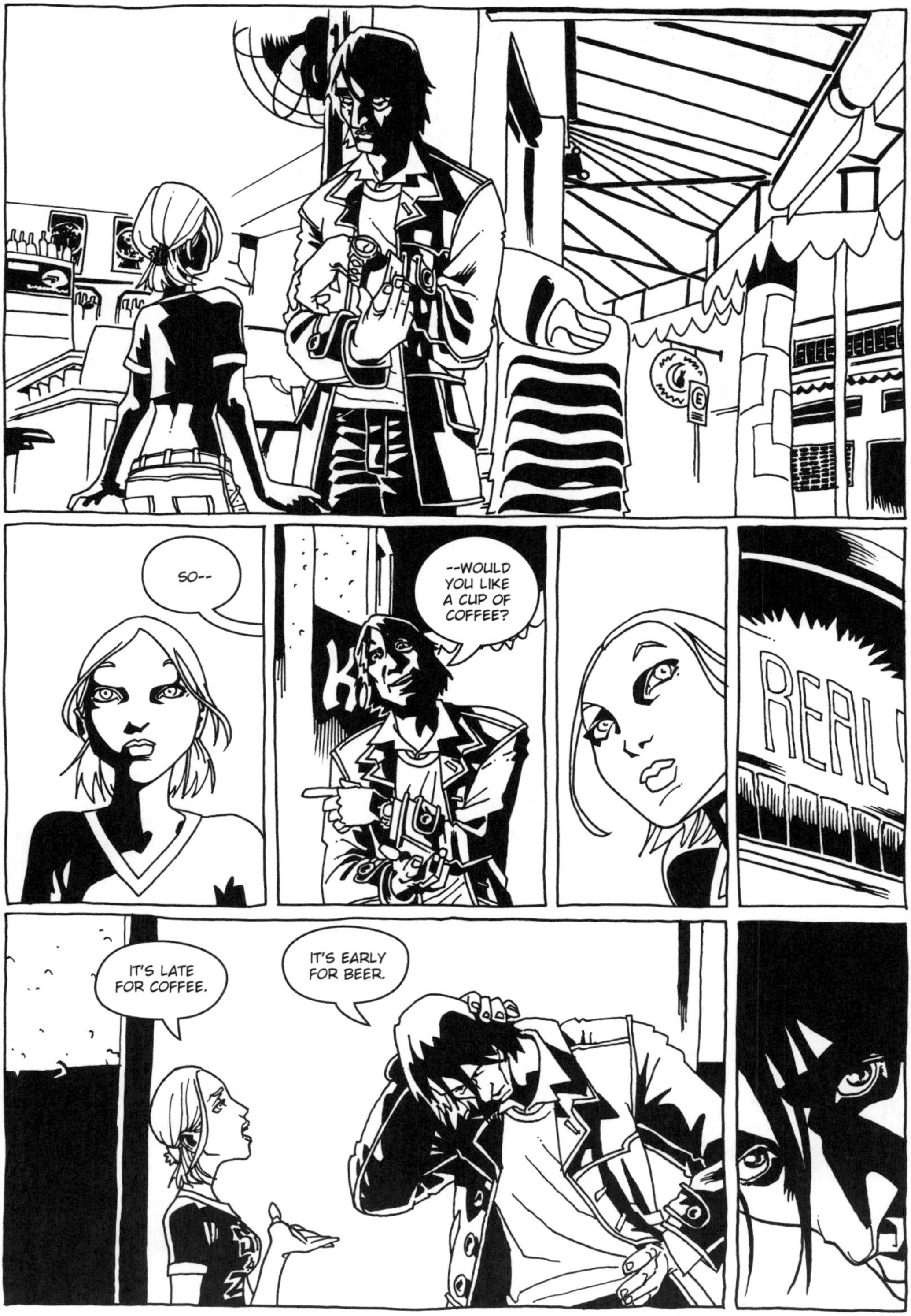
SO--
--WOULD YOU LIKE A CUP OF COFFEE?
REAL
IT'S LATE FOR COFFEE.
IT'S EARLY FOR BEER.

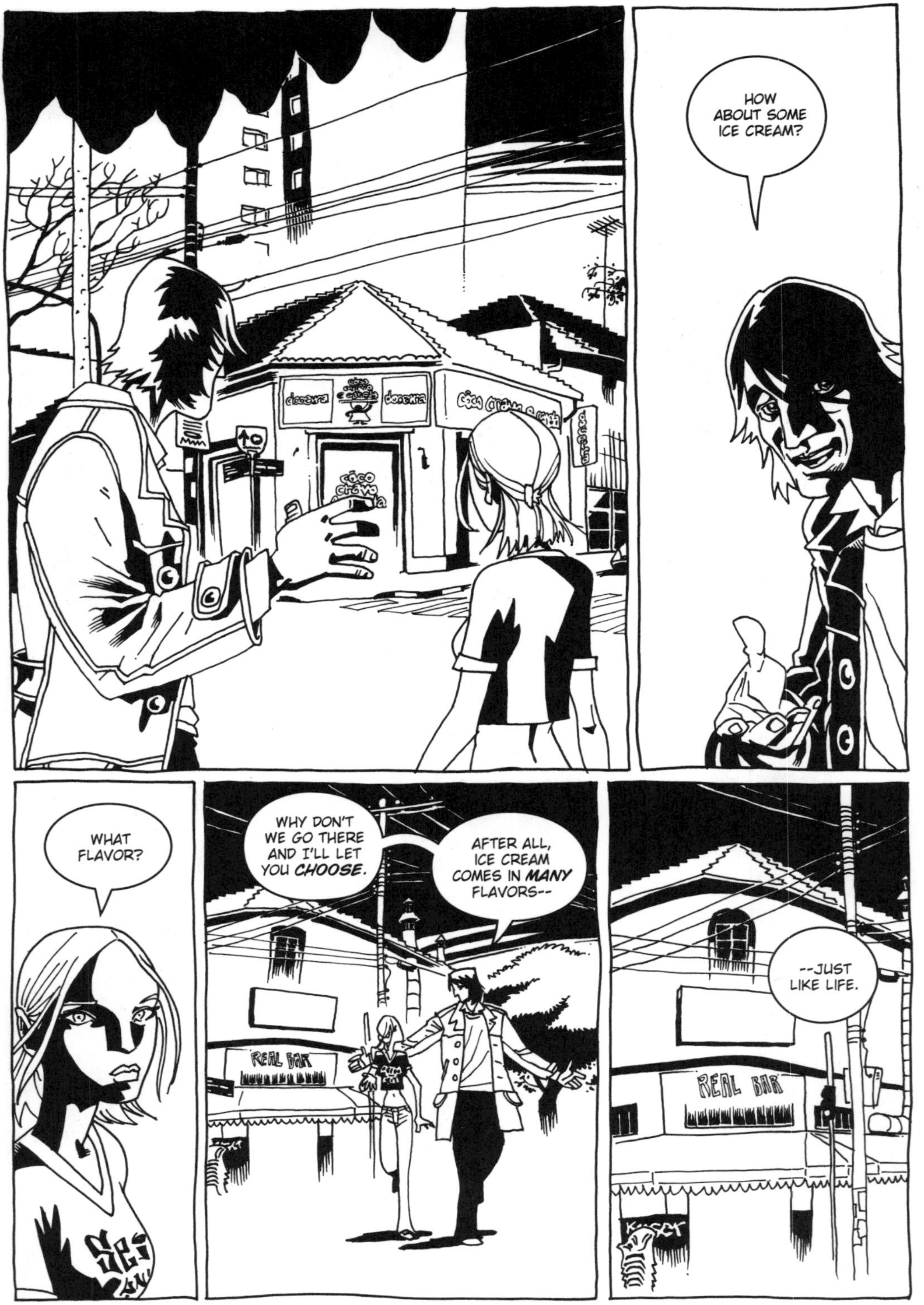
HOW ABOUT SOME ICE CREAM?
WHAT FLAVOR?
WHY DON'T WE GO THERE AND I'LL LET YOU *CHOOSE*.
AFTER ALL, ICE CREAM COMES IN *MANY* FLAVORS--
--JUST LIKE LIFE.
REAL BAR
REAL BAR

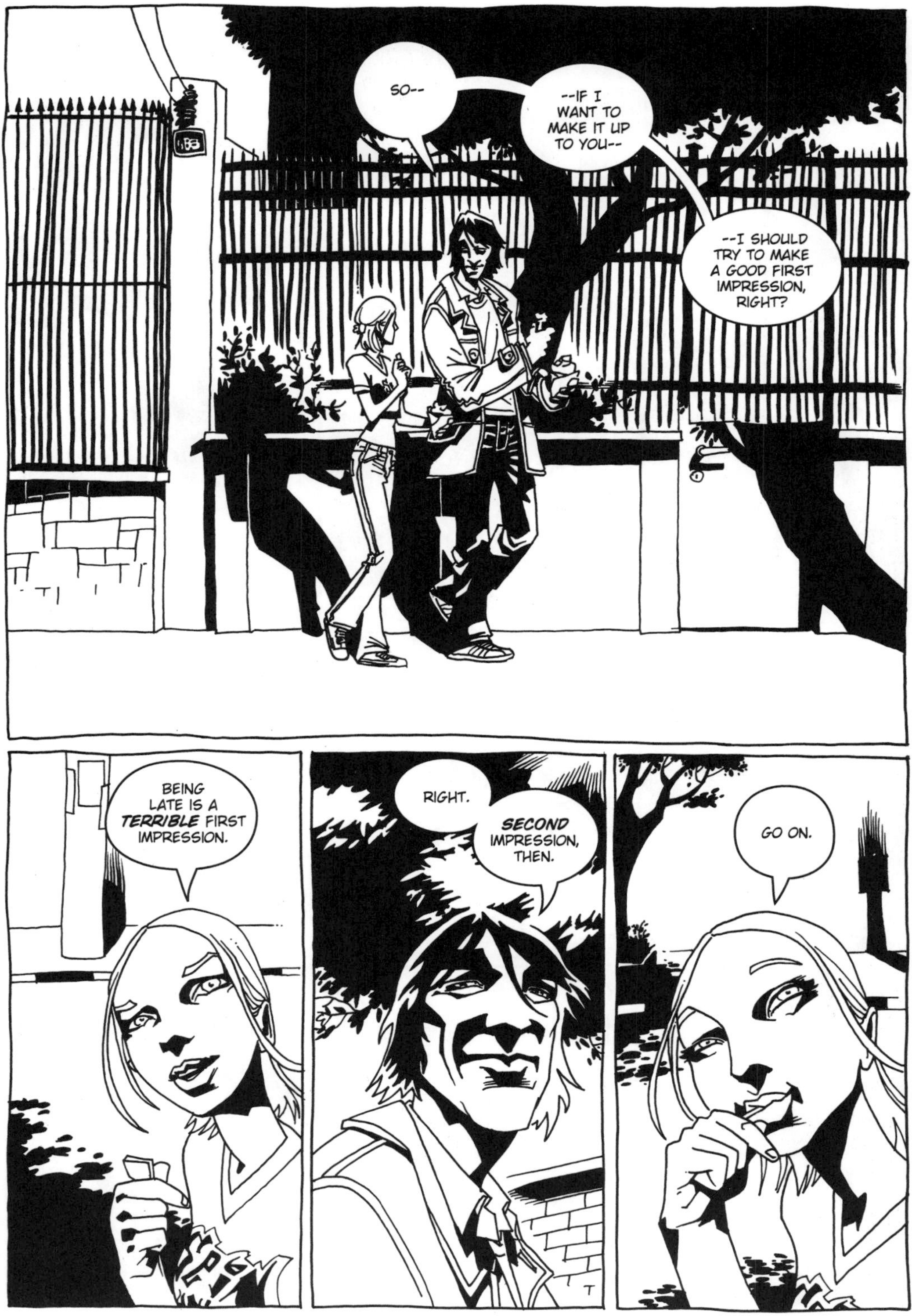
SO--
--IF I WANT TO MAKE IT UP TO YOU--
--I SHOULD TRY TO MAKE A GOOD FIRST IMPRESSION, RIGHT?
BEING LATE IS A *TERRIBLE* FIRST IMPRESSION.
RIGHT.
SECOND IMPRESSION, THEN.
GO ON.

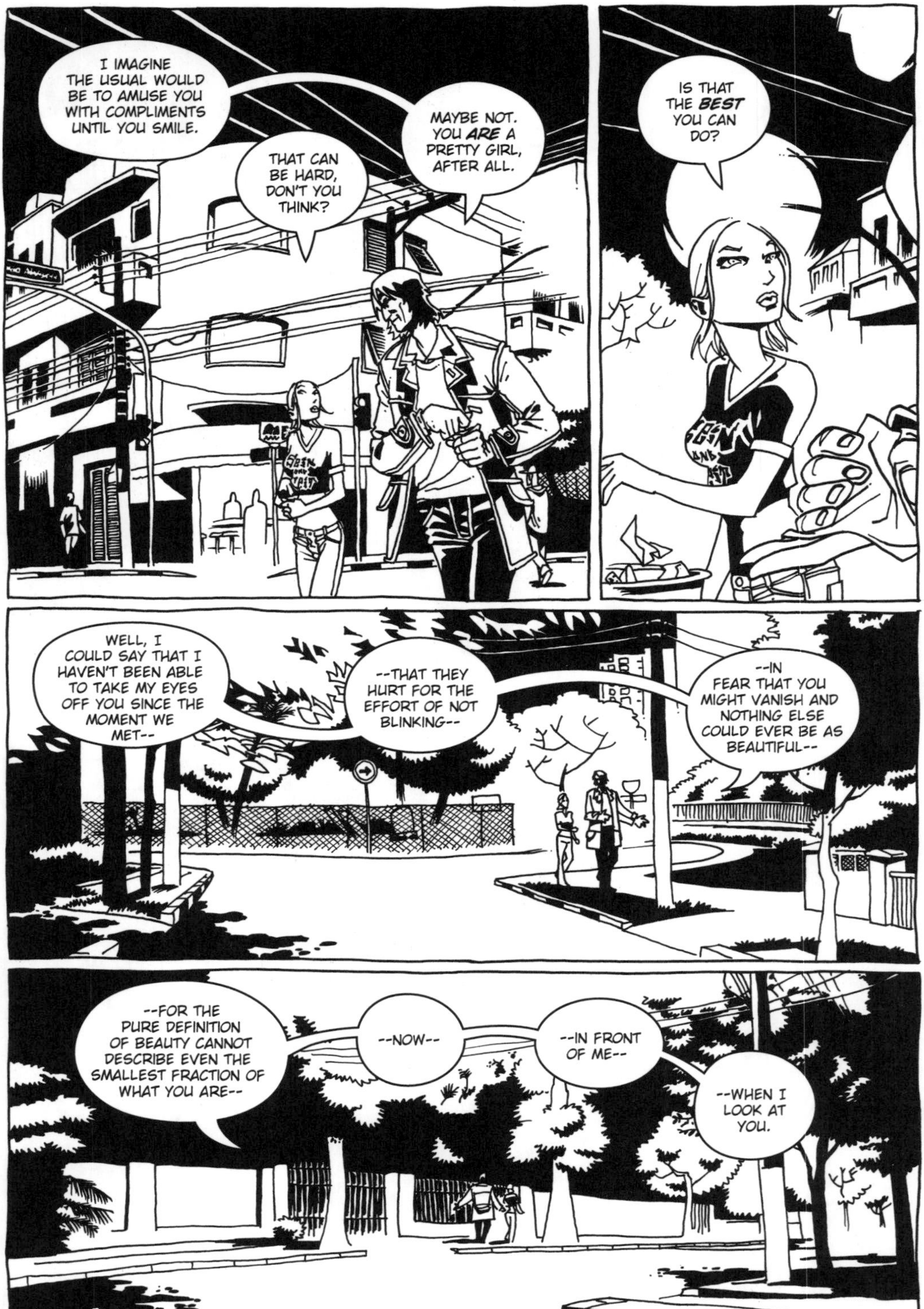
I IMAGINE THE USUAL WOULD BE TO AMUSE YOU WITH COMPLIMENTS UNTIL YOU SMILE.
THAT CAN BE HARD, DON'T YOU THINK?
MAYBE NOT. YOU **ARE** A PRETTY GIRL, AFTER ALL.
IS THAT THE **BEST** YOU CAN DO?
WELL, I COULD SAY THAT I HAVEN'T BEEN ABLE TO TAKE MY EYES OFF YOU SINCE THE MOMENT WE MET--
--THAT THEY HURT FOR THE EFFORT OF NOT BLINKING--
--IN FEAR THAT YOU MIGHT VANISH AND NOTHING ELSE COULD EVER BE AS BEAUTIFUL--
--FOR THE PURE DEFINITION OF BEAUTY CANNOT DESCRIBE EVEN THE SMALLEST FRACTION OF WHAT YOU ARE--
--NOW--
--IN FRONT OF ME--
--WHEN I LOOK AT YOU.

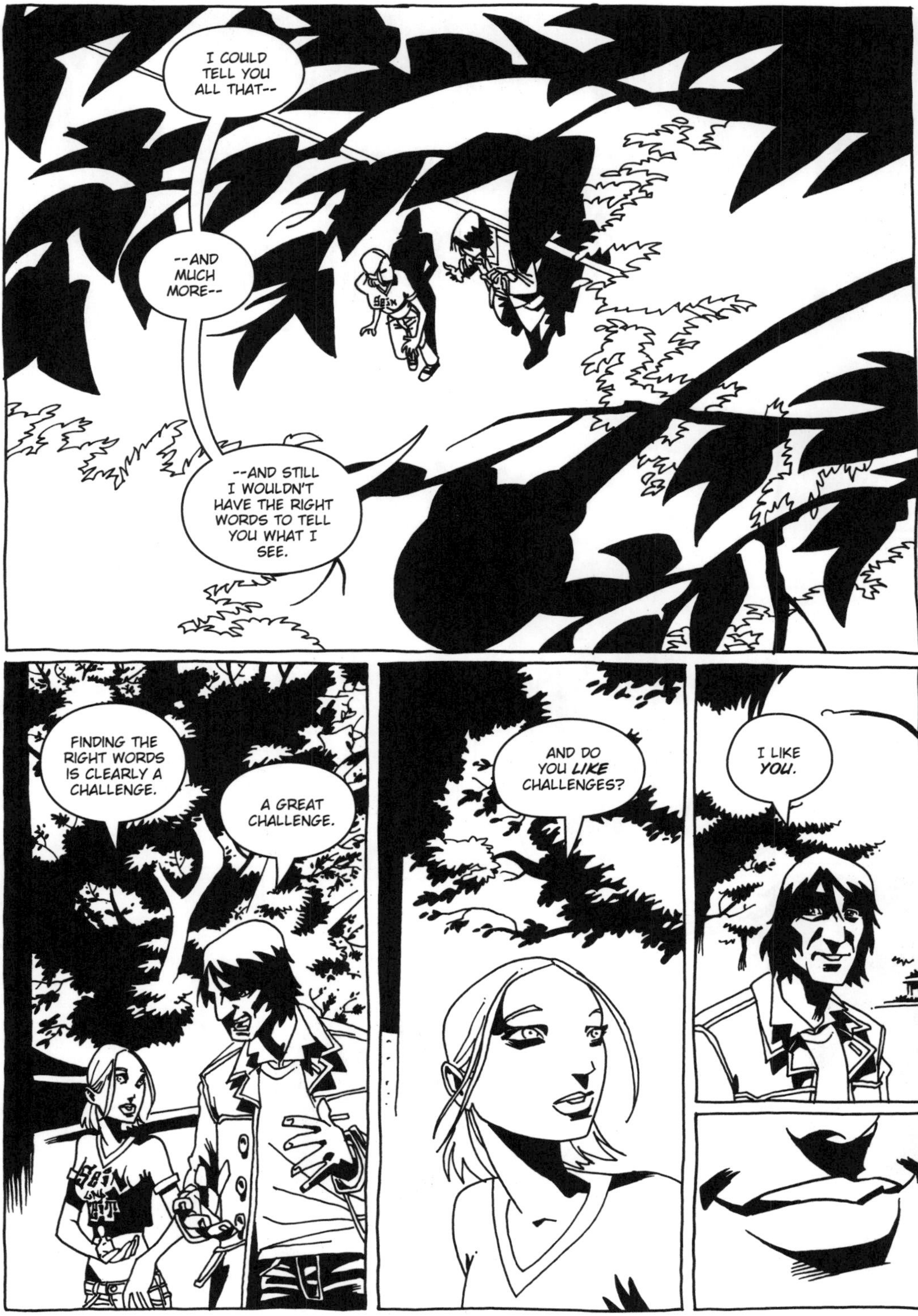
I COULD TELL YOU ALL THAT--
--AND MUCH MORE--
--AND STILL I WOULDN'T HAVE THE RIGHT WORDS TO TELL YOU WHAT I SEE.
FINDING THE RIGHT WORDS IS CLEARLY A CHALLENGE.
A GREAT CHALLENGE.
AND DO YOU LIKE CHALLENGES?
I LIKE YOU.

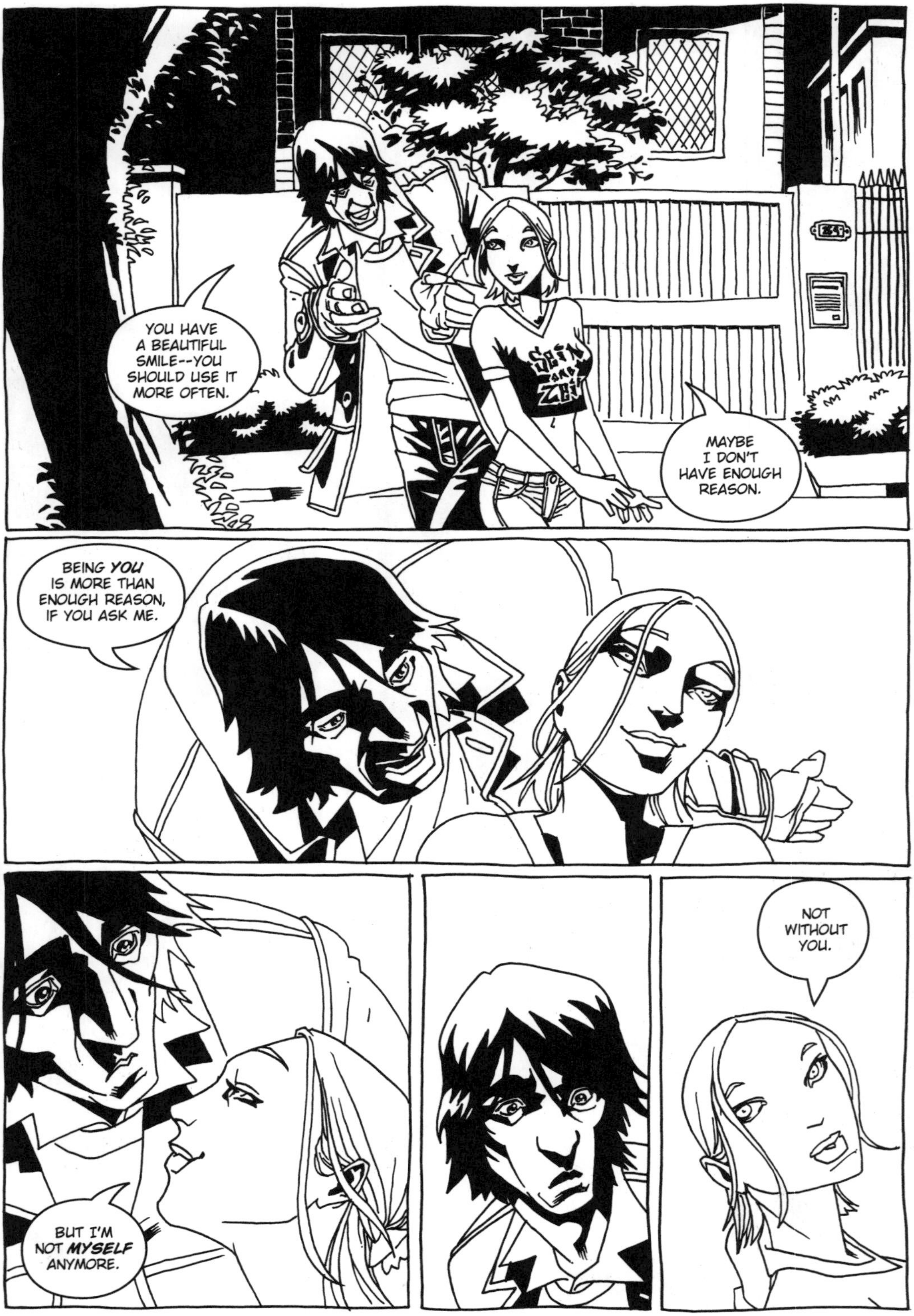
YOU HAVE A BEAUTIFUL SMILE--YOU SHOULD USE IT MORE OFTEN.
MAYBE I DON'T HAVE ENOUGH REASON.
BEING *YOU* IS MORE THAN ENOUGH REASON, IF YOU ASK ME.
BUT I'M NOT *MYSELF* ANYMORE.
NOT WITHOUT YOU.

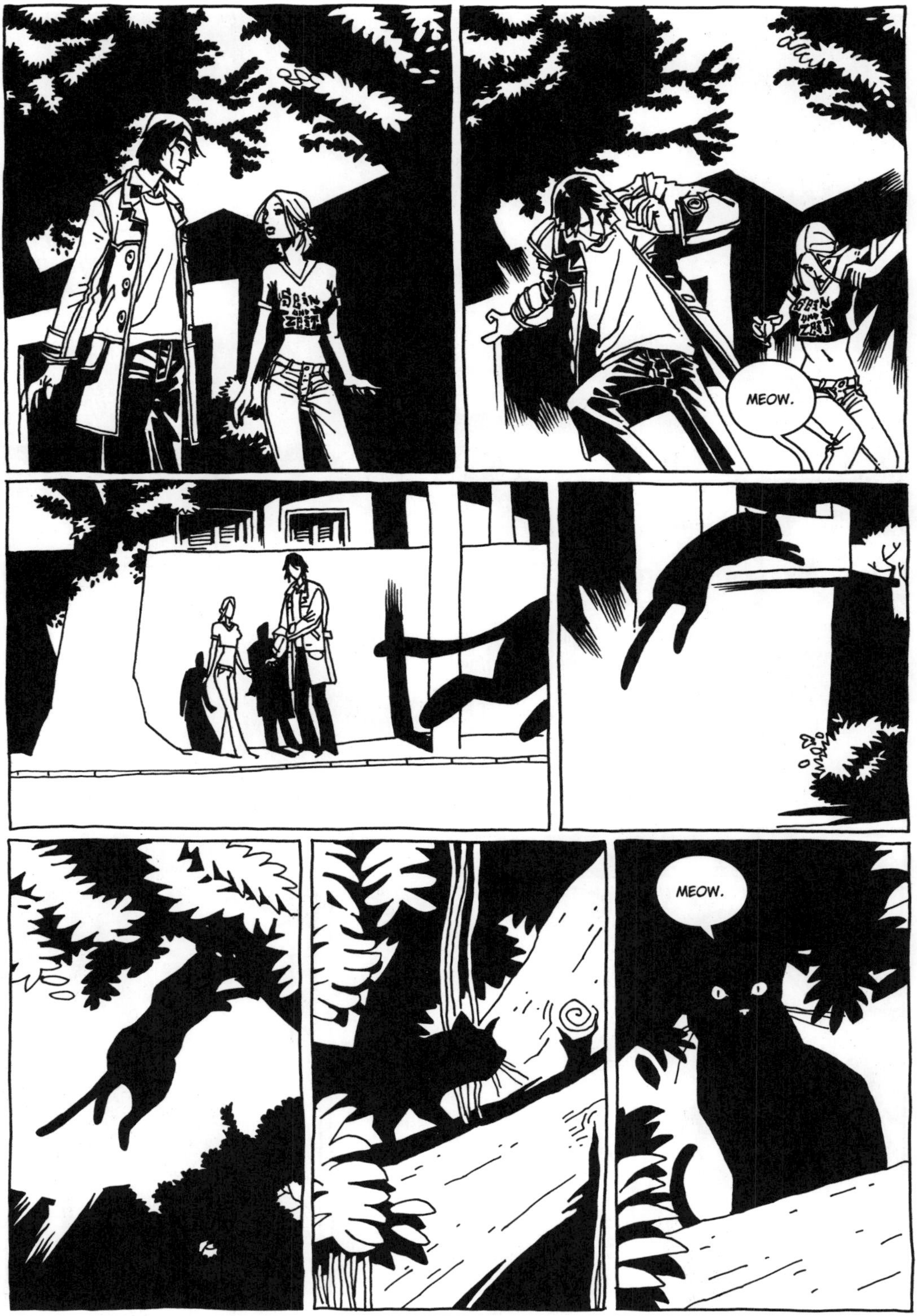
MEOW.
MEOW.

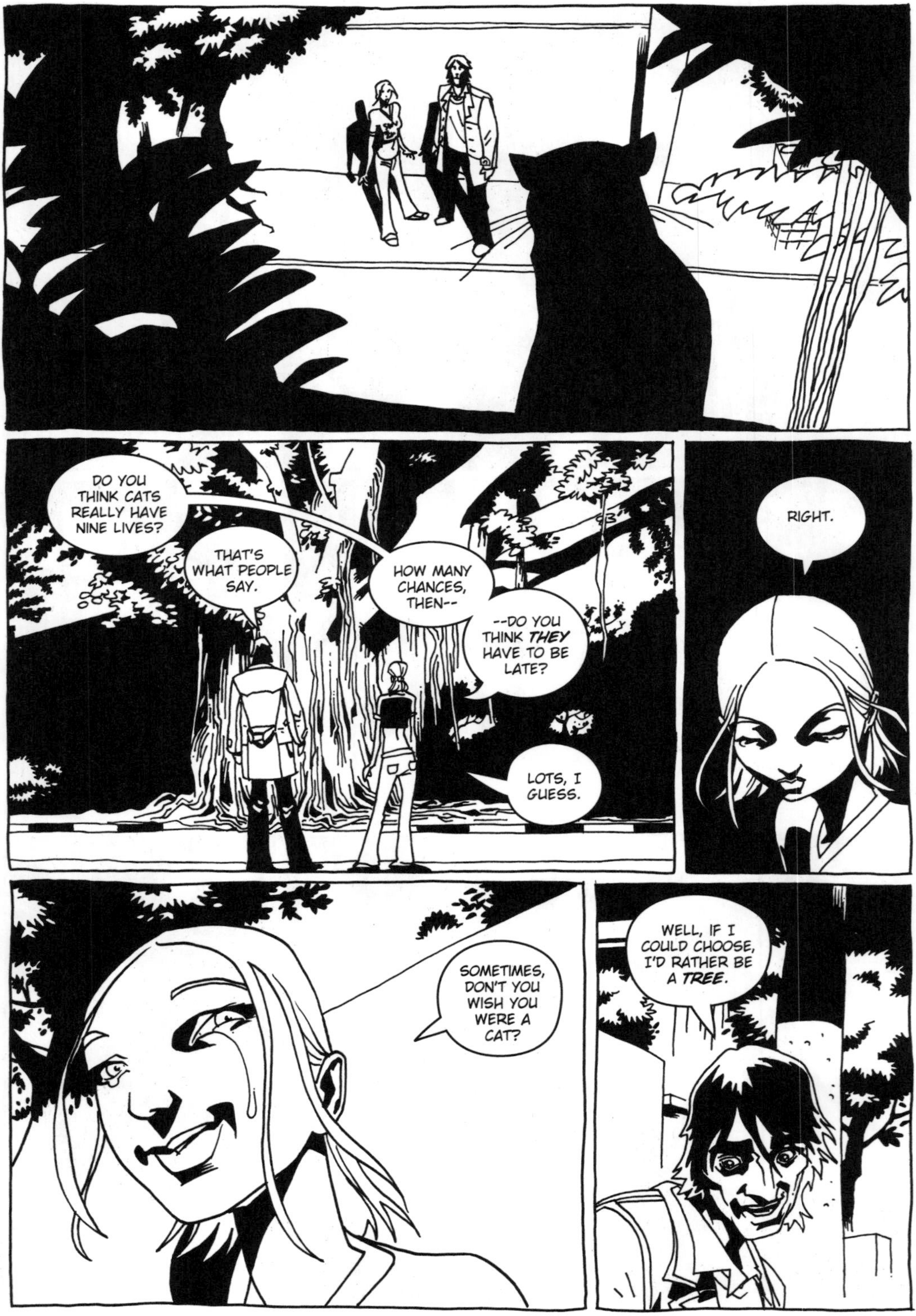
DO YOU THINK CATS REALLY HAVE NINE LIVES?
THAT'S WHAT PEOPLE SAY.
HOW MANY CHANCES, THEN--
--DO YOU THINK *THEY* HAVE TO BE LATE?
LOTS, I GUESS.
RIGHT.
SOMETIMES, DON'T YOU WISH YOU WERE A CAT?
WELL, IF I COULD CHOOSE, I'D RATHER BE A *TREE*.

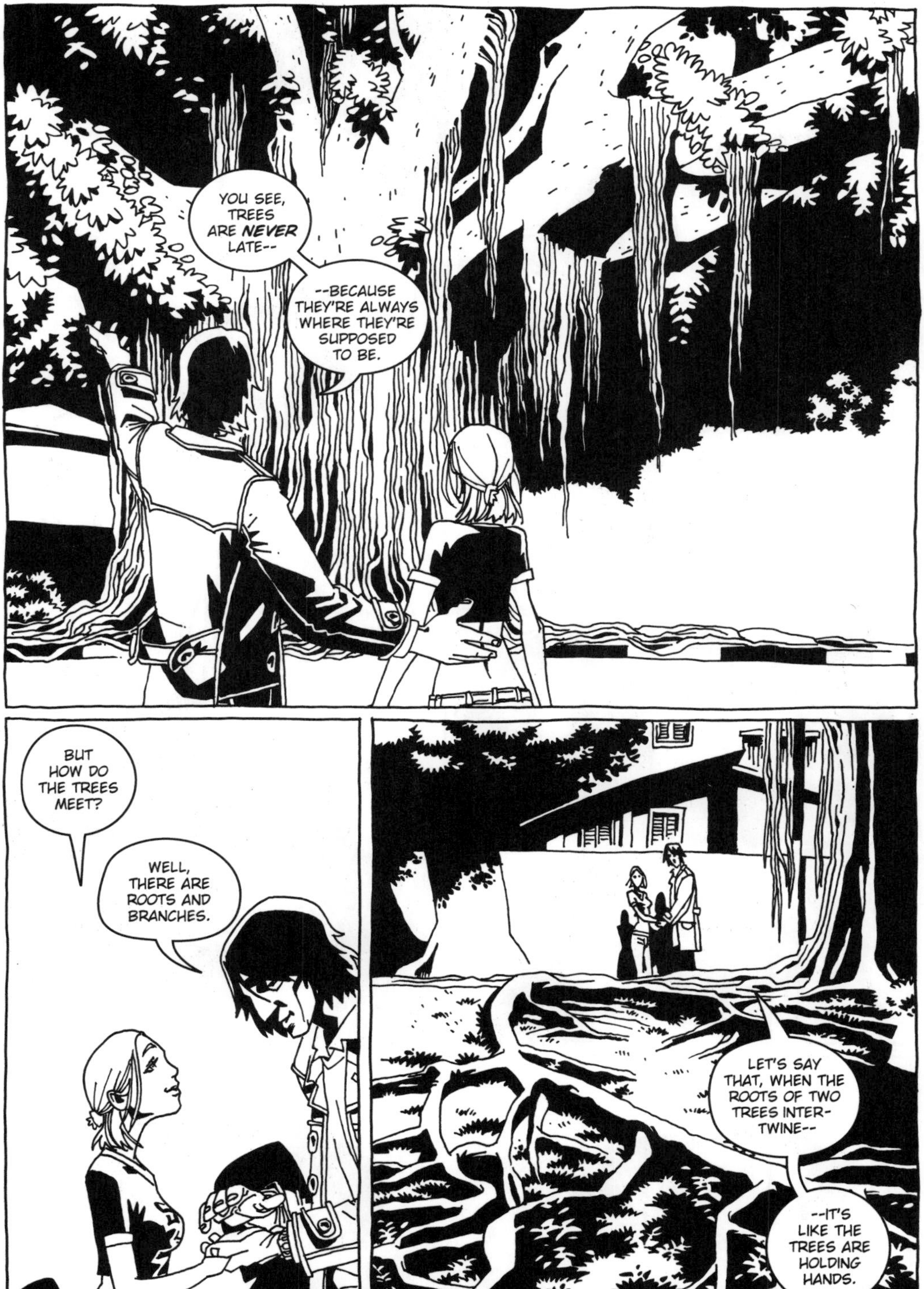
YOU SEE, TREES ARE NEVER LATE--
--BECAUSE THEY'RE ALWAYS WHERE THEY'RE SUPPOSED TO BE.
BUT HOW DO THE TREES MEET?
WELL, THERE ARE ROOTS AND BRANCHES.
LET'S SAY THAT, WHEN THE ROOTS OF TWO TREES INTER-TWINE--
--IT'S LIKE THE TREES ARE HOLDING HANDS.

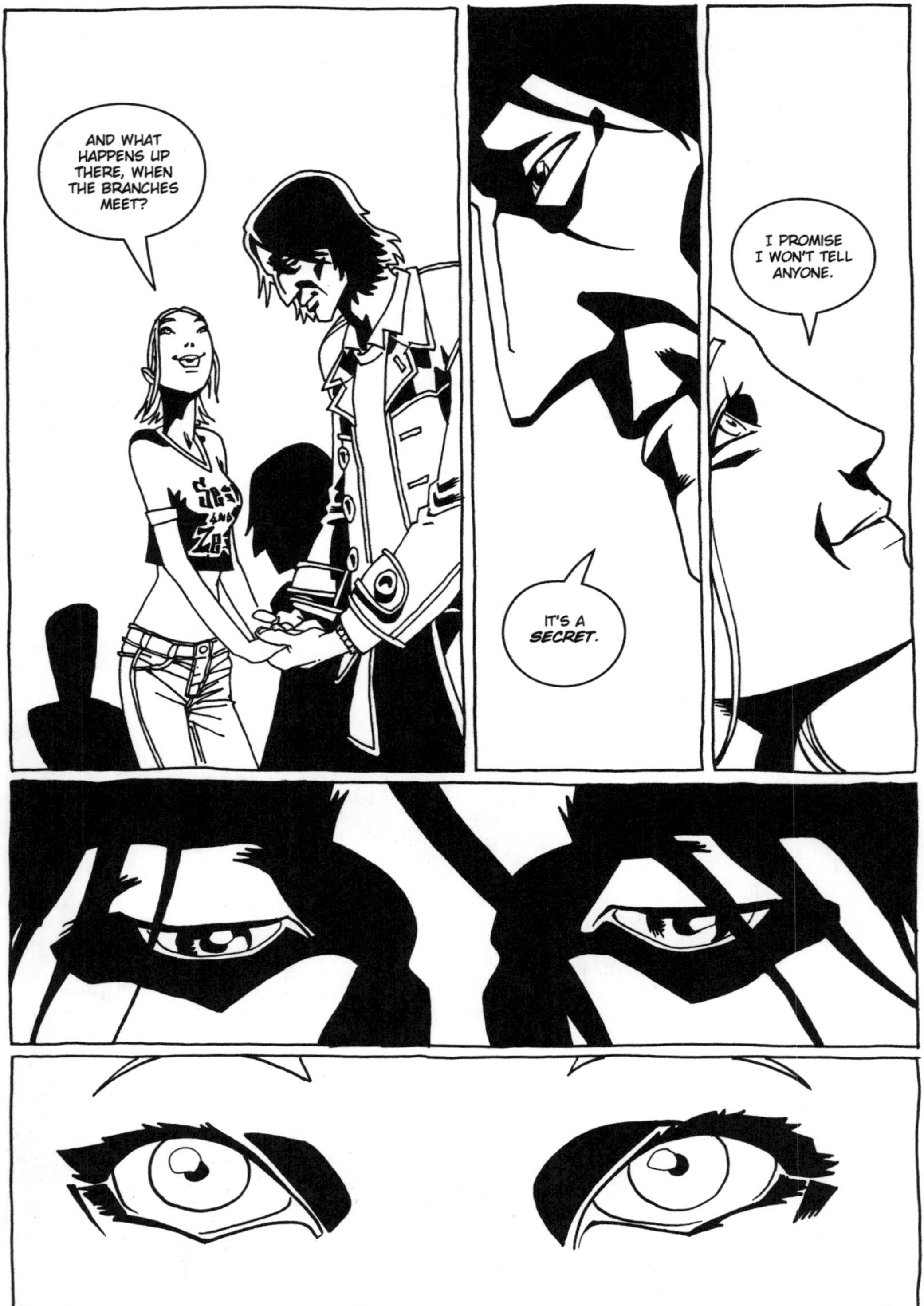
AND WHAT HAPPENS UP THERE, WHEN THE BRANCHES MEET?
IT'S A SECRET.
I PROMISE I WON'T TELL ANYONE.

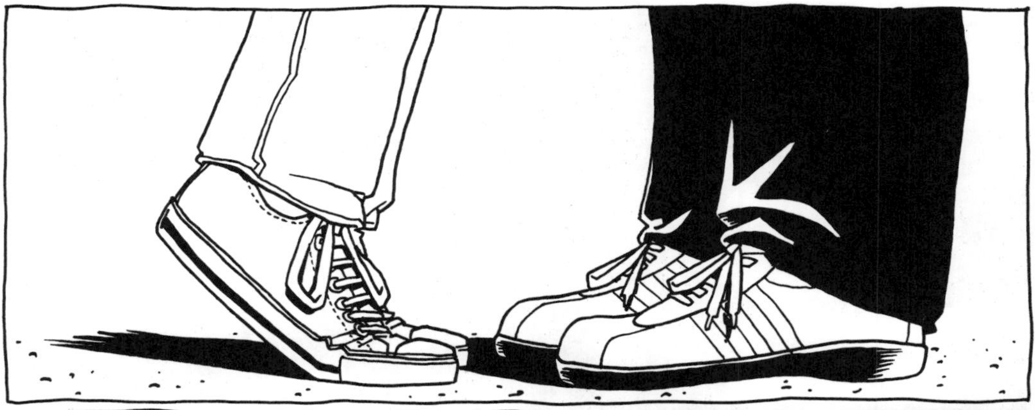

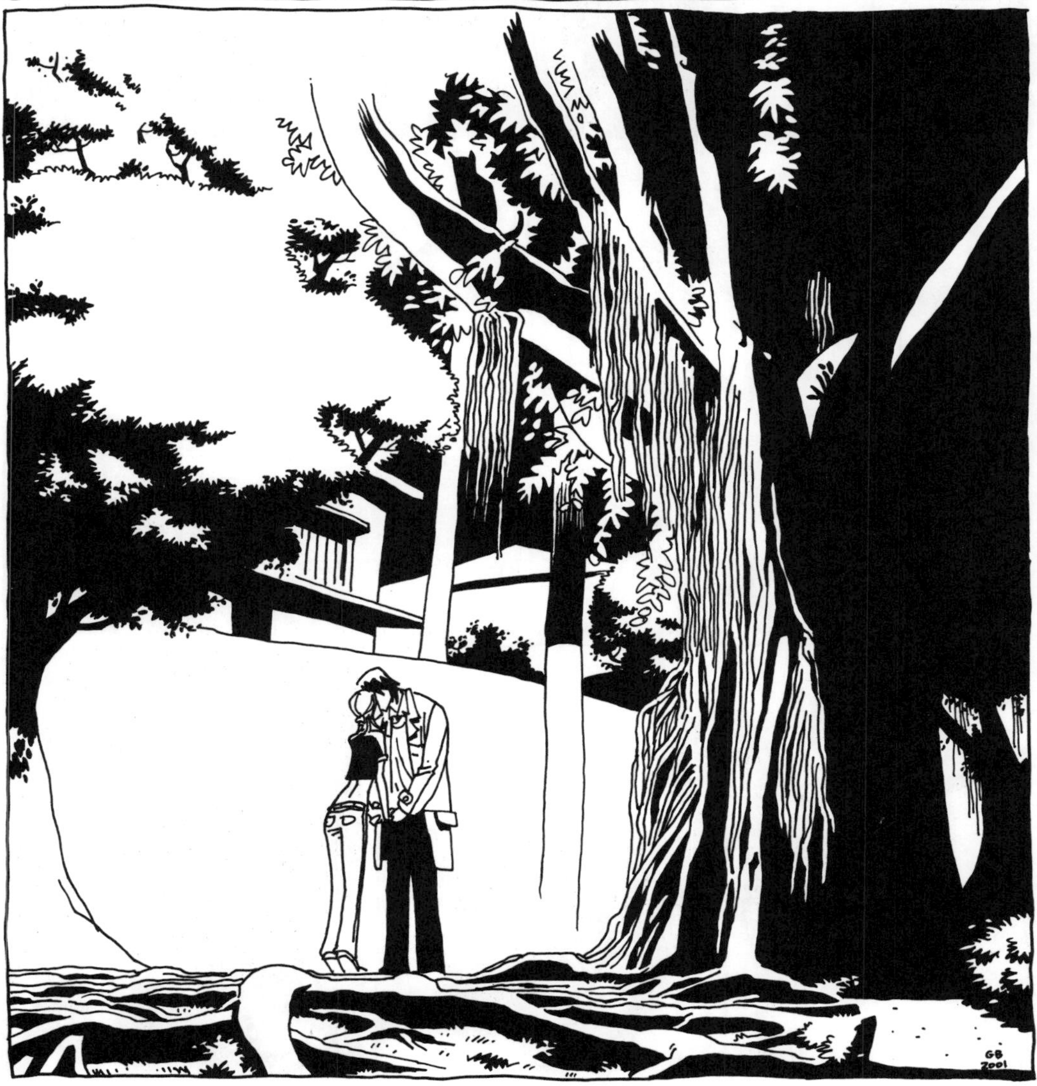
GB
2001

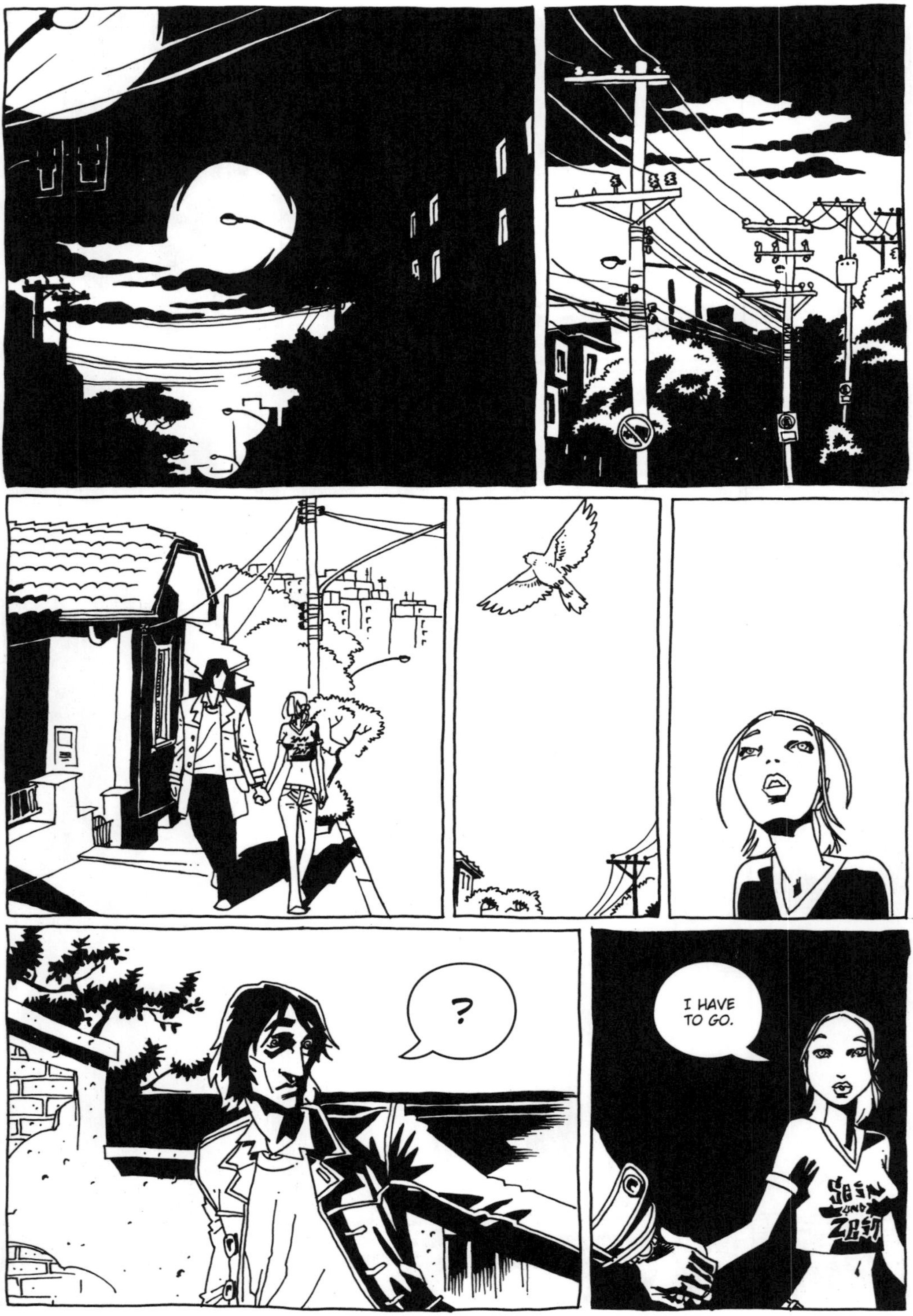
?
I HAVE TO GO.
SEIN UND ZEIT

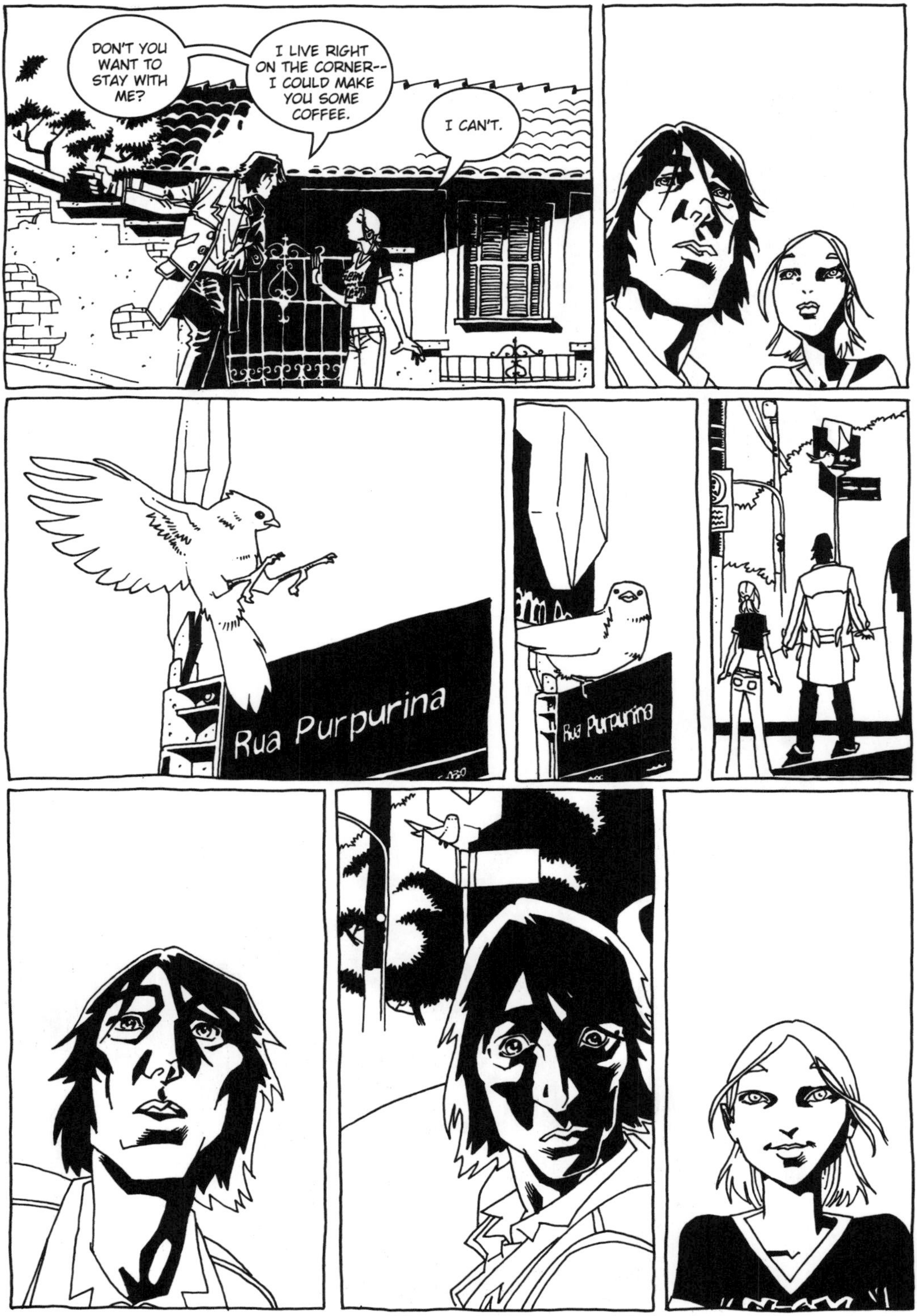
DON'T YOU WANT TO STAY WITH ME?
I LIVE RIGHT ON THE CORNER-- I COULD MAKE YOU SOME COFFEE.
I CAN'T.
Rua Purpurina
Rua Purpurina

I STILL DON'T KNOW YOUR NAME.

YOU STILL HAVEN'T ASKED.

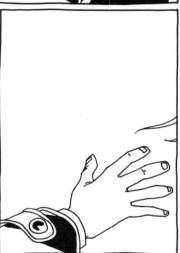

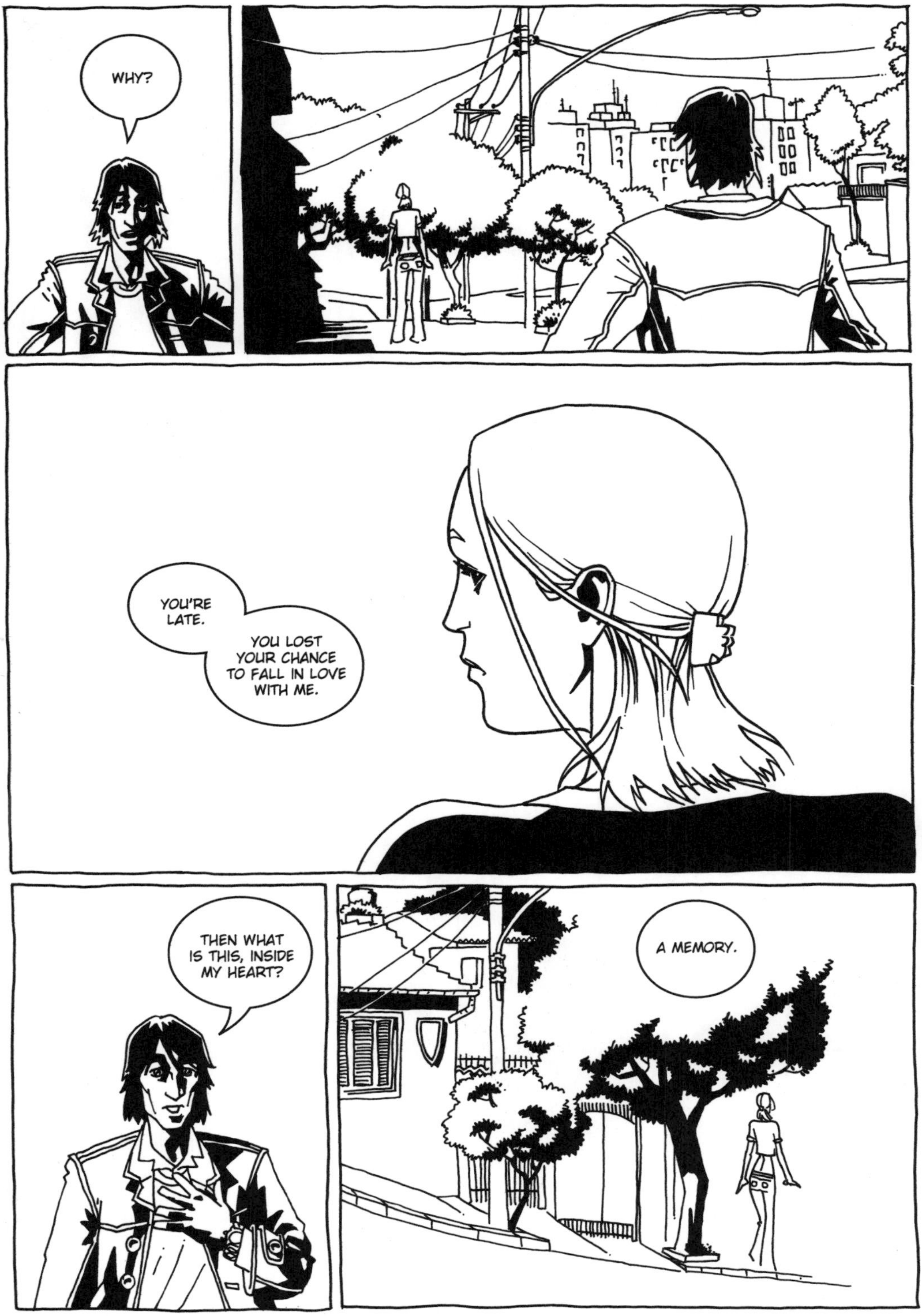
WHY?
YOU'RE LATE.
YOU LOST YOUR CHANCE TO FALL IN LOVE WITH ME.
THEN WHAT IS THIS, INSIDE MY HEART?
A MEMORY.

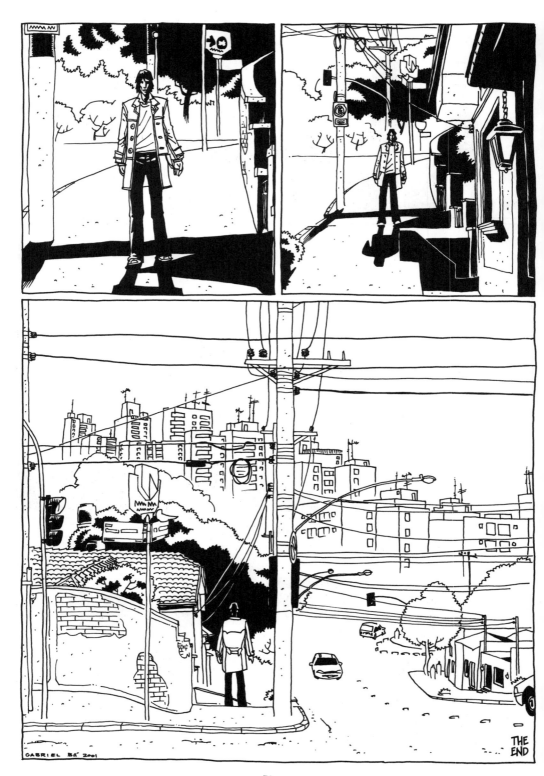

THE
END

GABRIEL BÁ 2001

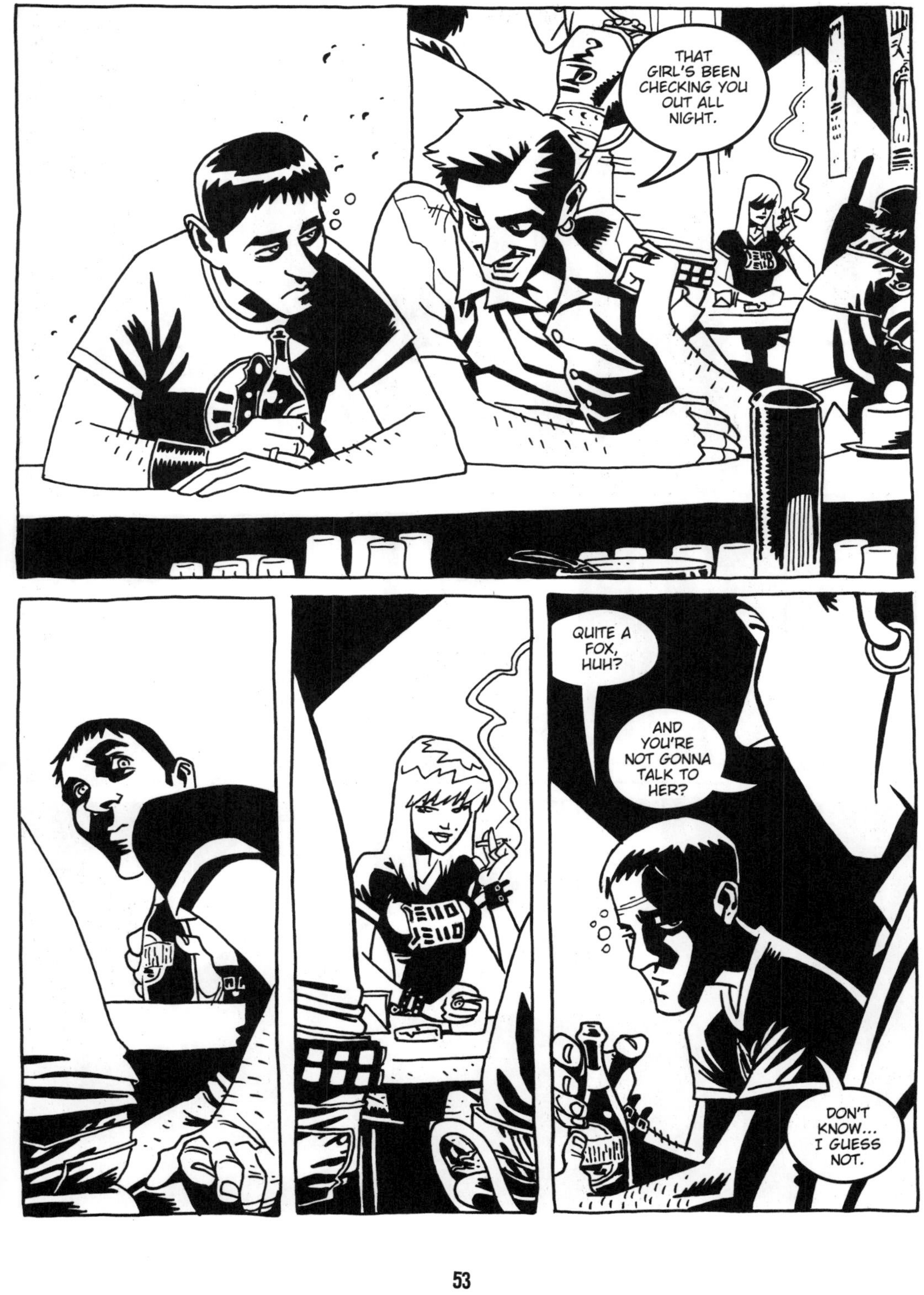
THAT GIRL'S BEEN CHECKING YOU OUT ALL NIGHT.
QUITE A FOX, HUH?
AND YOU'RE NOT GONNA TALK TO HER?
DON'T KNOW... I GUESS NOT.

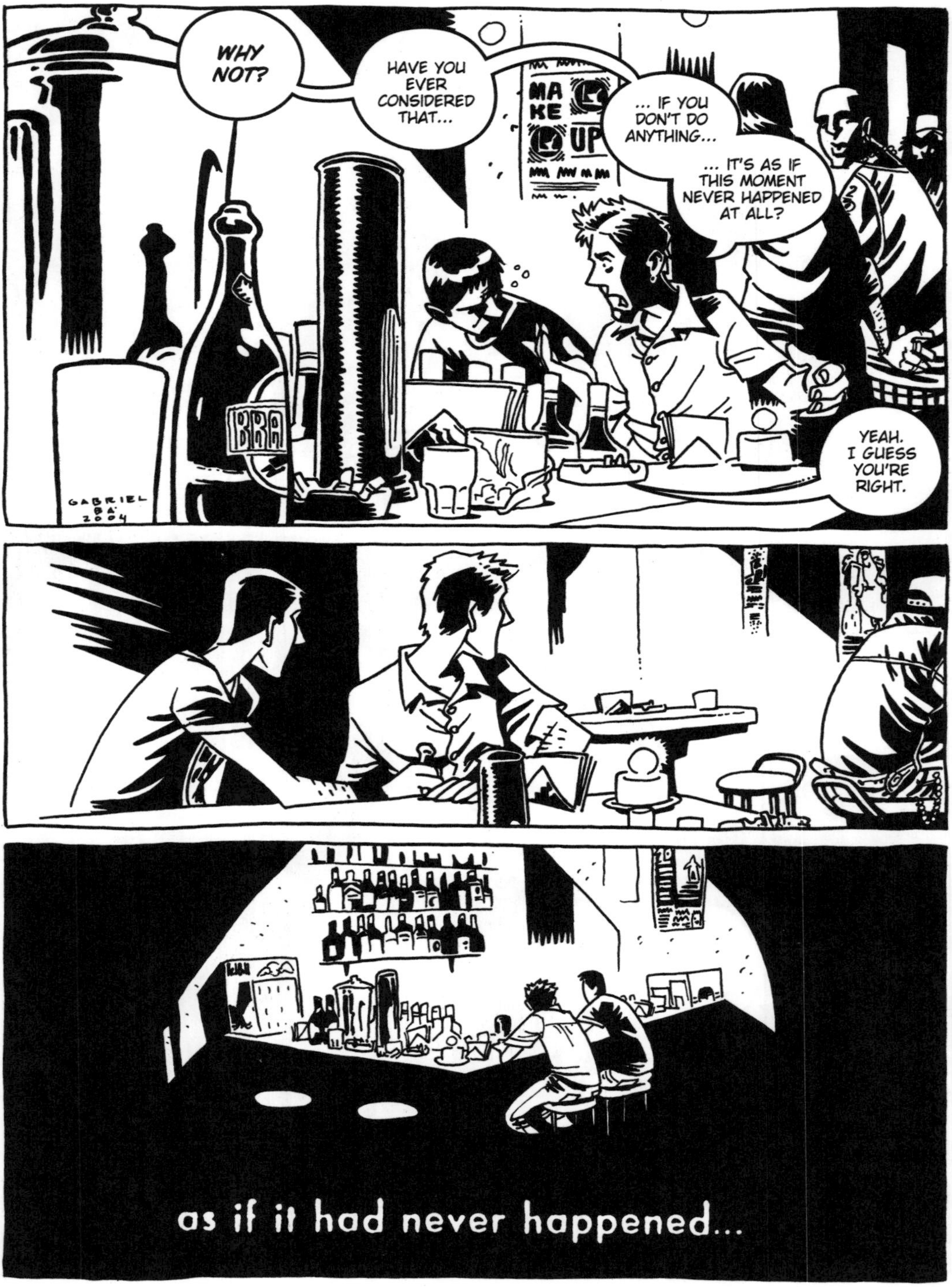
WHY NOT?
HAVE YOU EVER CONSIDERED THAT...
... IF YOU DON'T DO ANYTHING...
... IT'S AS IF THIS MOMENT NEVER HAPPENED AT ALL?
YEAH. I GUESS YOU'RE RIGHT.
GABRIEL BÁ 2004
as if it had never happened...

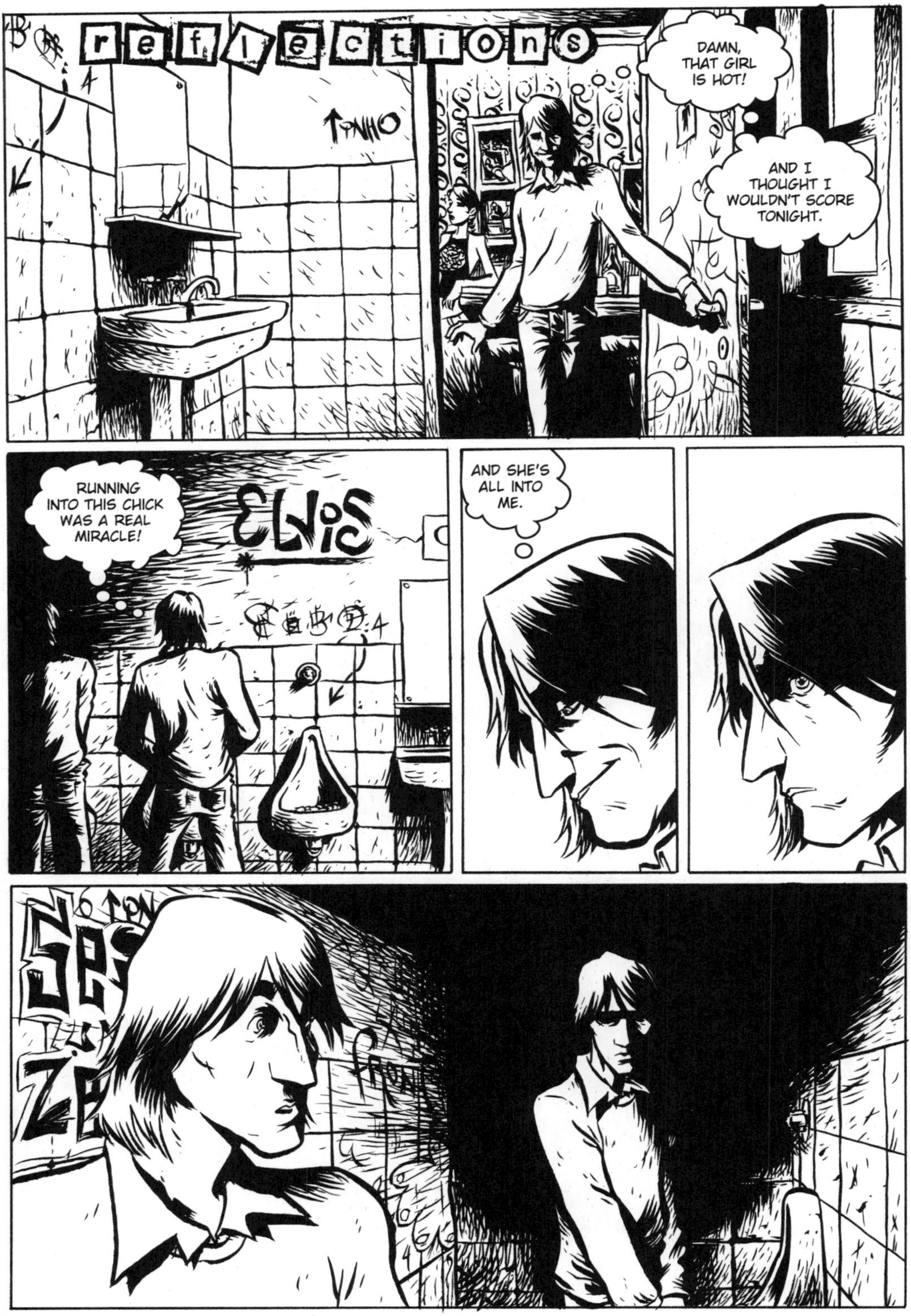
reflections
DAMN, THAT GIRL IS HOT!
AND I THOUGHT I WOULDN'T SCORE TONIGHT.
RUNNING INTO THIS CHICK WAS A REAL MIRACLE!
ELVIS
AND SHE'S ALL INTO ME.

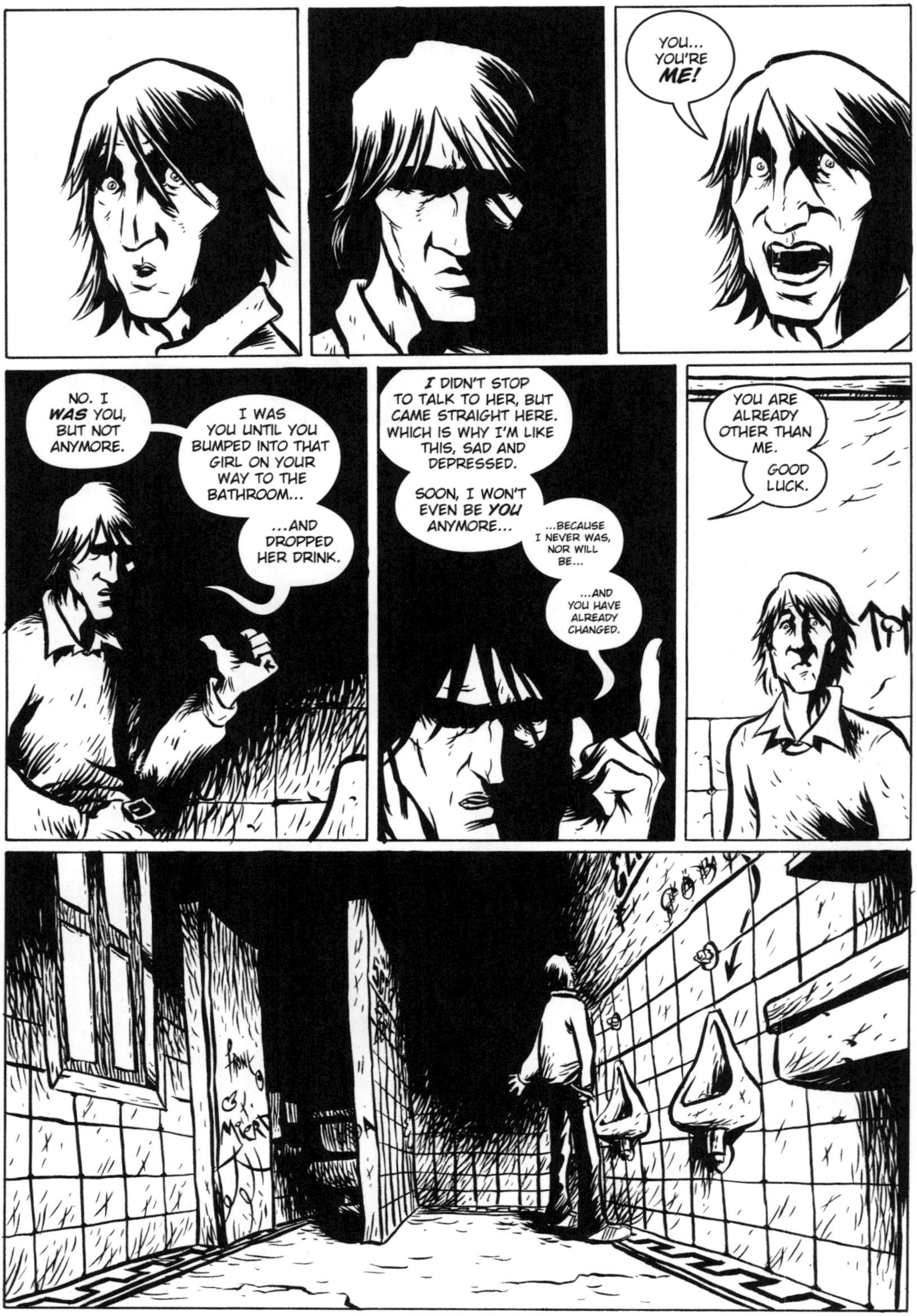
YOU... YOU'RE ME!
NO. I WAS YOU, BUT NOT ANYMORE.
I WAS YOU UNTIL YOU BUMPED INTO THAT GIRL ON YOUR WAY TO THE BATHROOM...
...AND DROPPED HER DRINK.
I DIDN'T STOP TO TALK TO HER, BUT CAME STRAIGHT HERE. WHICH IS WHY I'M LIKE THIS, SAD AND DEPRESSED.
SOON, I WON'T EVEN BE YOU ANYMORE...
...BECAUSE I NEVER WAS, NOR WILL BE...
...AND YOU HAVE ALREADY CHANGED.
YOU ARE ALREADY OTHER THAN ME.
GOOD LUCK.

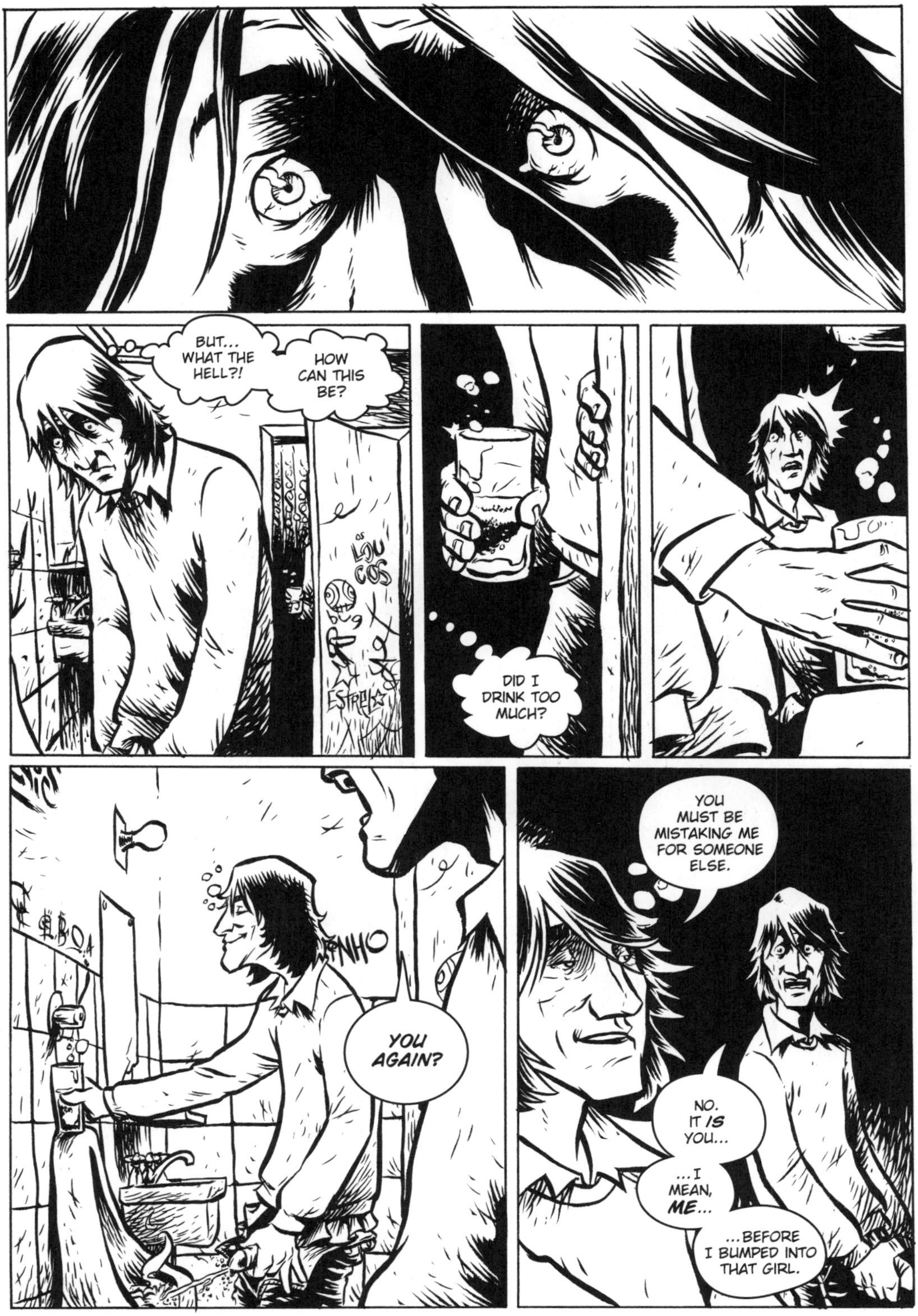
BUT... WHAT THE HELL?!
HOW CAN THIS BE?
LOU COS
ESTREL☆
DID I DRINK TOO MUCH?
YOU AGAIN?
YOU MUST BE MISTAKING ME FOR SOMEONE ELSE.
NO. IT *IS* YOU...
...I MEAN, ***ME***...
...BEFORE I BUMPED INTO THAT GIRL.

end of the first version.

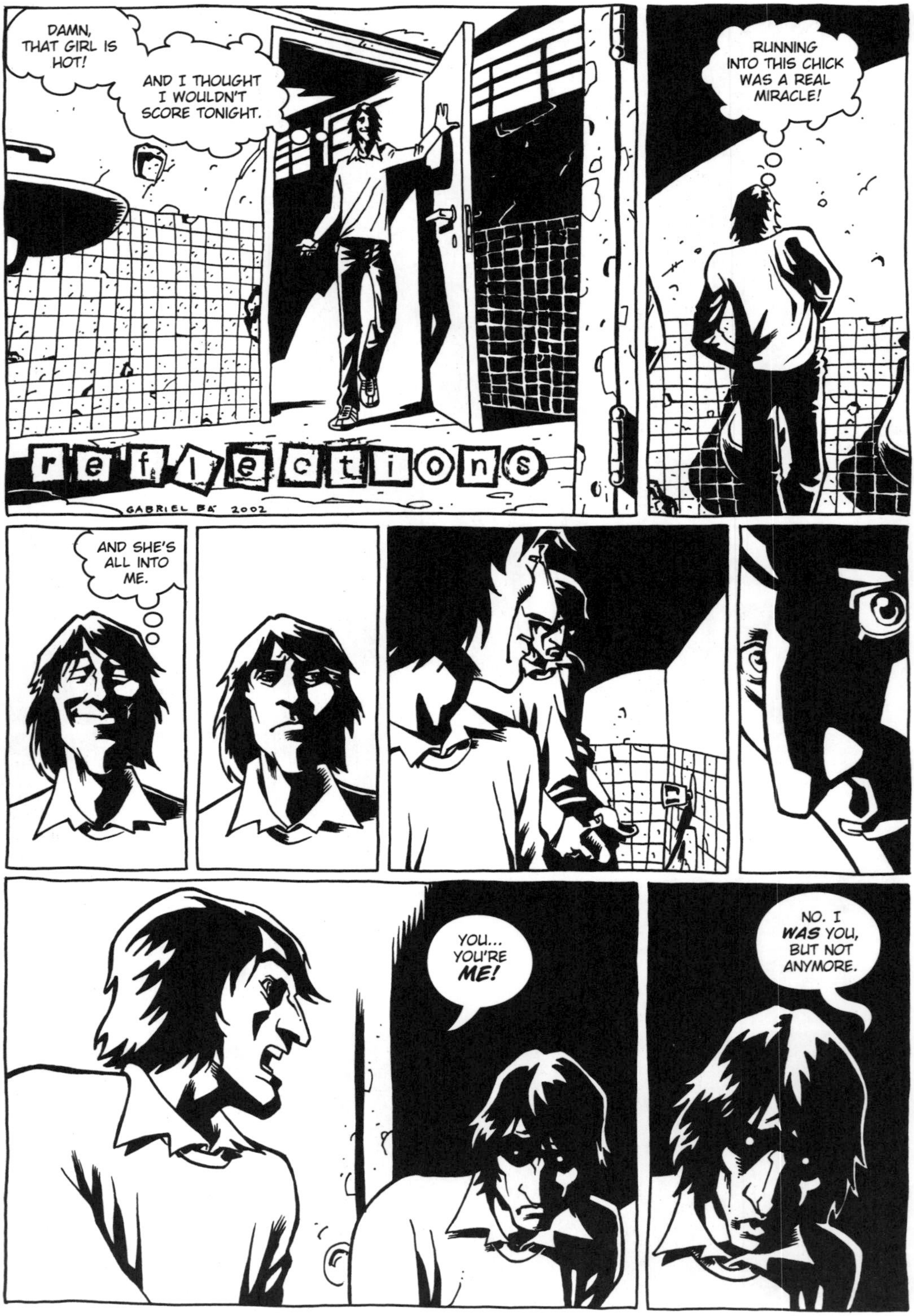
DAMN, THAT GIRL IS HOT!
AND I THOUGHT I WOULDN'T SCORE TONIGHT.
reflections
GABRIEL BÁ 2002
RUNNING INTO THIS CHICK WAS A REAL MIRACLE!
AND SHE'S ALL INTO ME.
YOU... YOU'RE **ME!**
NO. I **WAS** YOU, BUT NOT ANYMORE.

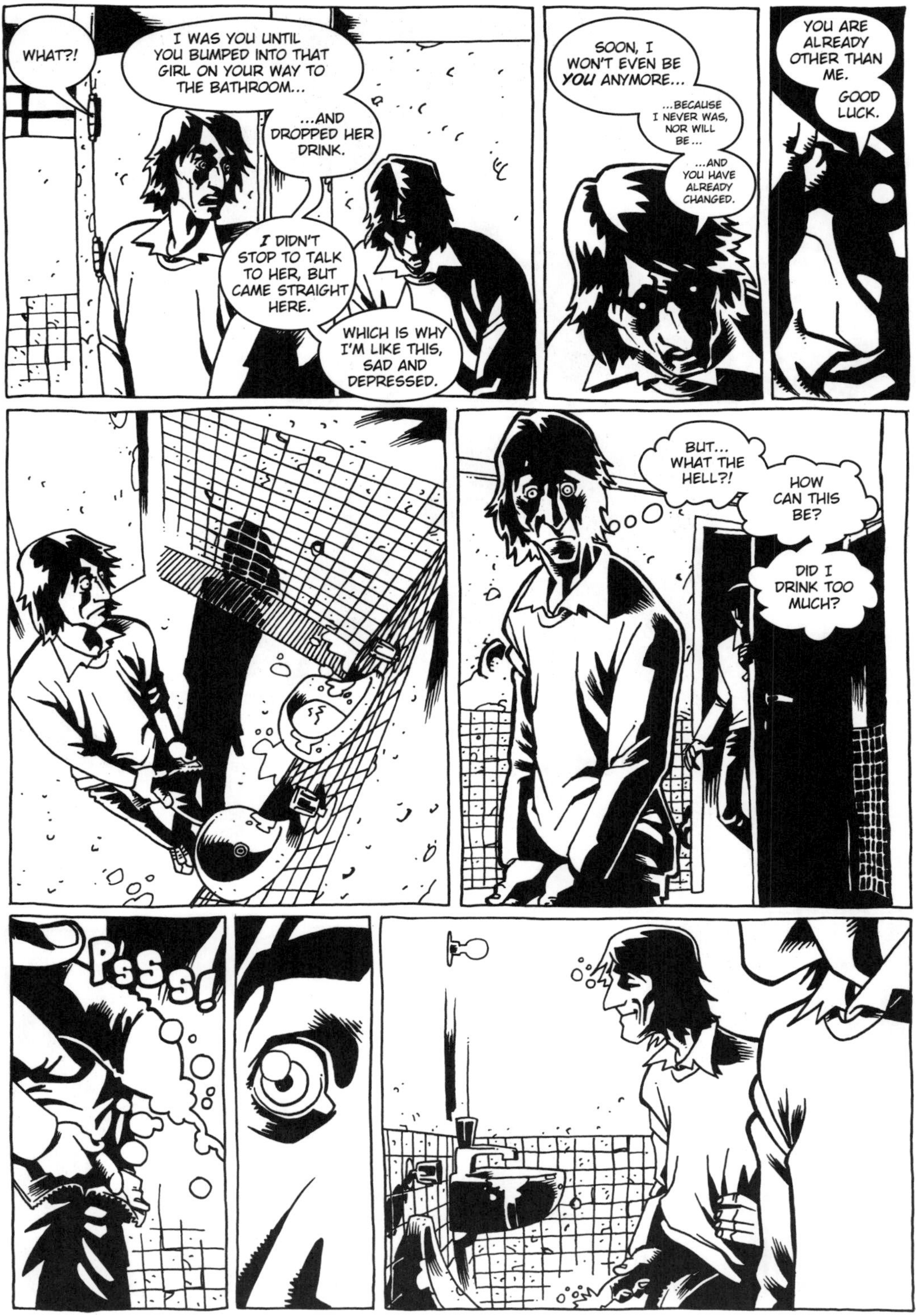
WHAT?!
I WAS YOU UNTIL YOU BUMPED INTO THAT GIRL ON YOUR WAY TO THE BATHROOM...
...AND DROPPED HER DRINK.
I DIDN'T STOP TO TALK TO HER, BUT CAME STRAIGHT HERE.
WHICH IS WHY I'M LIKE THIS, SAD AND DEPRESSED.
SOON, I WON'T EVEN BE YOU ANYMORE...
...BECAUSE I NEVER WAS, NOR WILL BE...
...AND YOU HAVE ALREADY CHANGED.
YOU ARE ALREADY OTHER THAN ME.
GOOD LUCK.
BUT... WHAT THE HELL?!
HOW CAN THIS BE?
DID I DRINK TOO MUCH?
PSSS!

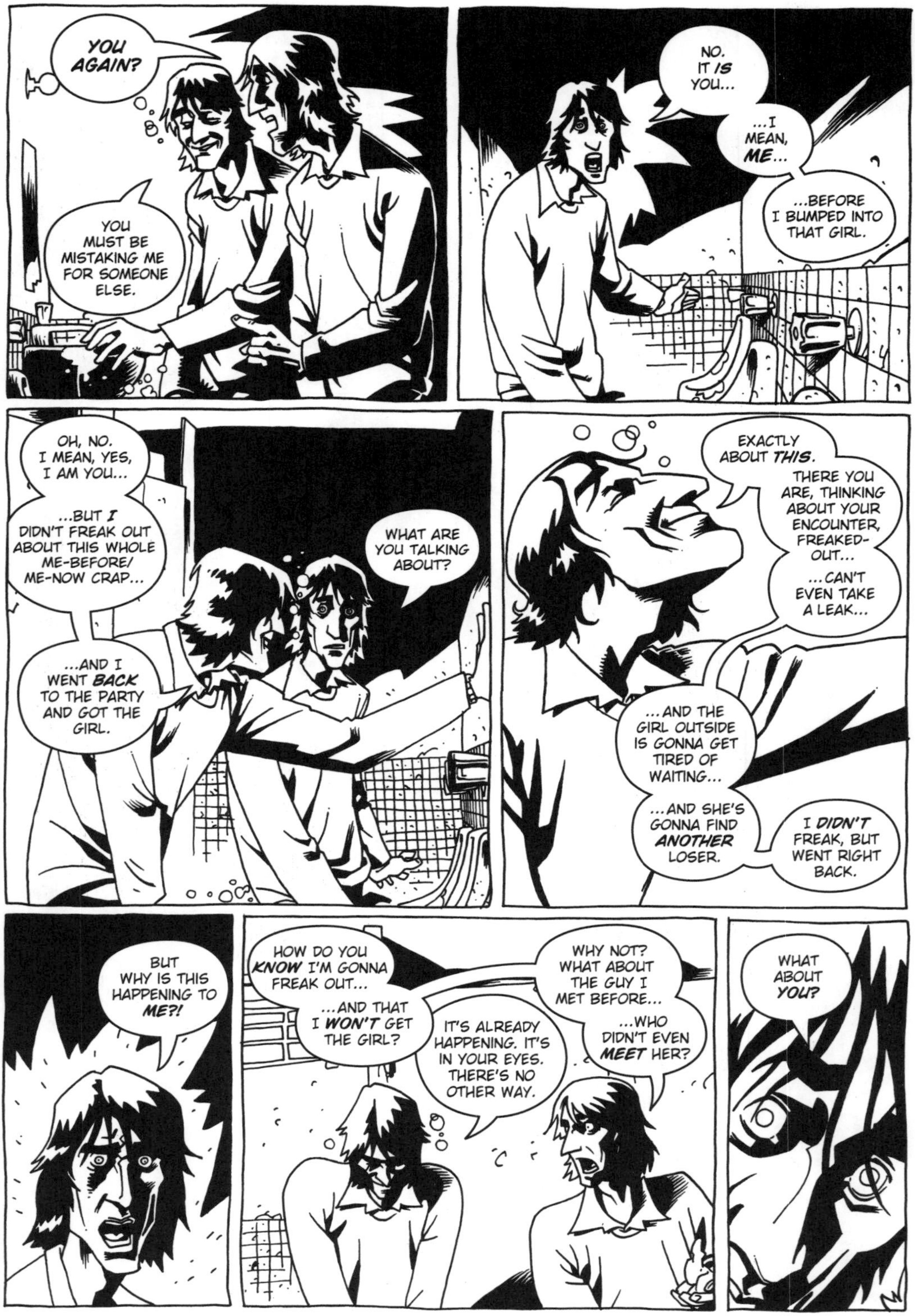
YOU AGAIN?
YOU MUST BE MISTAKING ME FOR SOMEONE ELSE.
NO. IT IS YOU...
...I MEAN, ME...
...BEFORE I BUMPED INTO THAT GIRL.
OH, NO. I MEAN, YES, I AM YOU...
...BUT I DIDN'T FREAK OUT ABOUT THIS WHOLE ME-BEFORE/ ME-NOW CRAP...
...AND I WENT BACK TO THE PARTY AND GOT THE GIRL.
WHAT ARE YOU TALKING ABOUT?
EXACTLY ABOUT THIS.
THERE YOU ARE, THINKING ABOUT YOUR ENCOUNTER, FREAKED-OUT...
...CAN'T EVEN TAKE A LEAK...
...AND THE GIRL OUTSIDE IS GONNA GET TIRED OF WAITING...
...AND SHE'S GONNA FIND ANOTHER LOSER.
I DIDN'T FREAK, BUT WENT RIGHT BACK.
BUT WHY IS THIS HAPPENING TO ME?!
HOW DO YOU KNOW I'M GONNA FREAK OUT...
...AND THAT I WON'T GET THE GIRL?
IT'S ALREADY HAPPENING. IT'S IN YOUR EYES. THERE'S NO OTHER WAY.
WHY NOT? WHAT ABOUT THE GUY I MET BEFORE...
...WHO DIDN'T EVEN MEET HER?
WHAT ABOUT YOU?

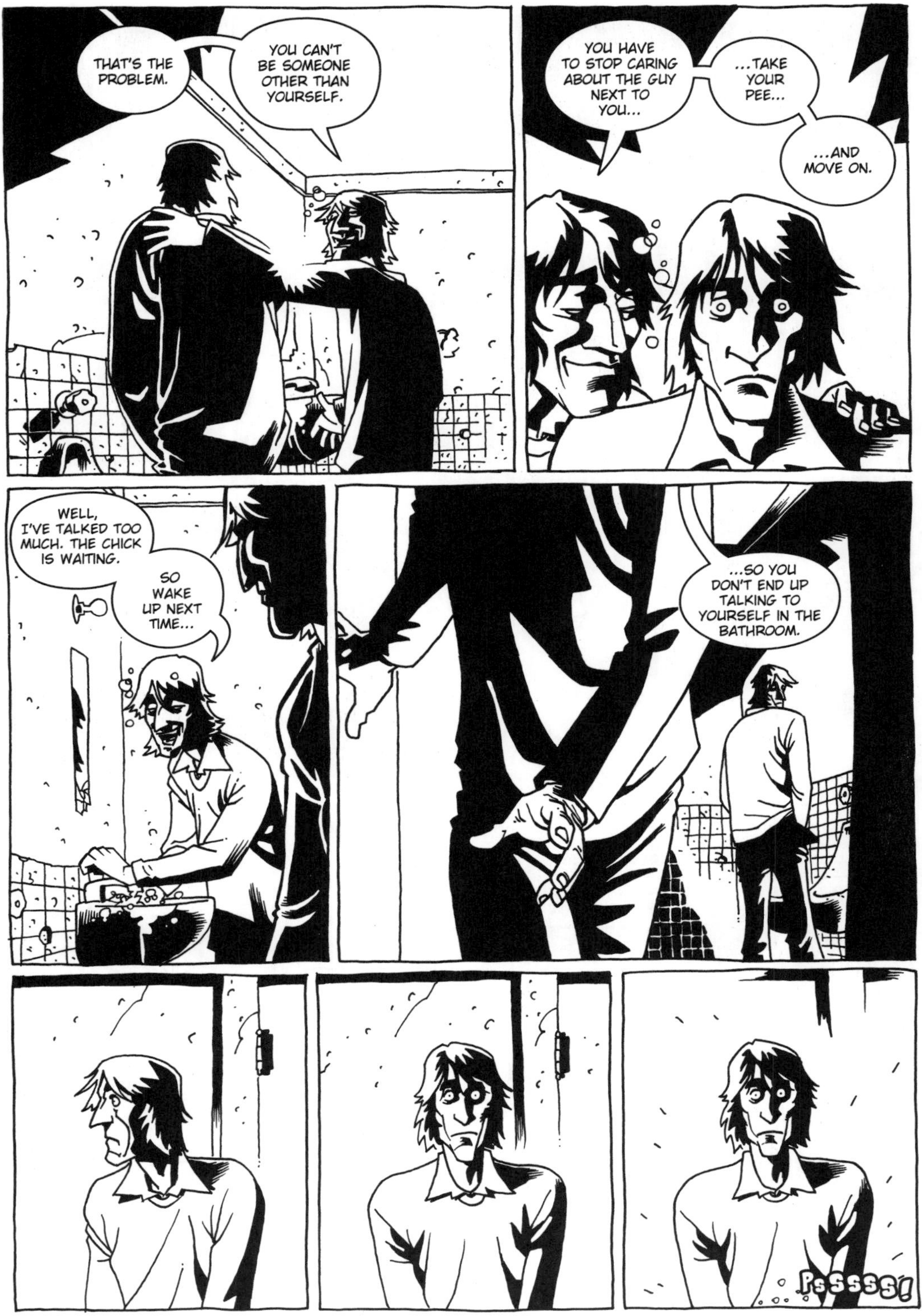
THAT'S THE PROBLEM.
YOU CAN'T BE SOMEONE OTHER THAN YOURSELF.
YOU HAVE TO STOP CARING ABOUT THE GUY NEXT TO YOU...
...TAKE YOUR PEE...
...AND MOVE ON.
WELL, I'VE TALKED TOO MUCH. THE CHICK IS WAITING.
SO WAKE UP NEXT TIME...
...SO YOU DON'T END UP TALKING TO YOURSELF IN THE BATHROOM.
PSSSSS!

end of the second version.

ALL YOU NEED IS LOVE

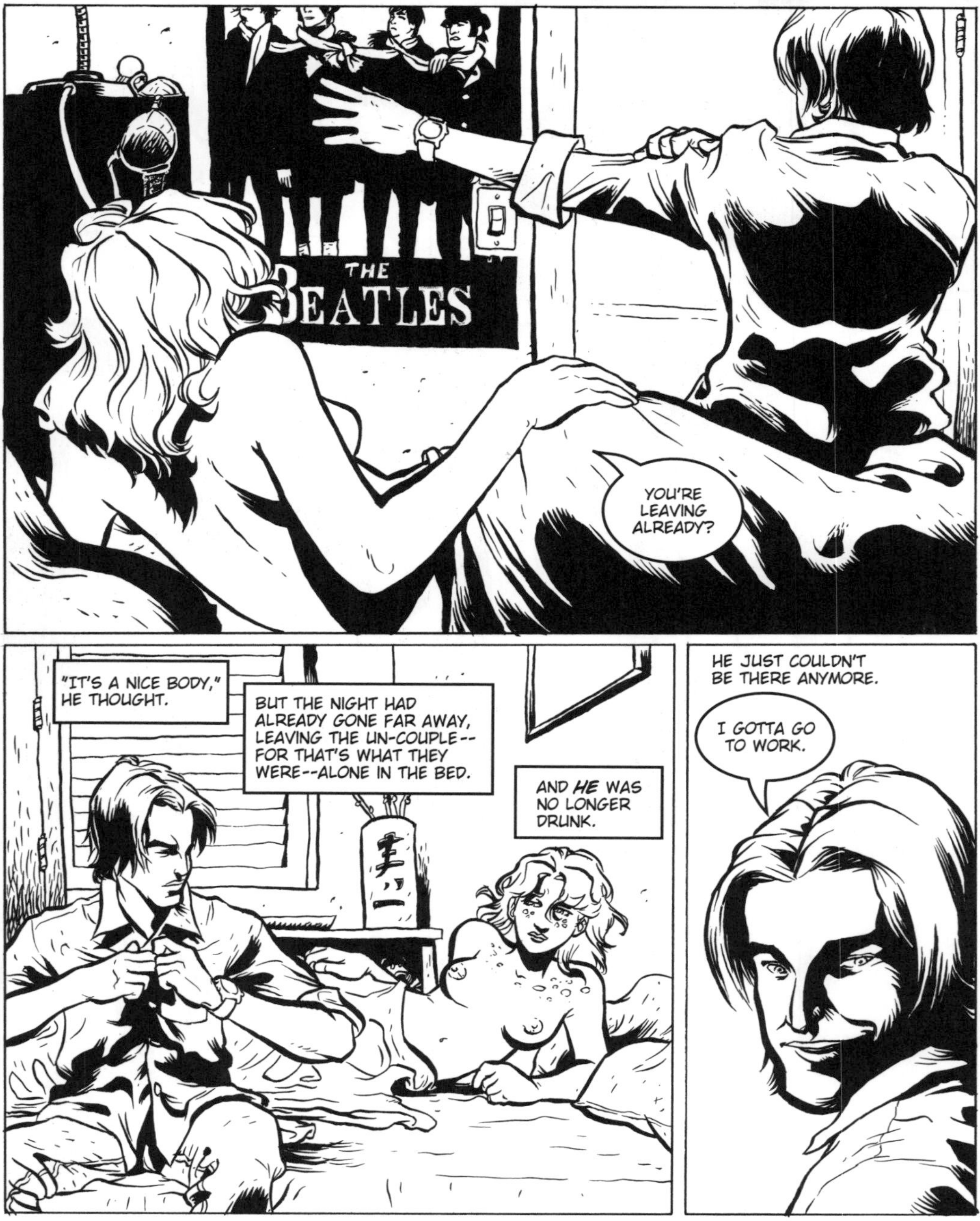

THE BEATLES
YOU'RE LEAVING ALREADY?
"IT'S A NICE BODY," HE THOUGHT.
BUT THE NIGHT HAD ALREADY GONE FAR AWAY, LEAVING THE UN-COUPLE--FOR THAT'S WHAT THEY WERE--ALONE IN THE BED.
AND *HE* WAS NO LONGER DRUNK.
HE JUST COULDN'T BE THERE ANYMORE.
I GOTTA GO TO WORK.

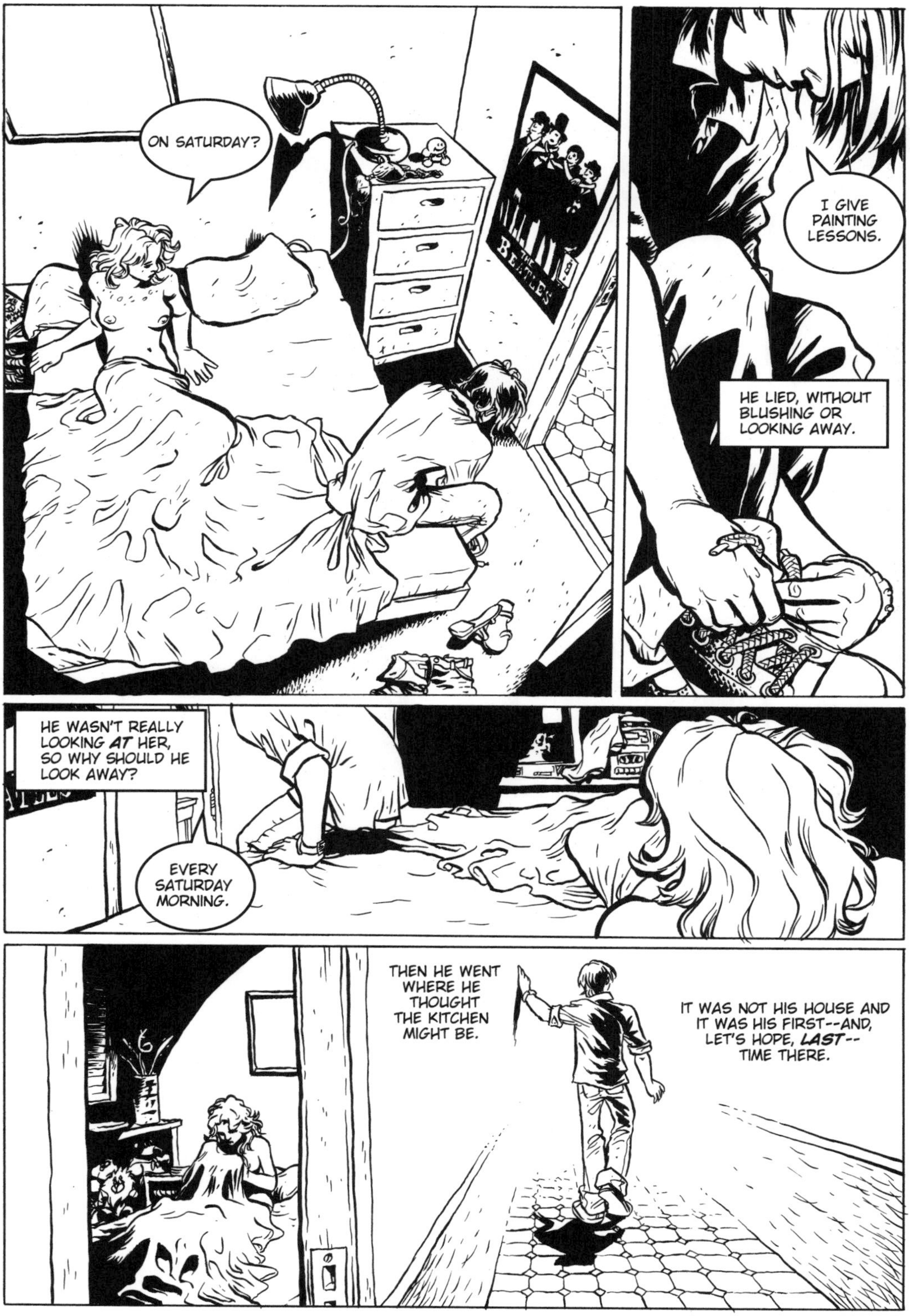
ON SATURDAY?
I GIVE PAINTING LESSONS.
HE LIED, WITHOUT BLUSHING OR LOOKING AWAY.
HE WASN'T REALLY LOOKING **AT** HER, SO WHY SHOULD HE LOOK AWAY?
EVERY SATURDAY MORNING.
THEN HE WENT WHERE HE THOUGHT THE KITCHEN MIGHT BE.
IT WAS NOT HIS HOUSE AND IT WAS HIS FIRST--AND, LET'S HOPE, **LAST**--TIME THERE.

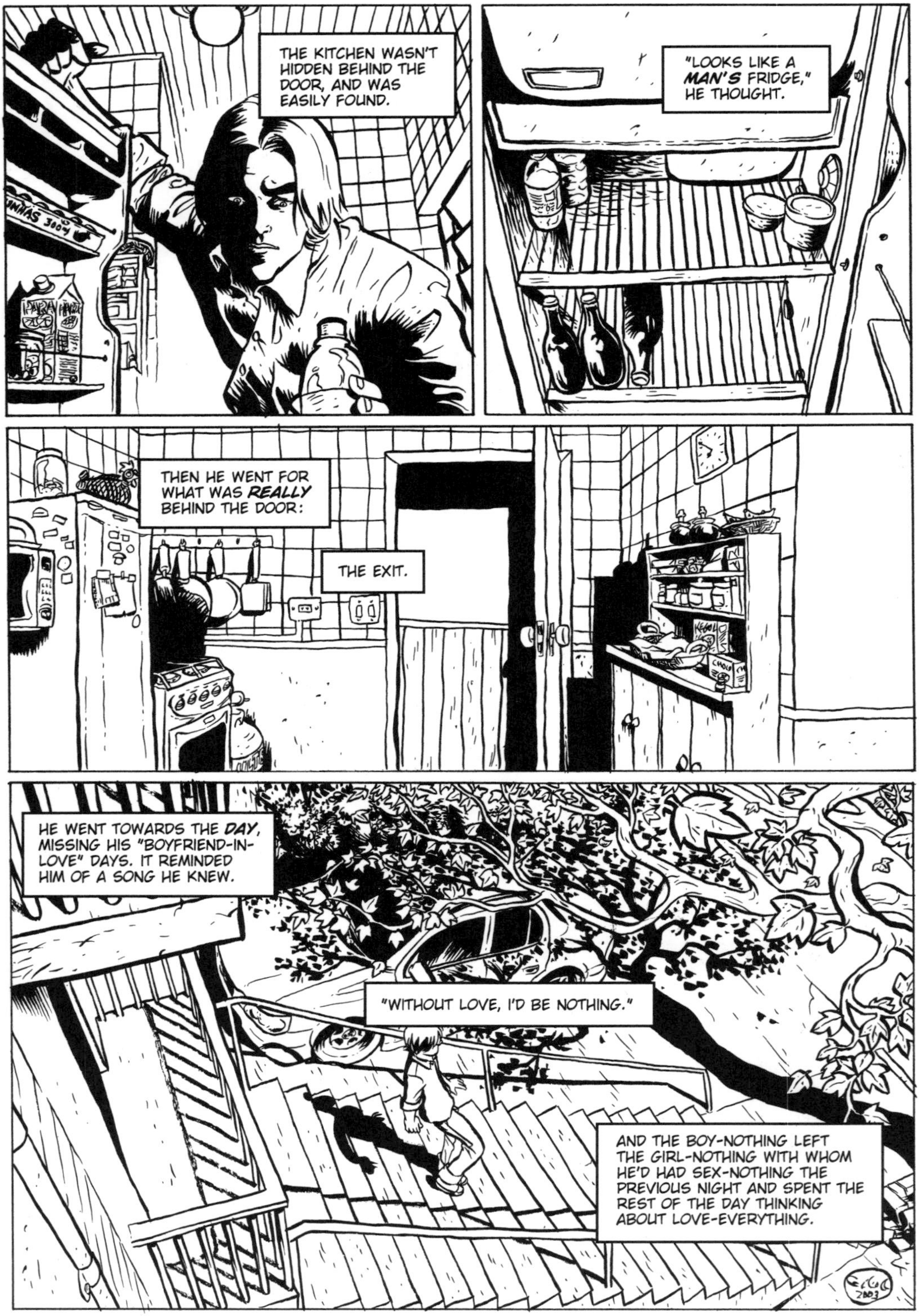
THE KITCHEN WASN'T HIDDEN BEHIND THE DOOR, AND WAS EASILY FOUND.
"LOOKS LIKE A *MAN'S* FRIDGE," HE THOUGHT.
THEN HE WENT FOR WHAT WAS *REALLY* BEHIND THE DOOR:
THE EXIT.
HE WENT TOWARDS THE *DAY*, MISSING HIS "BOYFRIEND-IN-LOVE" DAYS. IT REMINDED HIM OF A SONG HE KNEW.
"WITHOUT LOVE, I'D BE NOTHING."
AND THE BOY-NOTHING LEFT THE GIRL-NOTHING WITH WHOM HE'D HAD SEX-NOTHING THE PREVIOUS NIGHT AND SPENT THE REST OF THE DAY THINKING ABOUT LOVE-EVERYTHING.

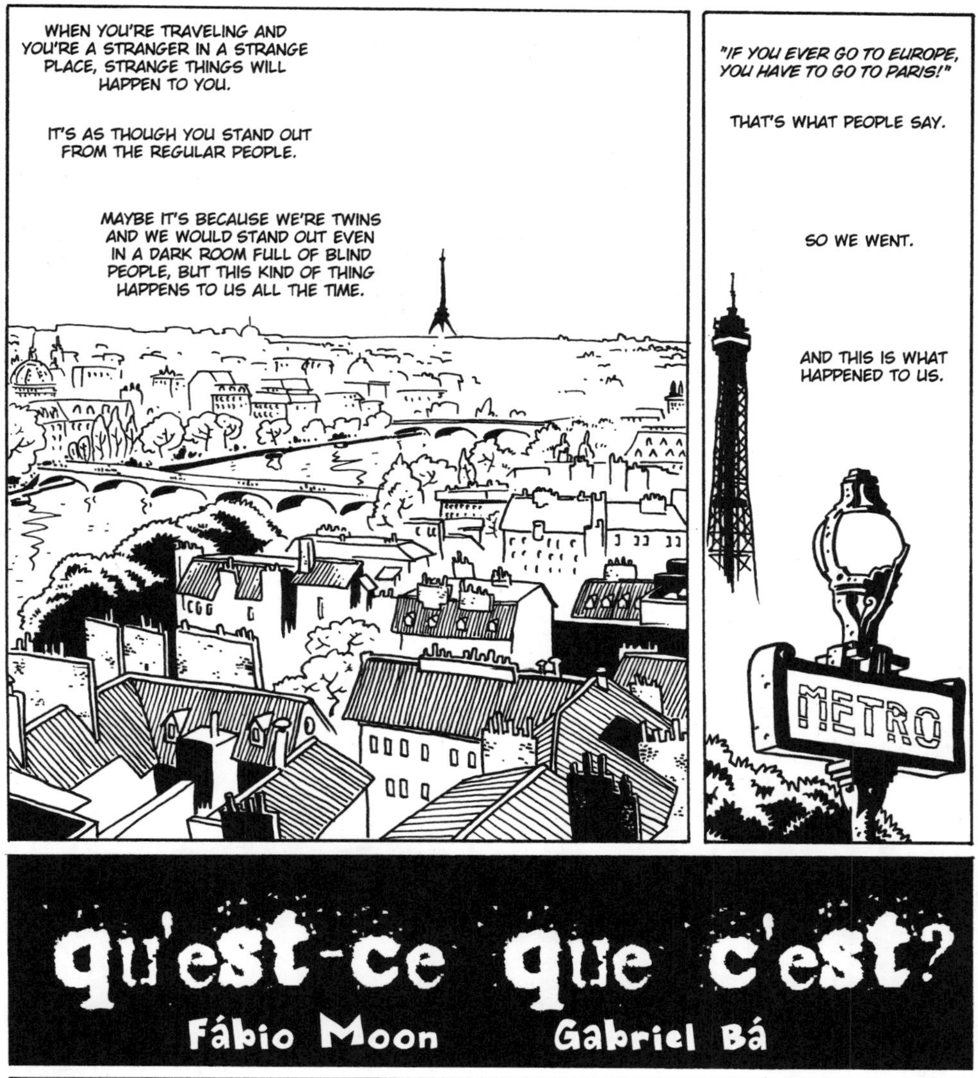
WHEN YOU'RE TRAVELING AND YOU'RE A STRANGER IN A STRANGE PLACE, STRANGE THINGS WILL HAPPEN TO YOU.
IT'S AS THOUGH YOU STAND OUT FROM THE REGULAR PEOPLE.
MAYBE IT'S BECAUSE WE'RE TWINS AND WE WOULD STAND OUT EVEN IN A DARK ROOM FULL OF BLIND PEOPLE, BUT THIS KIND OF THING HAPPENS TO US ALL THE TIME.
"IF YOU EVER GO TO EUROPE, YOU HAVE TO GO TO PARIS!"
THAT'S WHAT PEOPLE SAY.
SO WE WENT.
AND THIS IS WHAT HAPPENED TO US.
METRO

qu'est-ce que c'est?

Fábio Moon Gabriel Bá

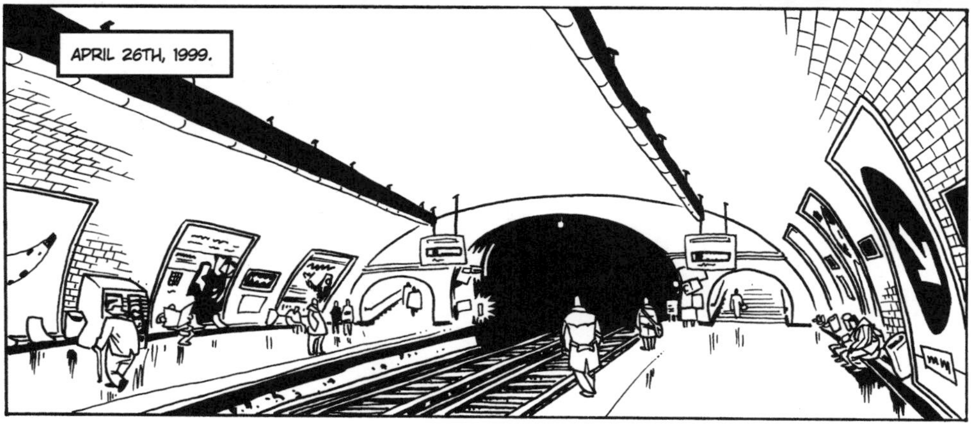
APRIL 26TH, 1999.

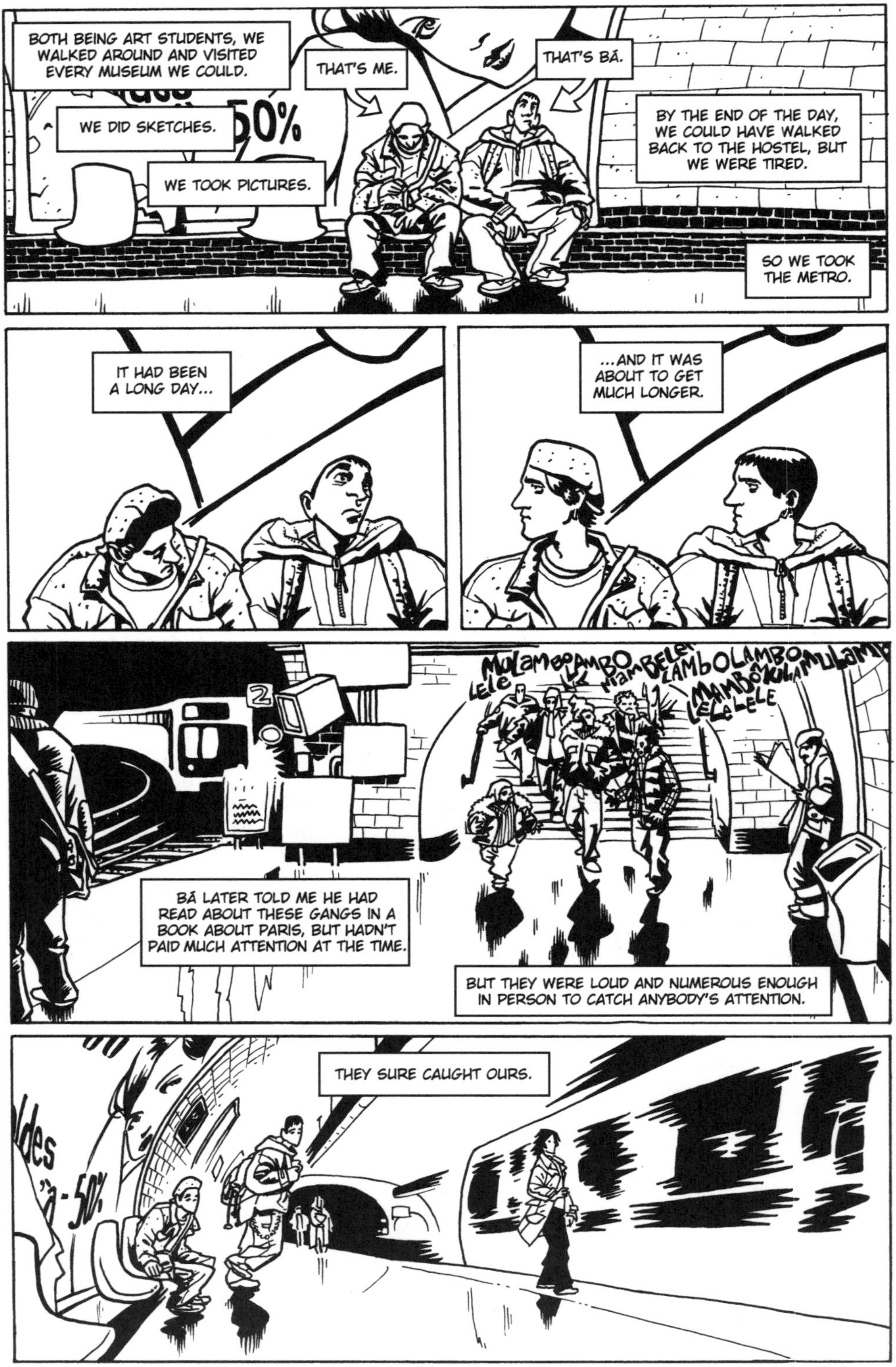
BOTH BEING ART STUDENTS, WE WALKED AROUND AND VISITED EVERY MUSEUM WE COULD.
WE DID SKETCHES.
WE TOOK PICTURES.
THAT'S ME.
THAT'S BÁ.
BY THE END OF THE DAY, WE COULD HAVE WALKED BACK TO THE HOSTEL, BUT WE WERE TIRED.
SO WE TOOK THE METRO.
IT HAD BEEN A LONG DAY...
...AND IT WAS ABOUT TO GET MUCH LONGER.
LELE
LAMBOLAMBO
LELELELE
BÁ LATER TOLD ME HE HAD READ ABOUT THESE GANGS IN A BOOK ABOUT PARIS, BUT HADN'T PAID MUCH ATTENTION AT THE TIME.
BUT THEY WERE LOUD AND NUMEROUS ENOUGH IN PERSON TO CATCH ANYBODY'S ATTENTION.
THEY SURE CAUGHT OURS.

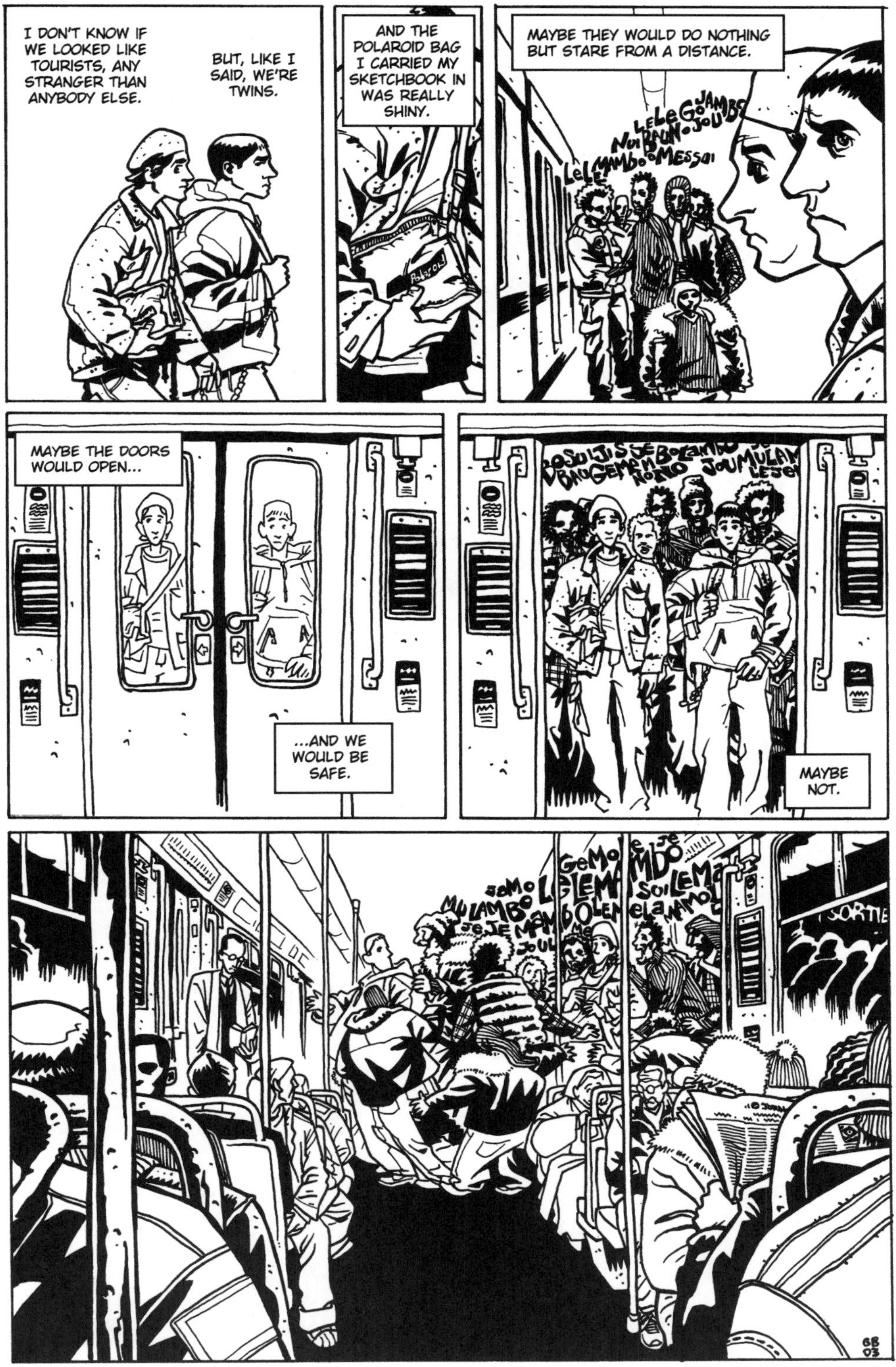
I DON'T KNOW IF WE LOOKED LIKE TOURISTS, ANY STRANGER THAN ANYBODY ELSE.
BUT, LIKE I SAID, WE'RE TWINS.
AND THE POLAROID BAG I CARRIED MY SKETCHBOOK IN WAS REALLY SHINY.
MAYBE THEY WOULD DO NOTHING BUT STARE FROM A DISTANCE.
MAYBE THE DOORS WOULD OPEN...
...AND WE WOULD BE SAFE.
MAYBE NOT.
SORTIE
GB 03

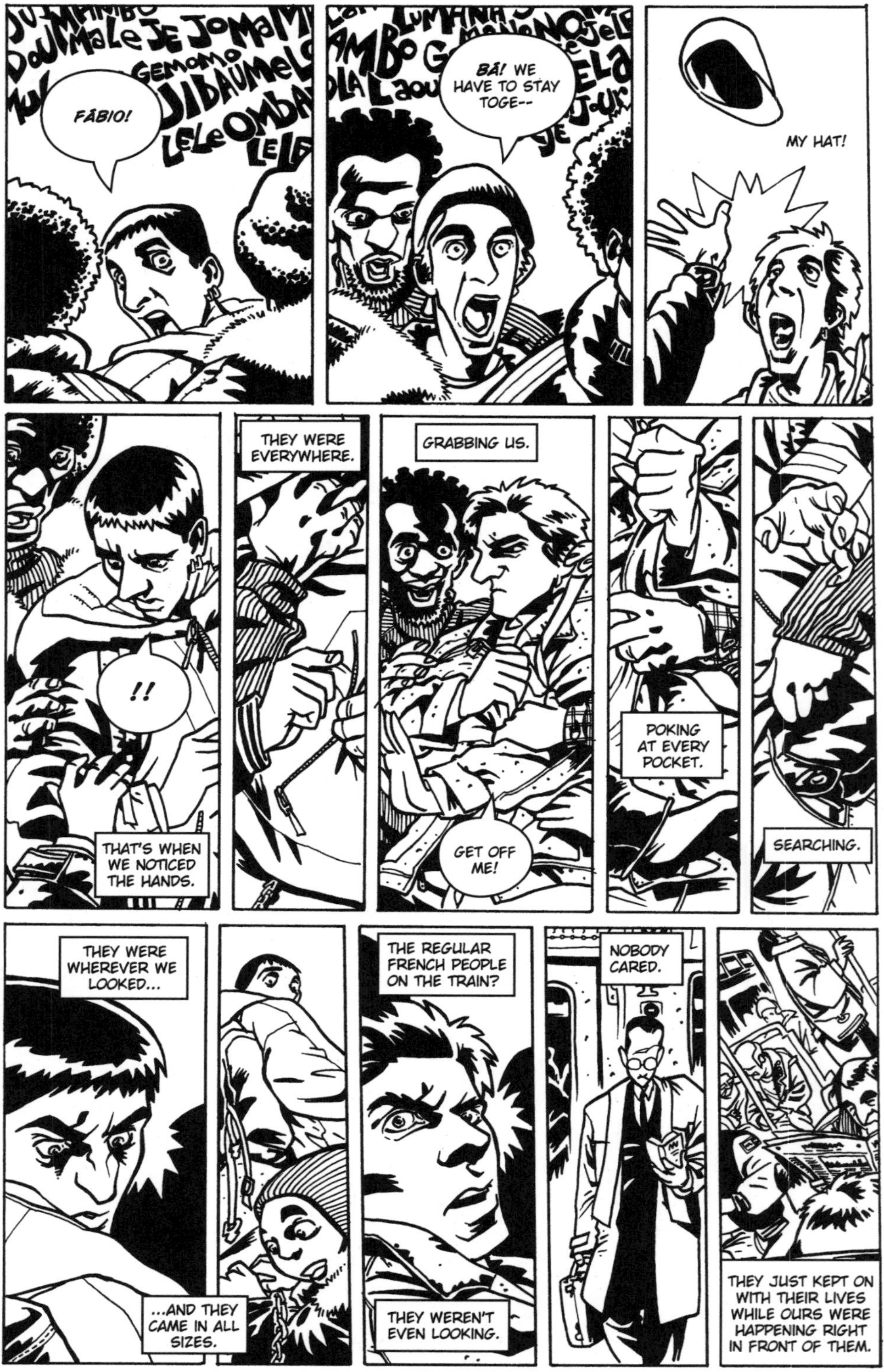
FÂBIO!
BÂ! WE HAVE TO STAY TOGE--
MY HAT!
!!
THAT'S WHEN WE NOTICED THE HANDS.
THEY WERE EVERYWHERE.
GRABBING US.
GET OFF ME!
POKING AT EVERY POCKET.
SEARCHING.
THEY WERE WHEREVER WE LOOKED...
...AND THEY CAME IN ALL SIZES.
THE REGULAR FRENCH PEOPLE ON THE TRAIN?
THEY WEREN'T EVEN LOOKING.
NOBODY CARED.
THEY JUST KEPT ON WITH THEIR LIVES WHILE OURS WERE HAPPENING RIGHT IN FRONT OF THEM.

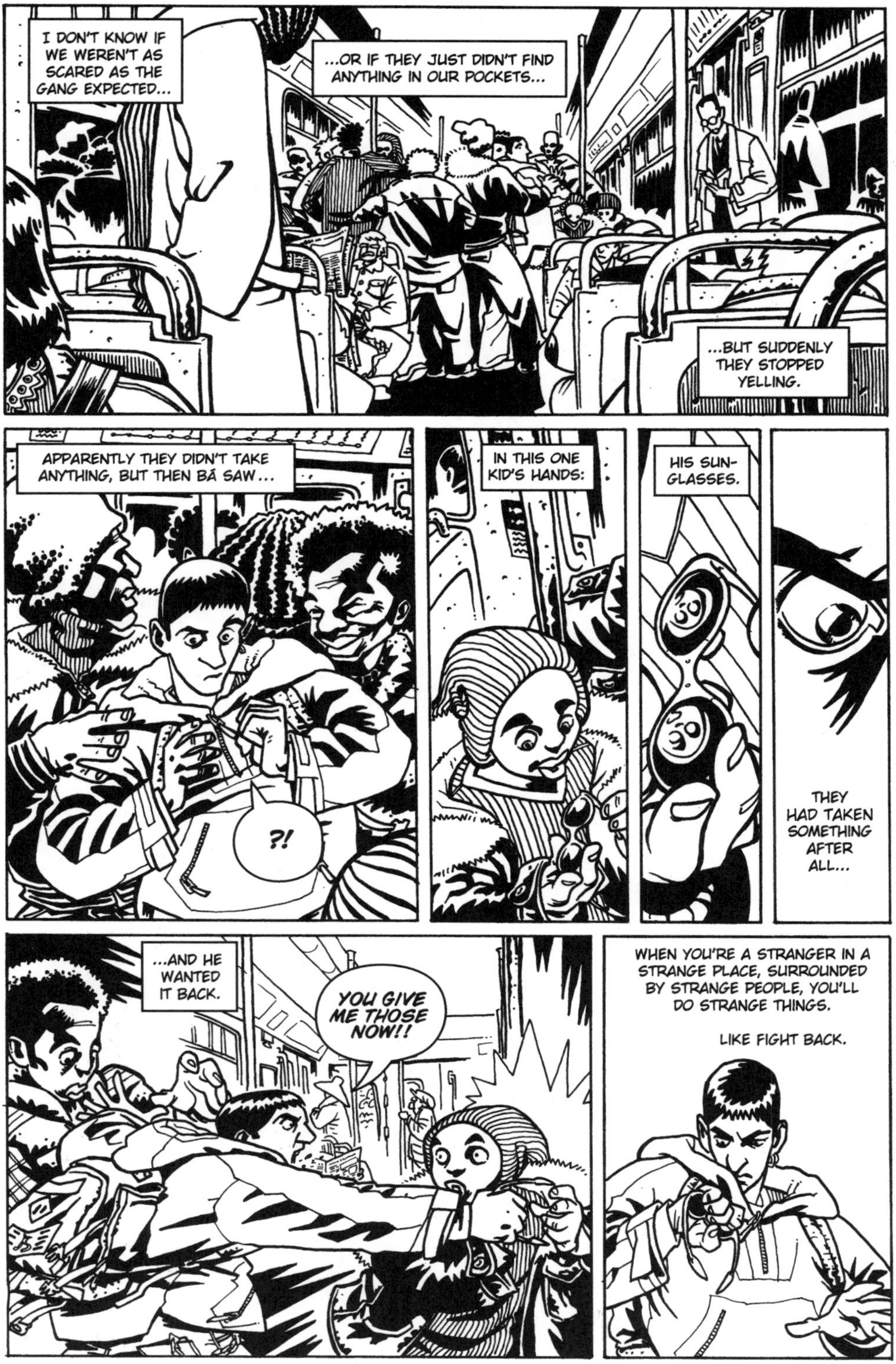
I DON'T KNOW IF WE WEREN'T AS SCARED AS THE GANG EXPECTED...
...OR IF THEY JUST DIDN'T FIND ANYTHING IN OUR POCKETS...
...BUT SUDDENLY THEY STOPPED YELLING.
APPARENTLY THEY DIDN'T TAKE ANYTHING, BUT THEN BÁ SAW...
?!
IN THIS ONE KID'S HANDS:
HIS SUN-GLASSES.
THEY HAD TAKEN SOMETHING AFTER ALL...
...AND HE WANTED IT BACK.
YOU GIVE ME THOSE NOW!!
WHEN YOU'RE A STRANGER IN A STRANGE PLACE, SURROUNDED BY STRANGE PEOPLE, YOU'LL DO STRANGE THINGS.
LIKE FIGHT BACK.

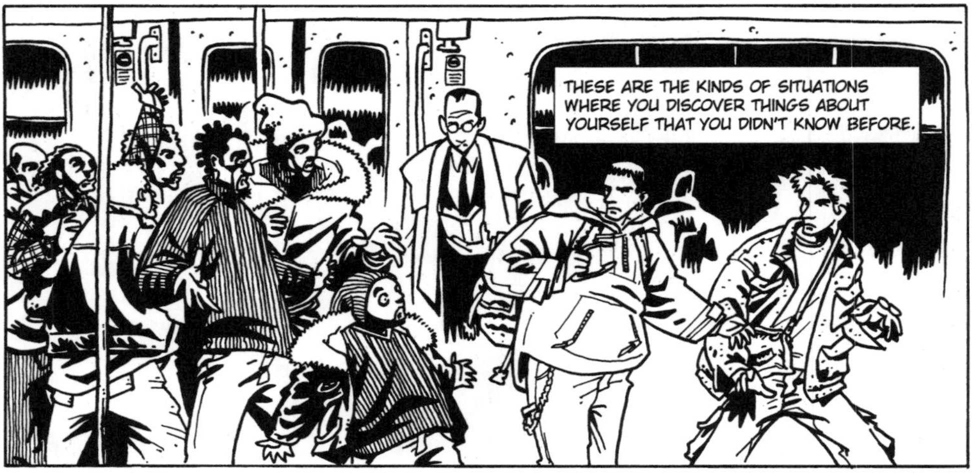
THESE ARE THE KINDS OF SITUATIONS WHERE YOU DISCOVER THINGS ABOUT YOURSELF THAT YOU DIDN'T KNOW BEFORE.

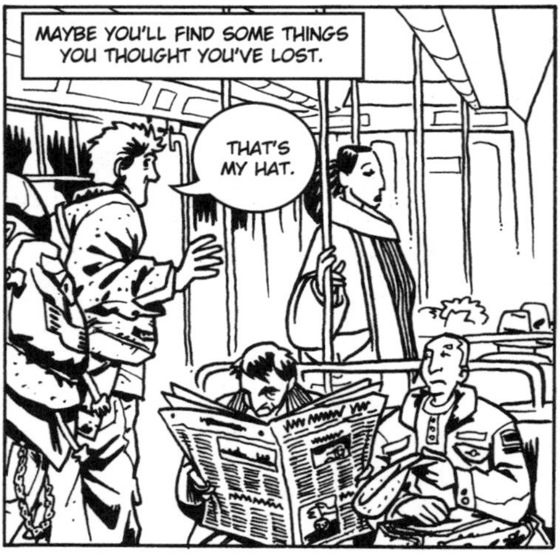
MAYBE YOU'LL FIND SOME THINGS YOU THOUGHT YOU'VE LOST.
THAT'S MY HAT.

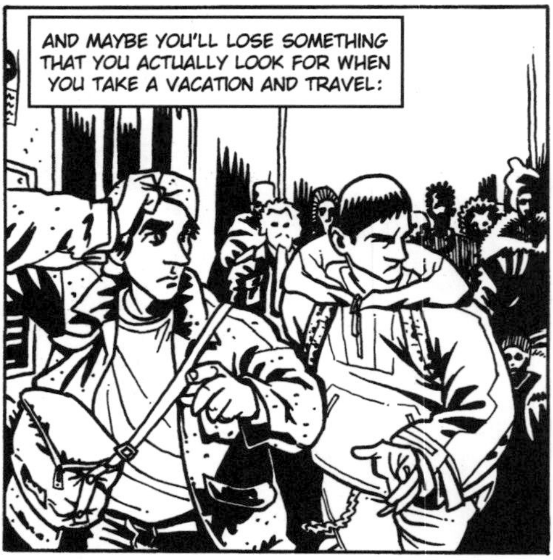
AND MAYBE YOU'LL LOSE SOMETHING THAT YOU ACTUALLY LOOK FOR WHEN YOU TAKE A VACATION AND TRAVEL:

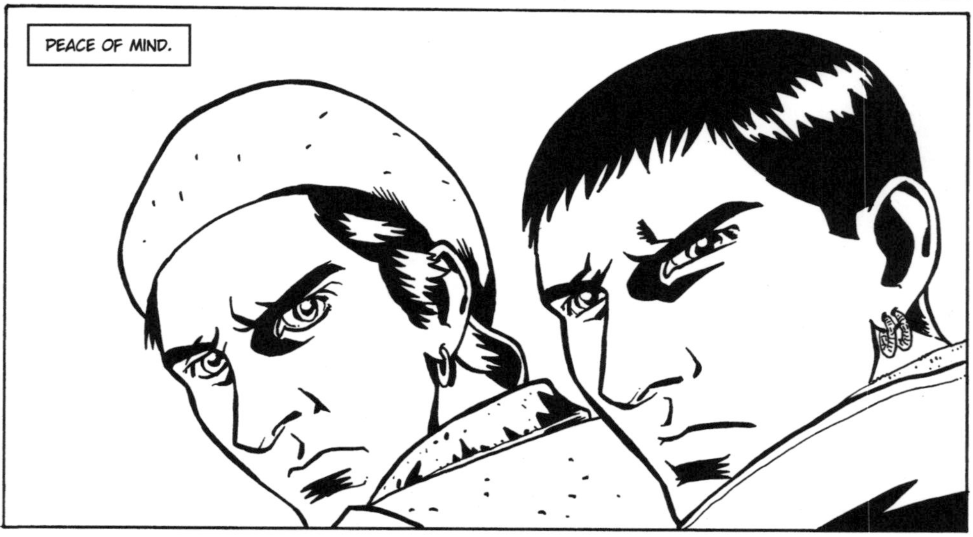
PEACE OF MIND.

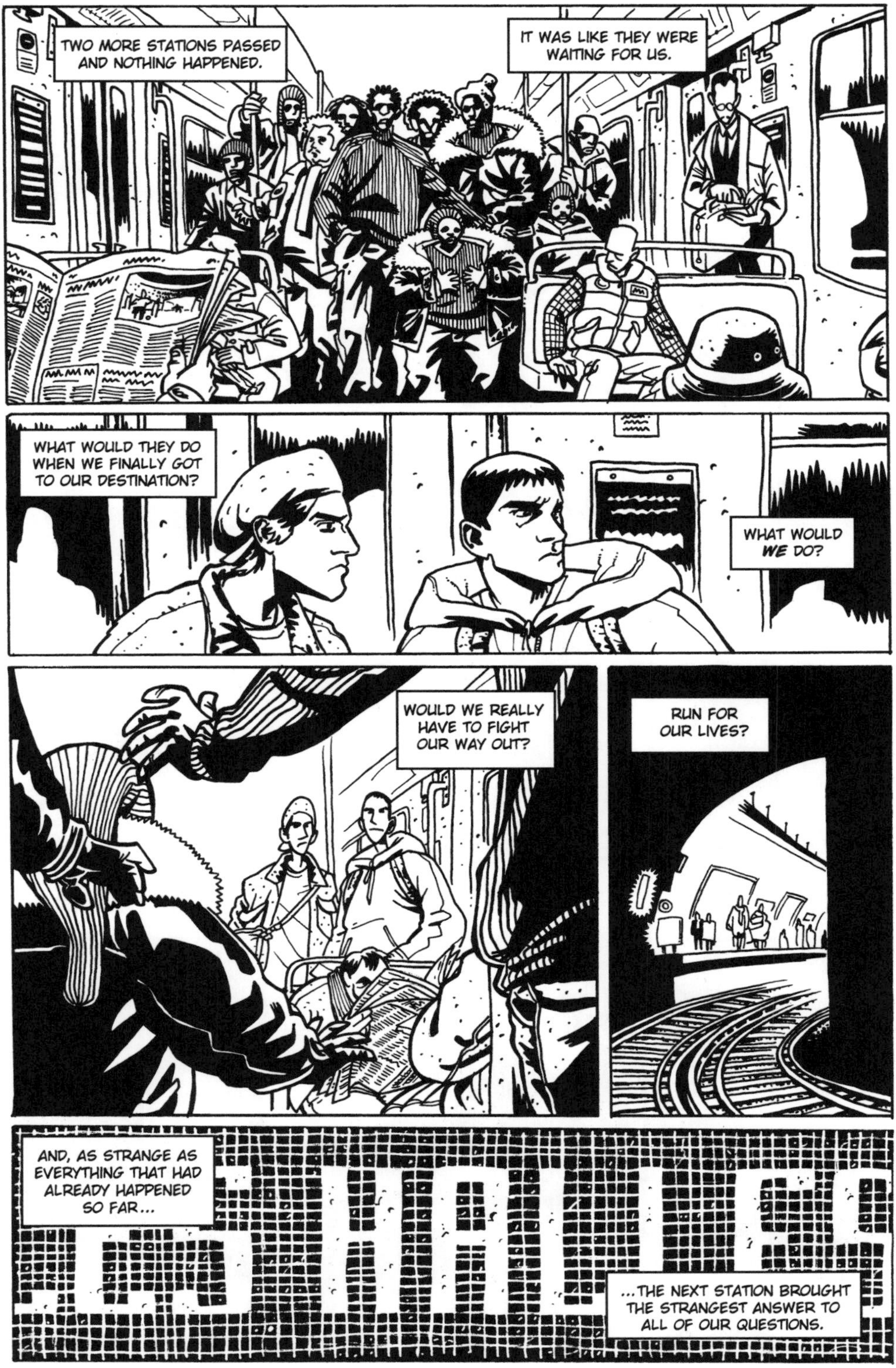
TWO MORE STATIONS PASSED AND NOTHING HAPPENED.
IT WAS LIKE THEY WERE WAITING FOR US.
WHAT WOULD THEY DO WHEN WE FINALLY GOT TO OUR DESTINATION?
WHAT WOULD *WE* DO?
WOULD WE REALLY HAVE TO FIGHT OUR WAY OUT?
RUN FOR OUR LIVES?
AND, AS STRANGE AS EVERYTHING THAT HAD ALREADY HAPPENED SO FAR...
...THE NEXT STATION BROUGHT THE STRANGEST ANSWER TO ALL OF OUR QUESTIONS.

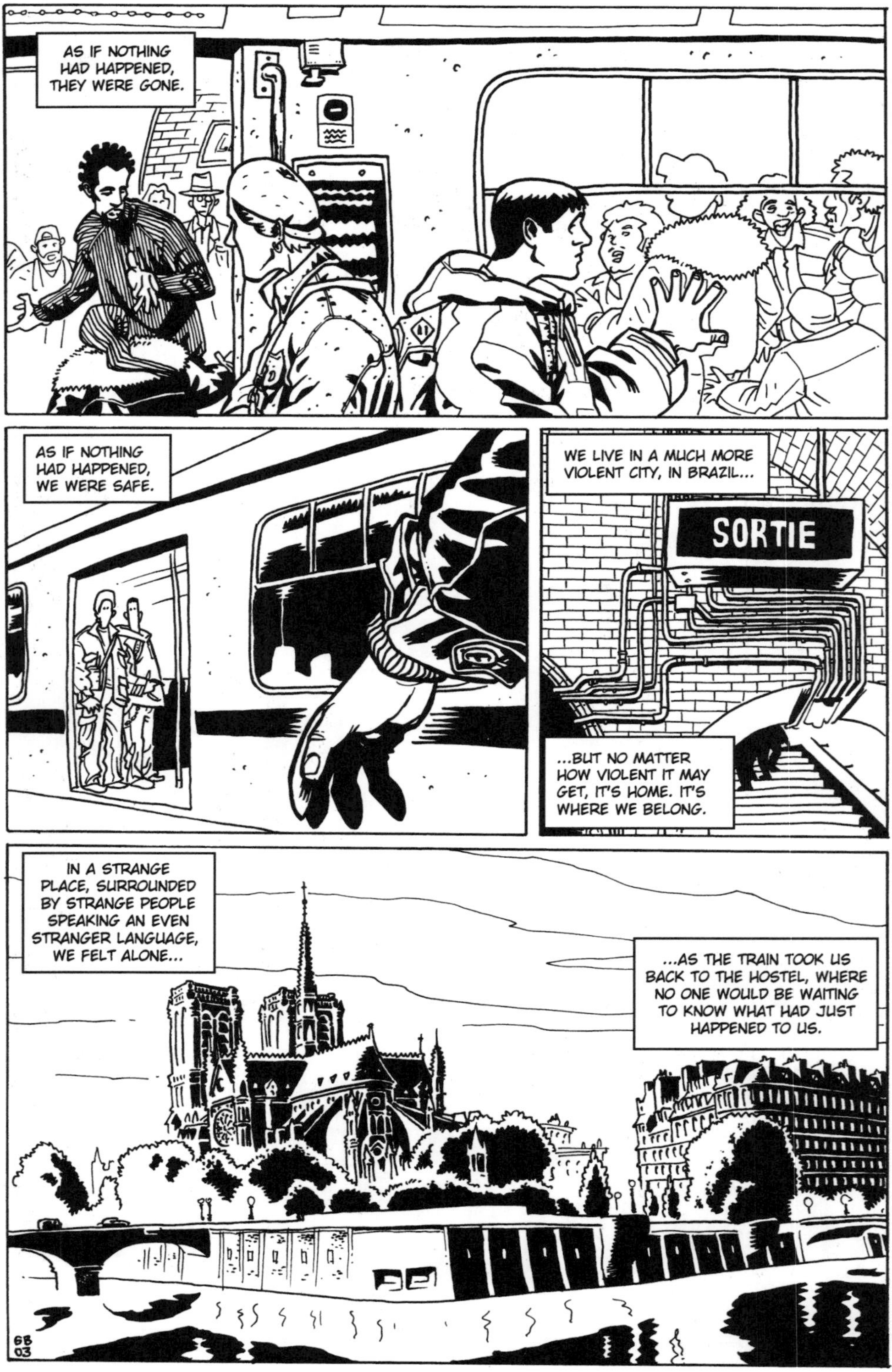
AS IF NOTHING HAD HAPPENED, THEY WERE GONE.
AS IF NOTHING HAD HAPPENED, WE WERE SAFE.
WE LIVE IN A MUCH MORE VIOLENT CITY, IN BRAZIL...
SORTIE
...BUT NO MATTER HOW VIOLENT IT MAY GET, IT'S HOME. IT'S WHERE WE BELONG.
IN A STRANGE PLACE, SURROUNDED BY STRANGE PEOPLE SPEAKING AN EVEN STRANGER LANGUAGE, WE FELT ALONE...
...AS THE TRAIN TOOK US BACK TO THE HOSTEL, WHERE NO ONE WOULD BE WAITING TO KNOW WHAT HAD JUST HAPPENED TO US.
GB 03

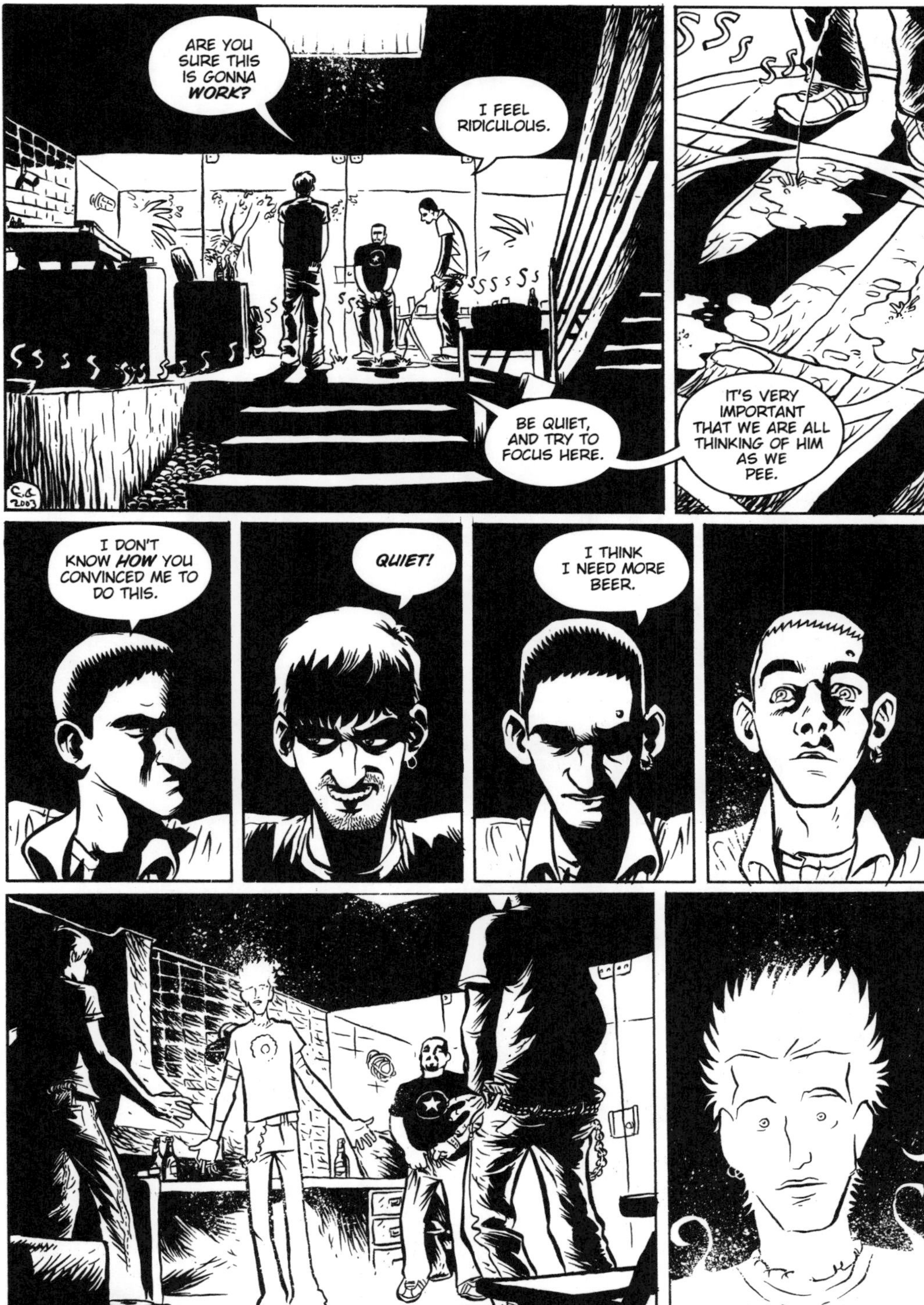
ARE YOU SURE THIS IS GONNA *WORK?*
I FEEL RIDICULOUS.
BE QUIET, AND TRY TO FOCUS HERE.
IT'S VERY IMPORTANT THAT WE ARE ALL THINKING OF HIM AS WE PEE.
I DON'T KNOW *HOW* YOU CONVINCED ME TO DO THIS.
QUIET!
I THINK I NEED MORE BEER.

HAPPY BIRTHDAY, MY FRIEND!

by Fábio Moon and Gabriel Bá

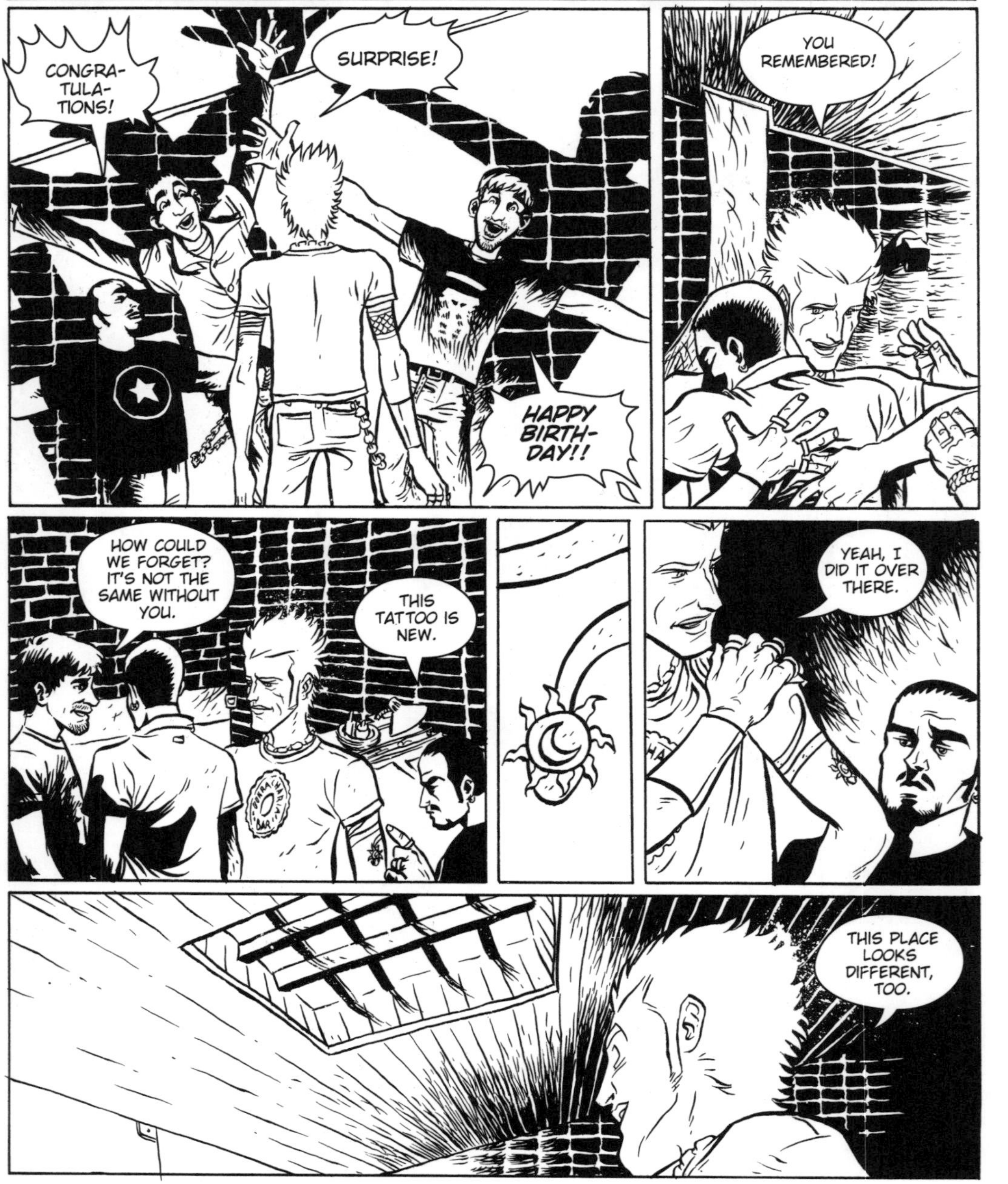
CONGRATULATIONS!
SURPRISE!
HAPPY BIRTHDAY!!
YOU REMEMBERED!
HOW COULD WE FORGET? IT'S NOT THE SAME WITHOUT YOU.
THIS TATTOO IS NEW.
YEAH, I DID IT OVER THERE.
THIS PLACE LOOKS DIFFERENT, TOO.

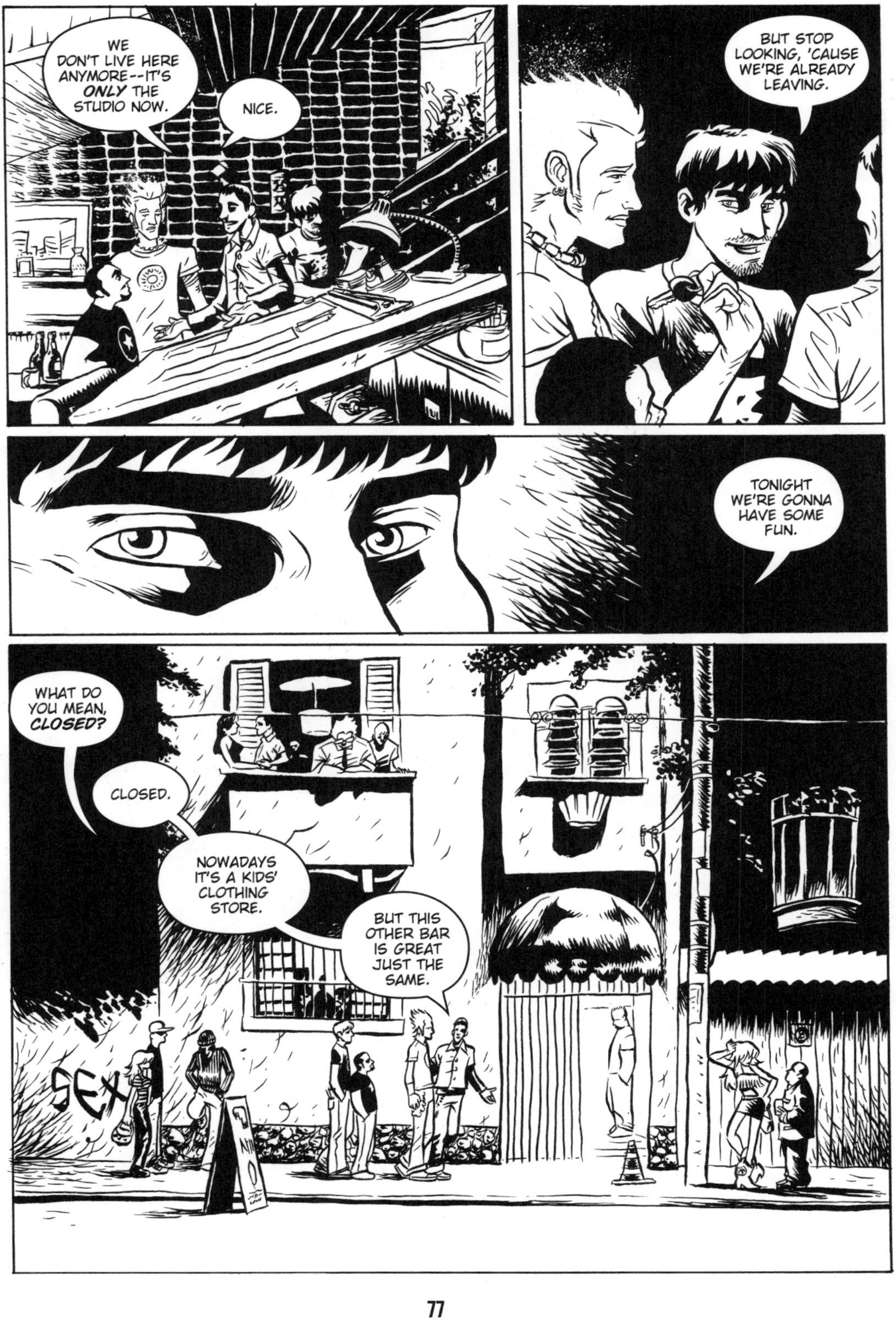

WE DON'T LIVE HERE ANYMORE--IT'S *ONLY* THE STUDIO NOW.
NICE.
BUT STOP LOOKING, 'CAUSE WE'RE ALREADY LEAVING.
TONIGHT WE'RE GONNA HAVE SOME FUN.
WHAT DO YOU MEAN, *CLOSED?*
CLOSED.
NOWADAYS IT'S A KIDS' CLOTHING STORE.
BUT THIS OTHER BAR IS GREAT JUST THE SAME.
SEX

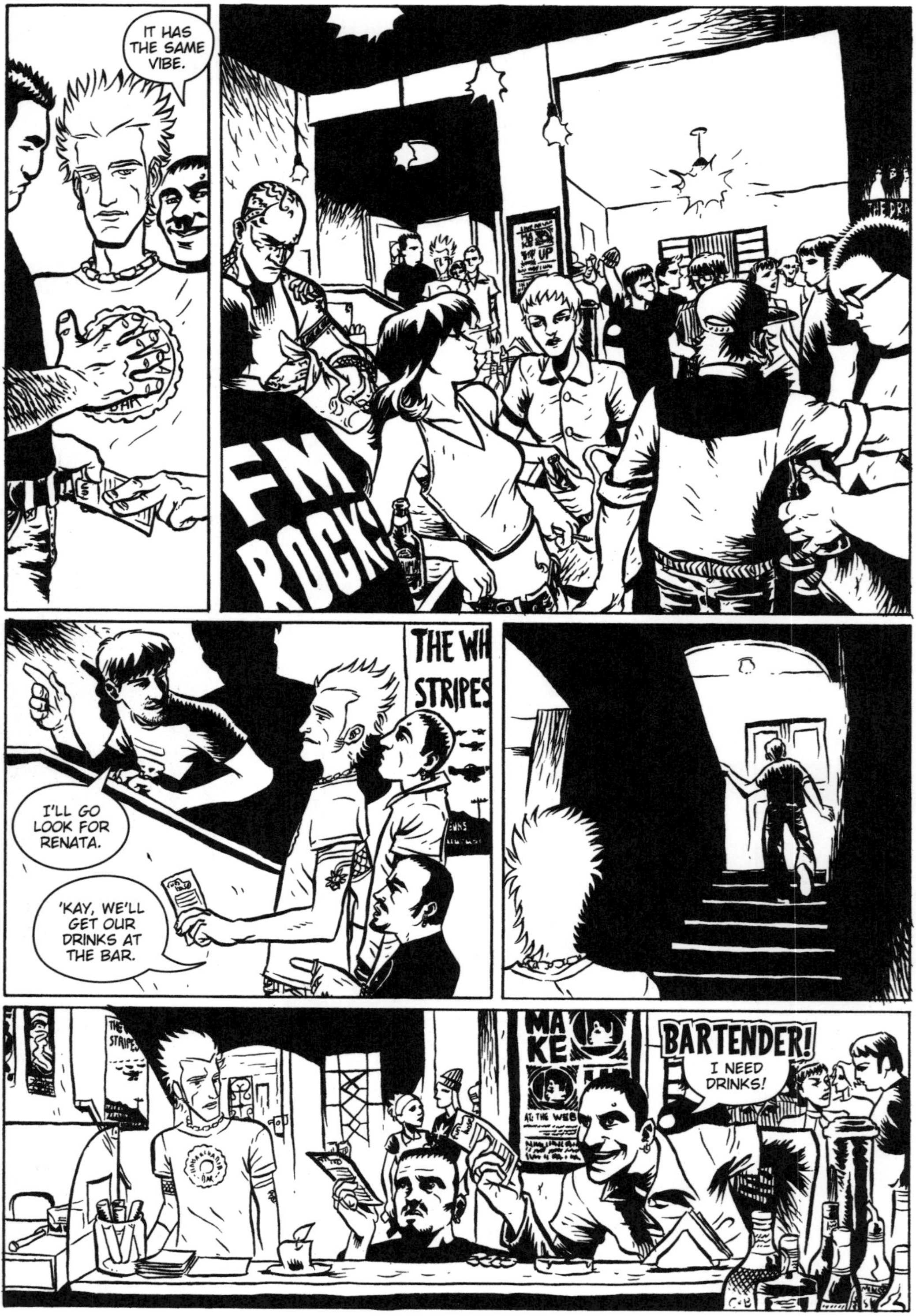
IT HAS THE SAME VIBE.
FM
I'LL GO LOOK FOR RENATA.
'KAY, WE'LL GET OUR DRINKS AT THE BAR.
THE WH
STRIPES
MA
KE
AT THE WEB
BARTENDER!
I NEED DRINKS!

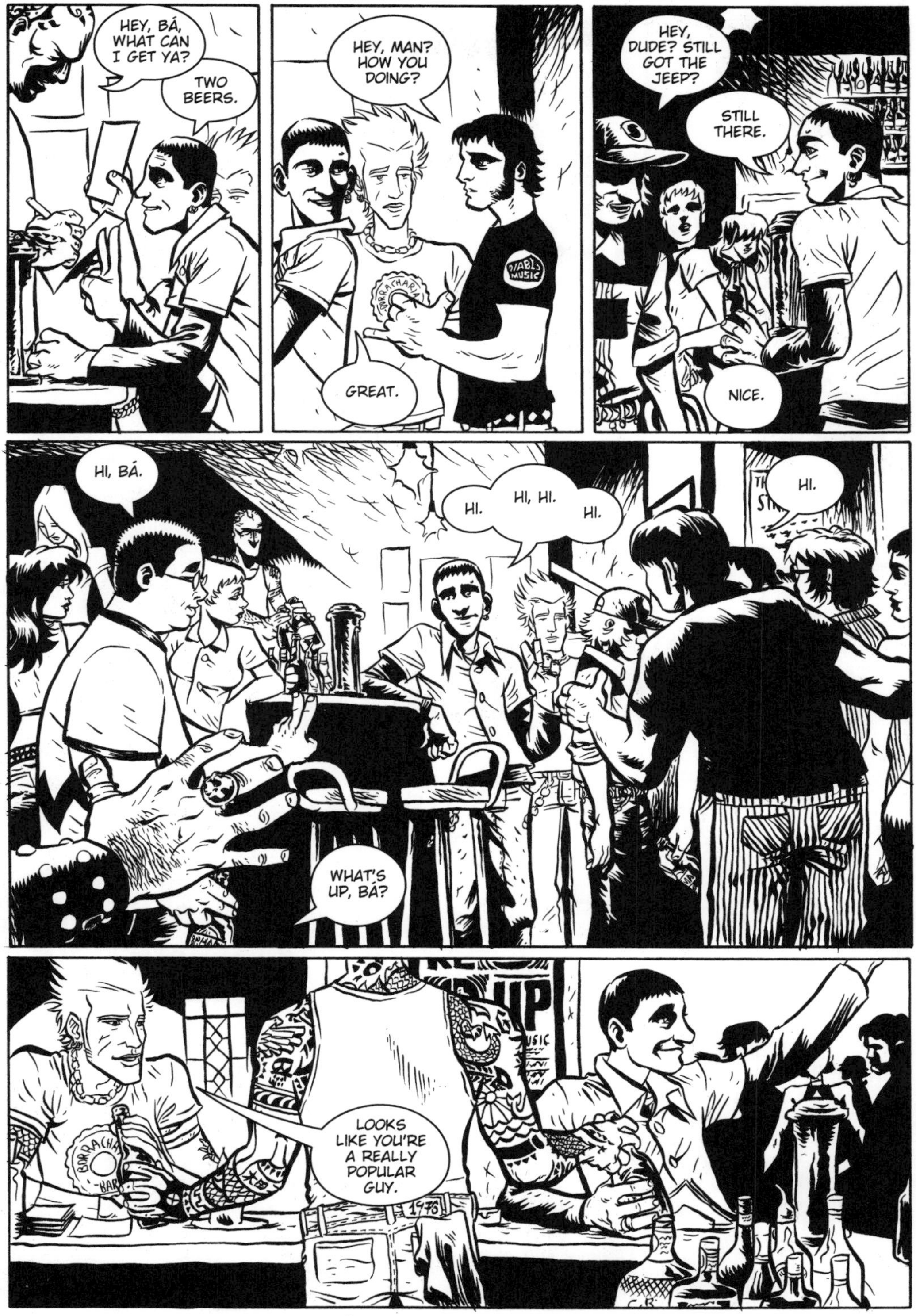
HEY, BÁ, WHAT CAN I GET YA?
TWO BEERS.
HEY, MAN? HOW YOU DOING?
GREAT.
HEY, DUDE? STILL GOT THE JEEP?
STILL THERE.
NICE.
HI, BÁ.
HI.
HI, HI.
HI.
HI.
WHAT'S UP, BÁ?
LOOKS LIKE YOU'RE A REALLY POPULAR GUY.

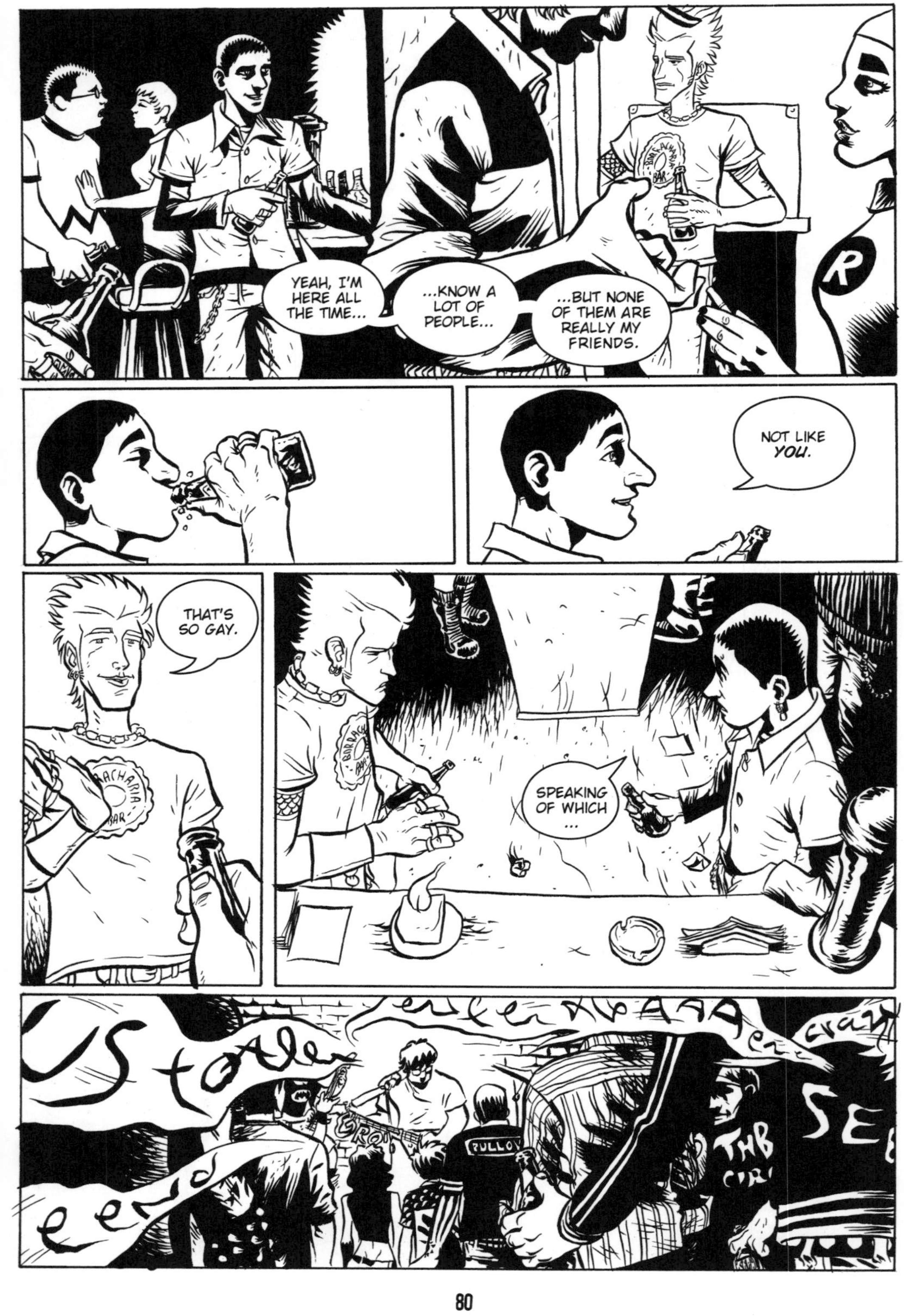
YEAH, I'M HERE ALL THE TIME...
...KNOW A LOT OF PEOPLE...
...BUT NONE OF THEM ARE REALLY MY FRIENDS.
NOT LIKE *YOU*.
THAT'S SO GAY.
SPEAKING OF WHICH ...

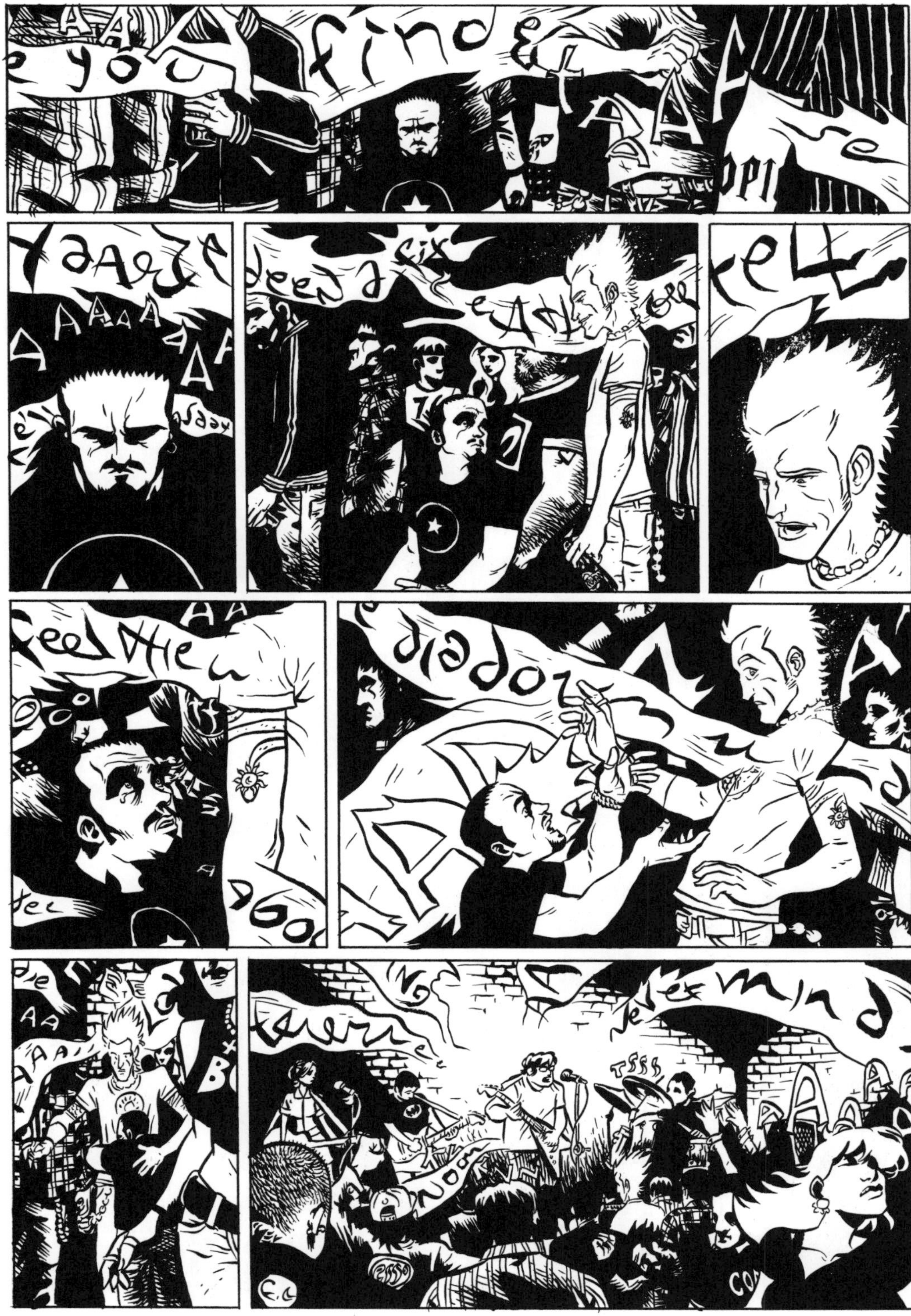

you
find
six
TSSS
mind

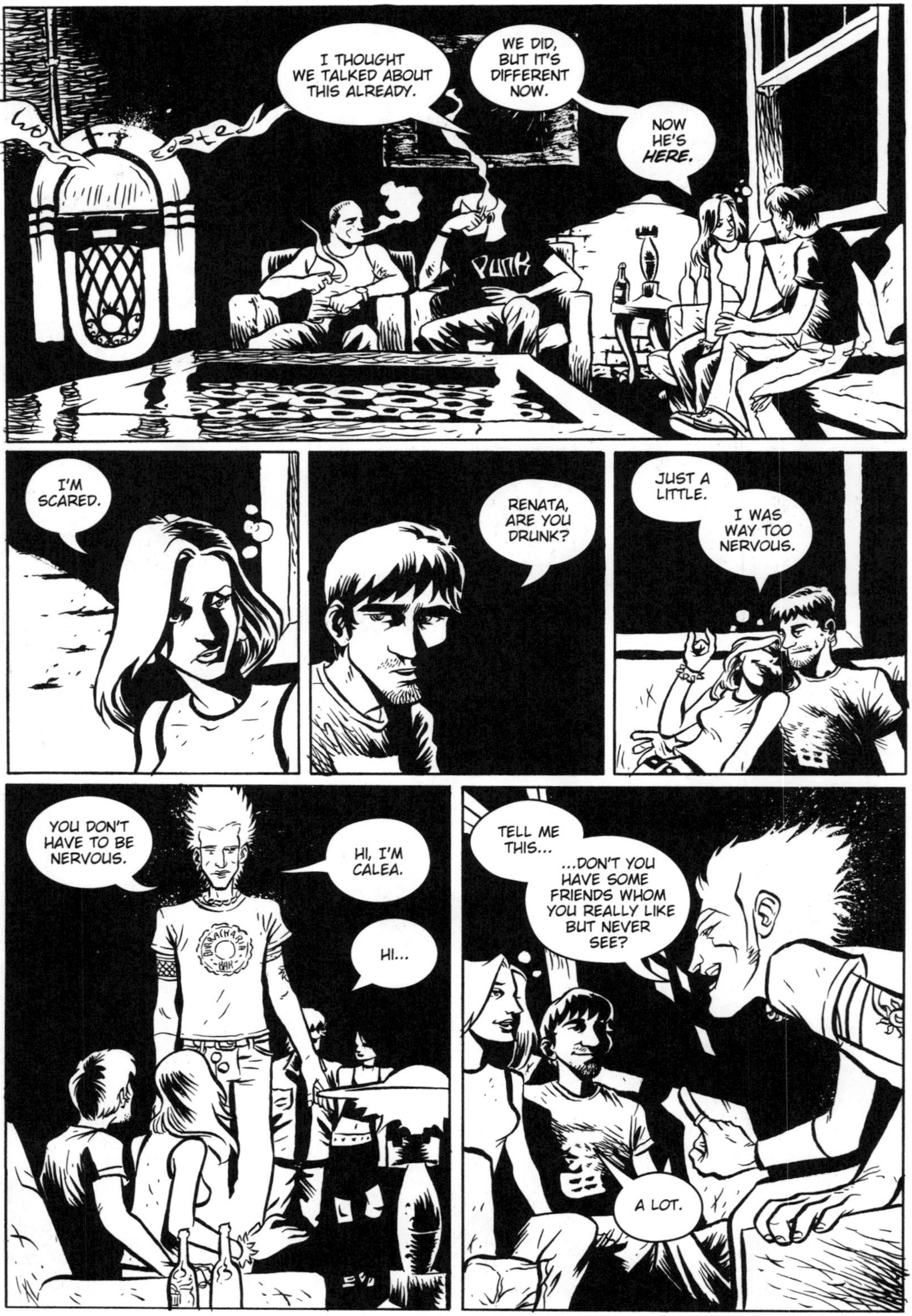
I THOUGHT WE TALKED ABOUT THIS ALREADY.
WE DID, BUT IT'S DIFFERENT NOW.
NOW HE'S *HERE.*
I'M SCARED.
RENATA, ARE YOU DRUNK?
JUST A LITTLE.
I WAS WAY TOO NERVOUS.
YOU DON'T HAVE TO BE NERVOUS.
HI, I'M CALEA.
HI...
TELL ME THIS...
...DON'T YOU HAVE SOME FRIENDS WHOM YOU REALLY LIKE BUT NEVER SEE?
A LOT.

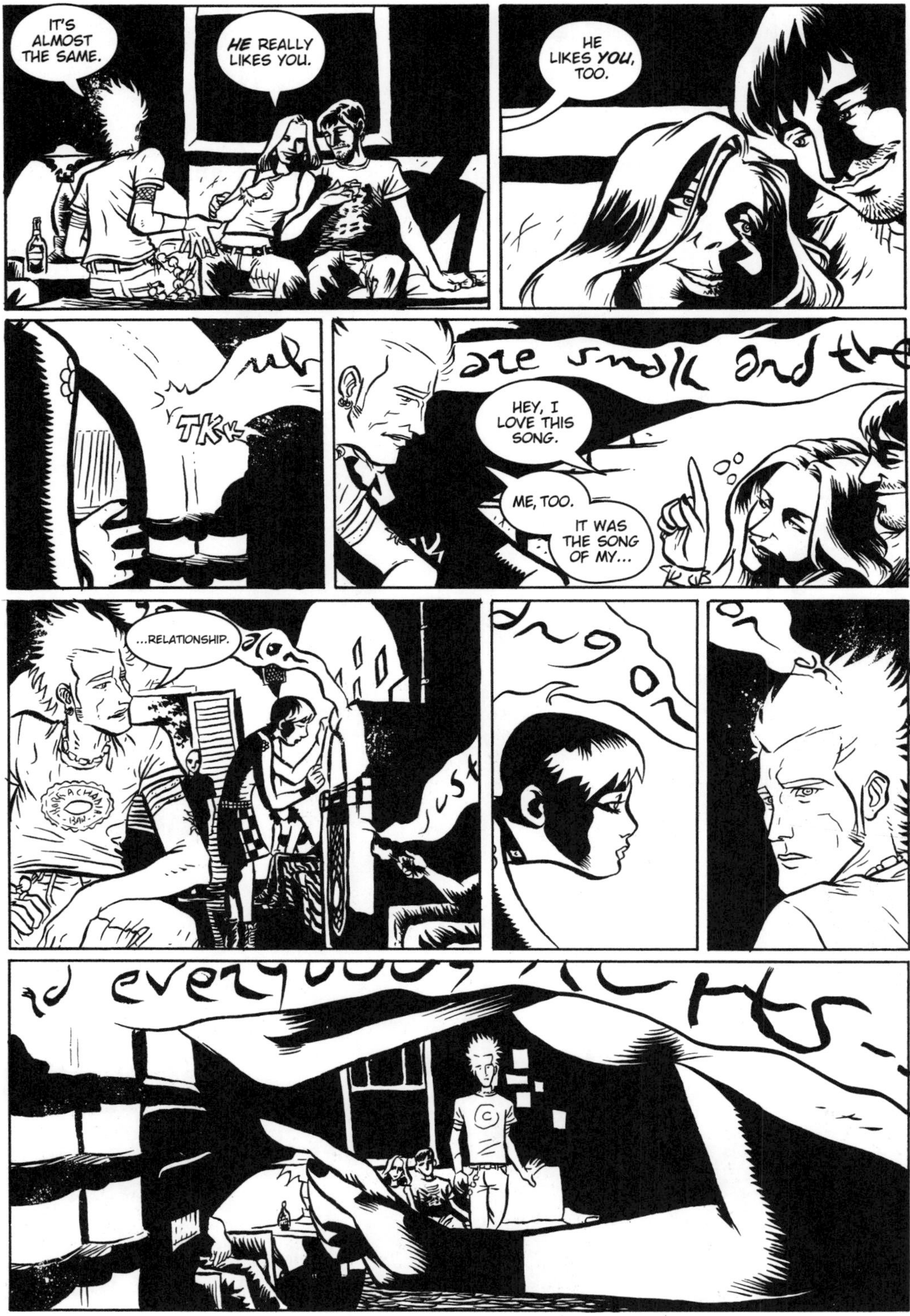
IT'S ALMOST THE SAME.
HE REALLY LIKES YOU.
HE LIKES YOU, TOO.
TKK
are small and the
HEY, I LOVE THIS SONG.
ME, TOO.
IT WAS THE SONG OF MY...
...RELATIONSHIP.

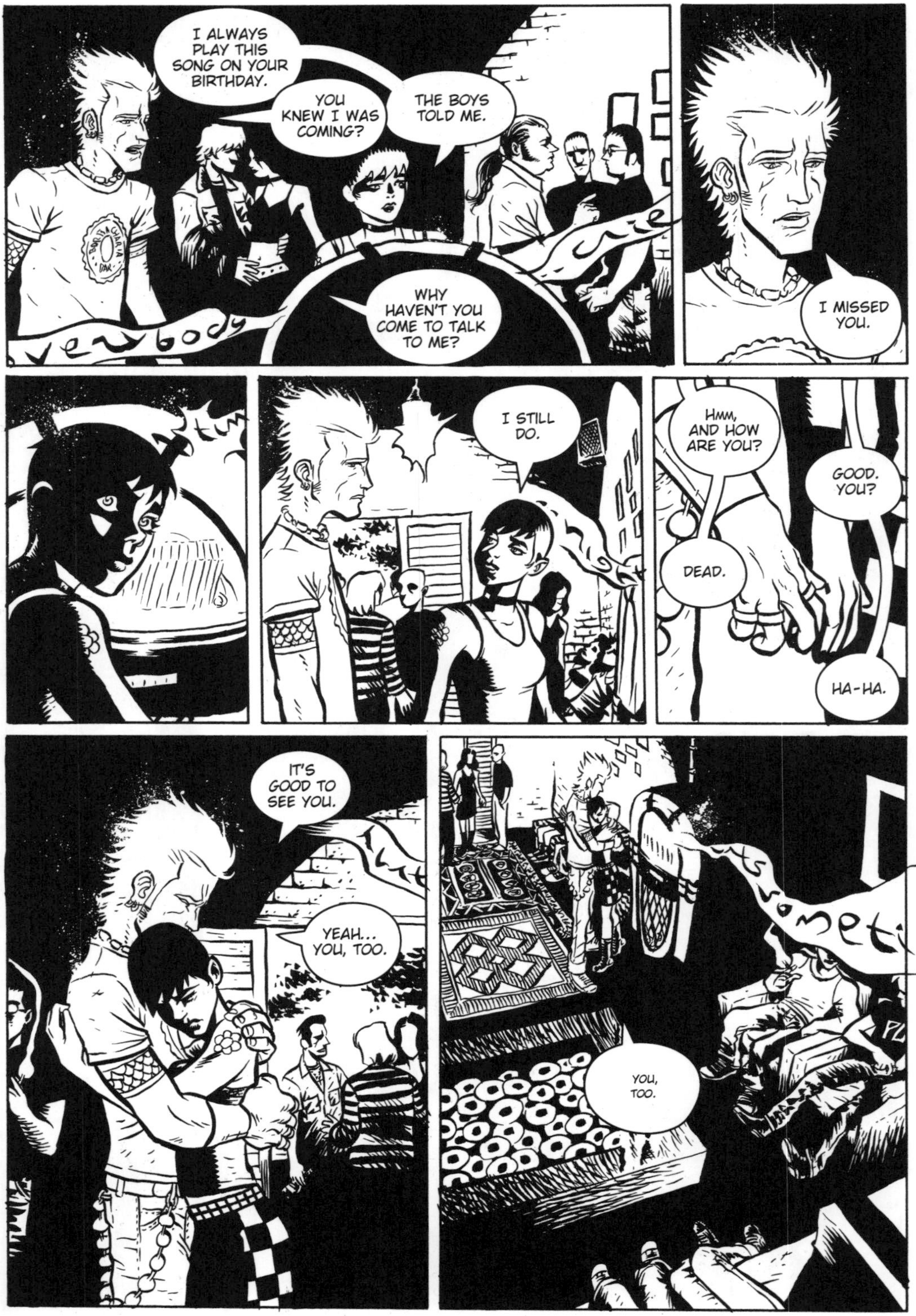
I ALWAYS PLAY THIS SONG ON YOUR BIRTHDAY.
YOU KNEW I WAS COMING?
THE BOYS TOLD ME.
WHY HAVEN'T YOU COME TO TALK TO ME?
I MISSED YOU.
I STILL DO.
HMM, AND HOW ARE YOU?
GOOD. YOU?
DEAD.
HA-HA.
IT'S GOOD TO SEE YOU.
YEAH... YOU, TOO.
YOU, TOO.

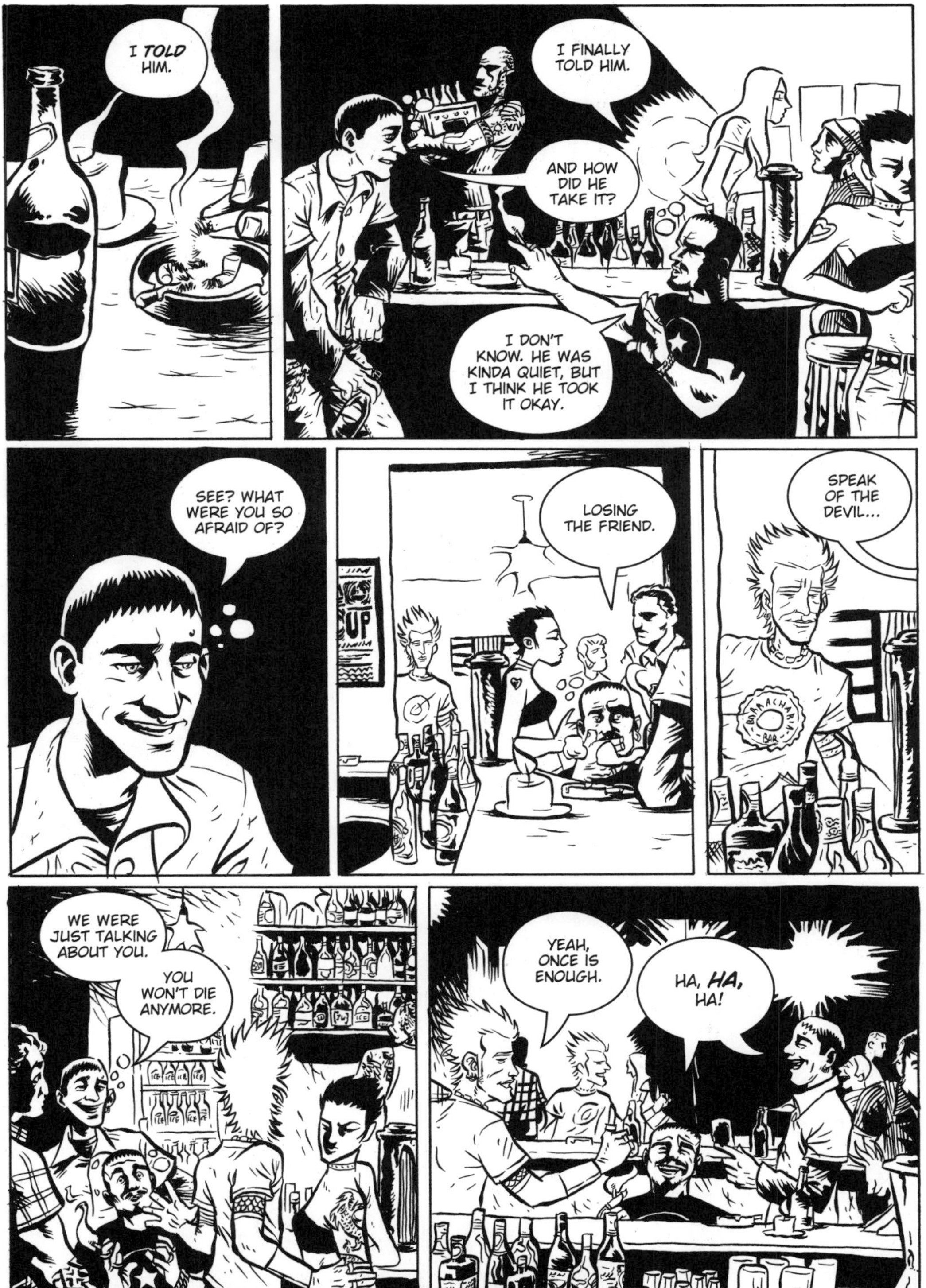
I TOLD HIM.
I FINALLY TOLD HIM.
AND HOW DID HE TAKE IT?
I DON'T KNOW. HE WAS KINDA QUIET, BUT I THINK HE TOOK IT OKAY.
SEE? WHAT WERE YOU SO AFRAID OF?
LOSING THE FRIEND.
SPEAK OF THE DEVIL...
BARRACHARIA BAR
WE WERE JUST TALKING ABOUT YOU.
YOU WON'T DIE ANYMORE.
YEAH, ONCE IS ENOUGH.
HA, HA, HA!

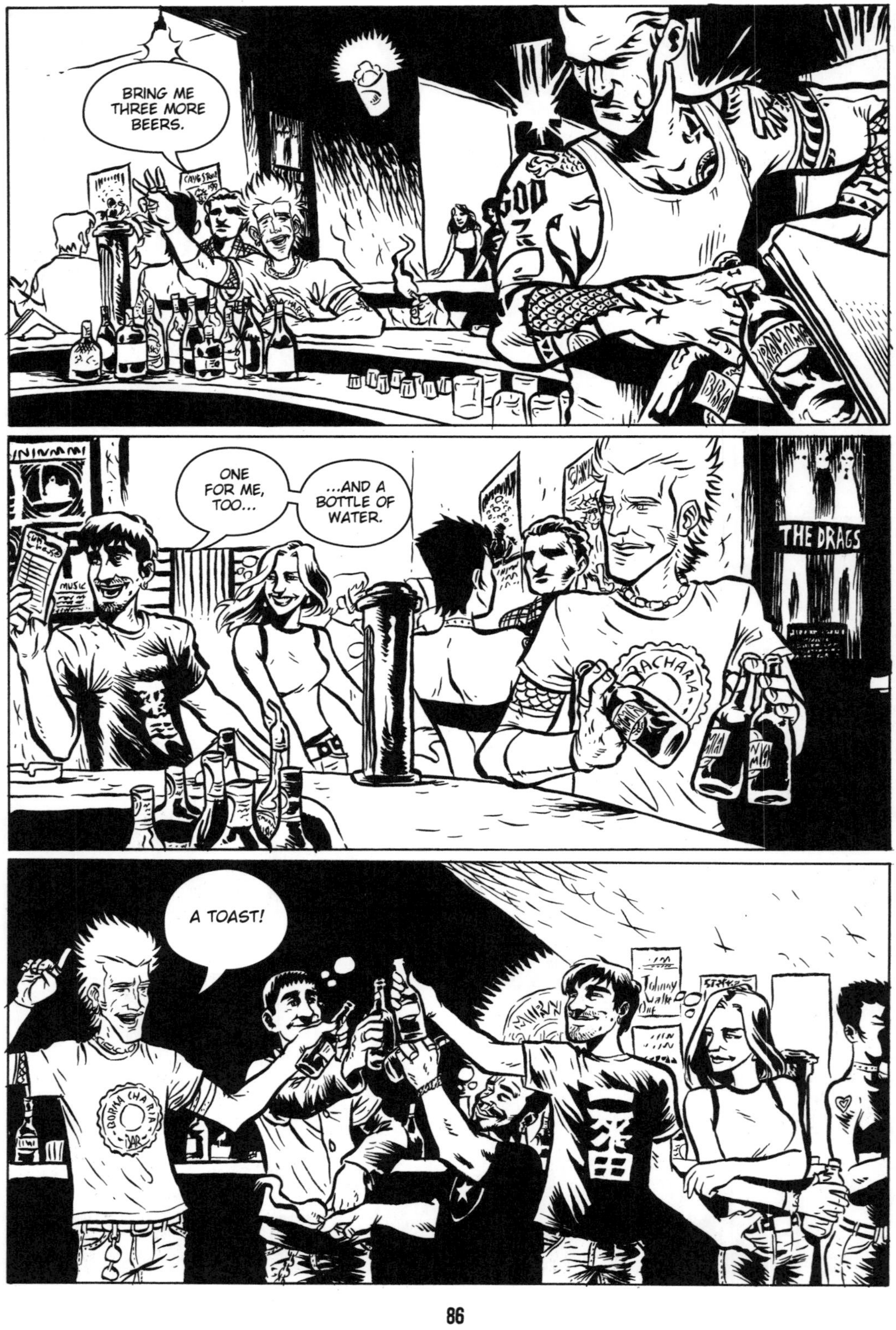
BRING ME THREE MORE BEERS.
ONE FOR ME, TOO...
...AND A BOTTLE OF WATER.
THE DRAGS
MUSIC
A TOAST!

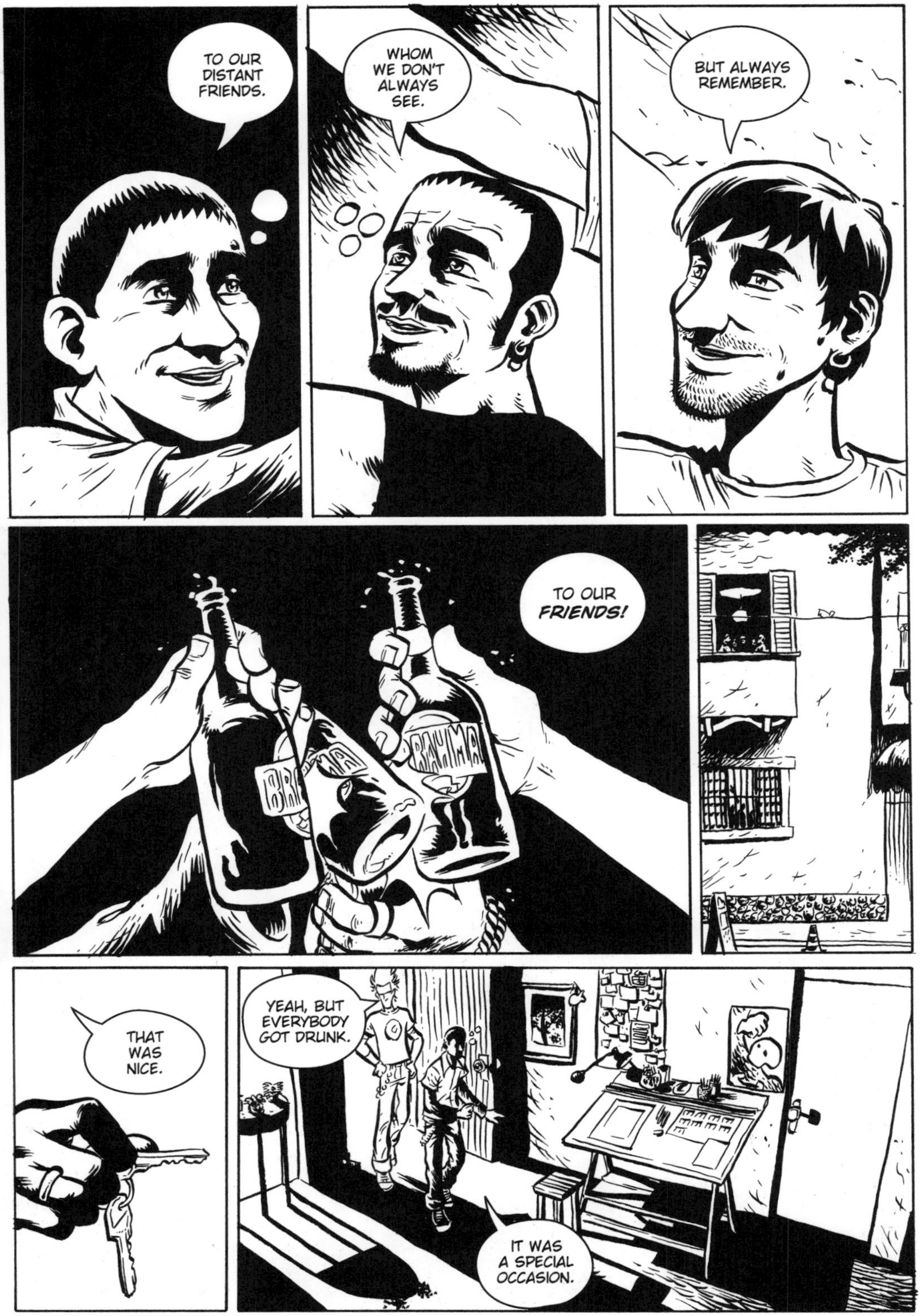
TO OUR DISTANT FRIENDS.
WHOM WE DON'T ALWAYS SEE.
BUT ALWAYS REMEMBER.
TO OUR FRIENDS!
BRAHMA
THAT WAS NICE.
YEAH, BUT EVERYBODY GOT DRUNK.
IT WAS A SPECIAL OCCASION.

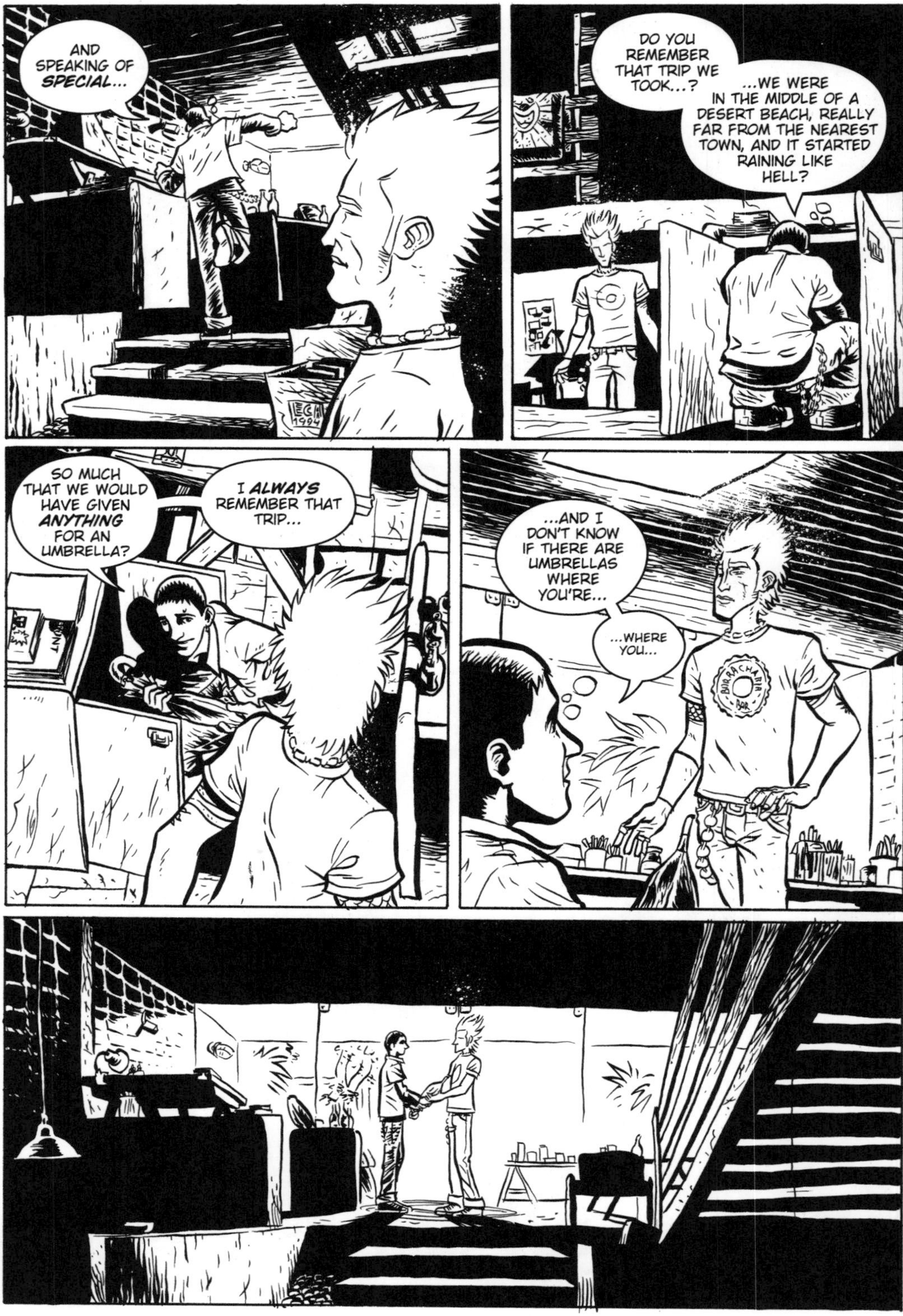
AND SPEAKING OF *SPECIAL*...
DO YOU REMEMBER THAT TRIP WE TOOK...?
...WE WERE IN THE MIDDLE OF A DESERT BEACH, REALLY FAR FROM THE NEAREST TOWN, AND IT STARTED RAINING LIKE HELL?
SO MUCH THAT WE WOULD HAVE GIVEN *ANYTHING* FOR AN UMBRELLA?
I *ALWAYS* REMEMBER THAT TRIP...
...AND I DON'T KNOW IF THERE ARE UMBRELLAS WHERE YOU'RE...
...WHERE YOU...
BORRACHARIA BAR

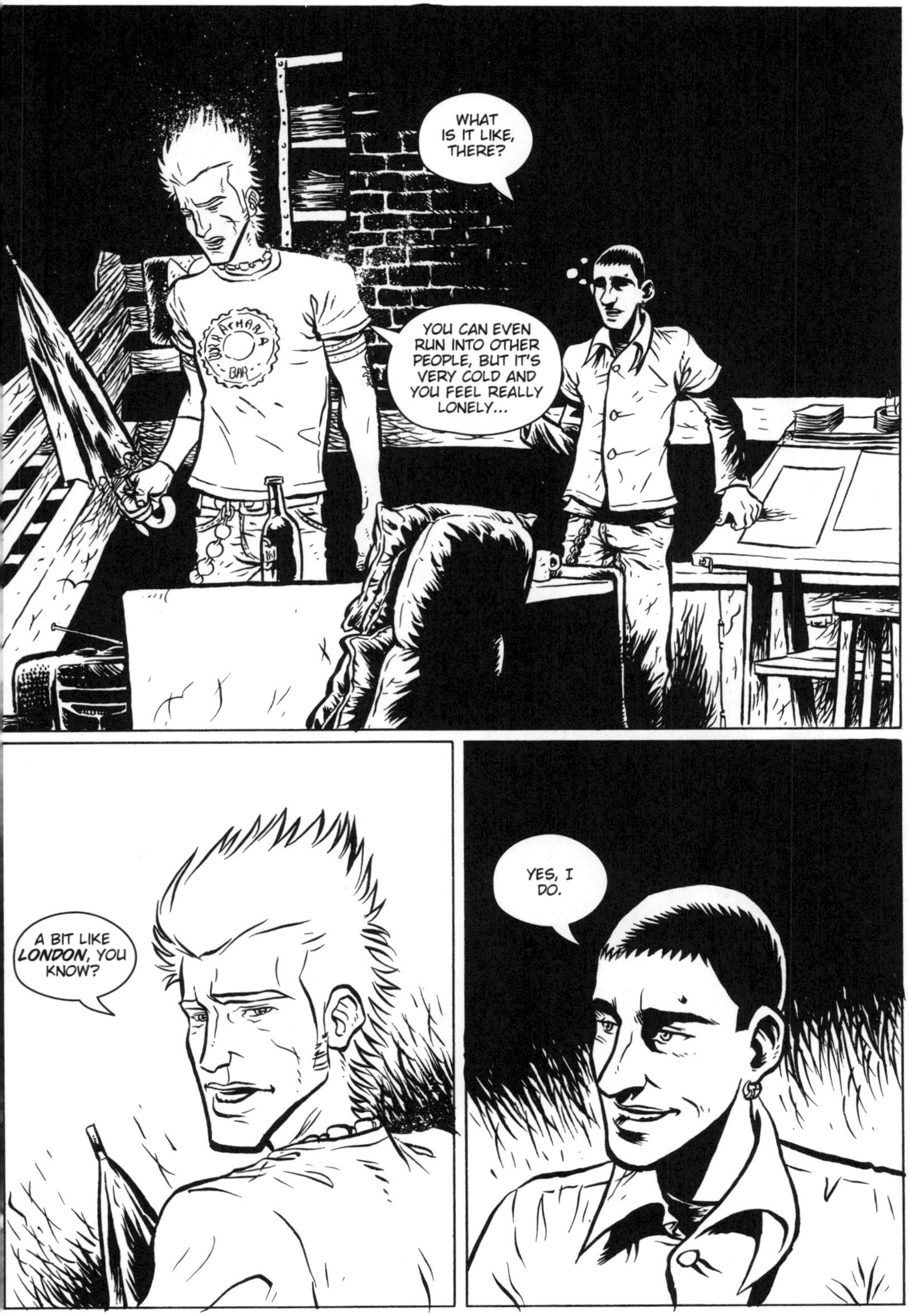
WHAT IS IT LIKE, THERE?
YOU CAN EVEN RUN INTO OTHER PEOPLE, BUT IT'S VERY COLD AND YOU FEEL REALLY LONELY...
A BIT LIKE *LONDON*, YOU KNOW?
YES, I DO.

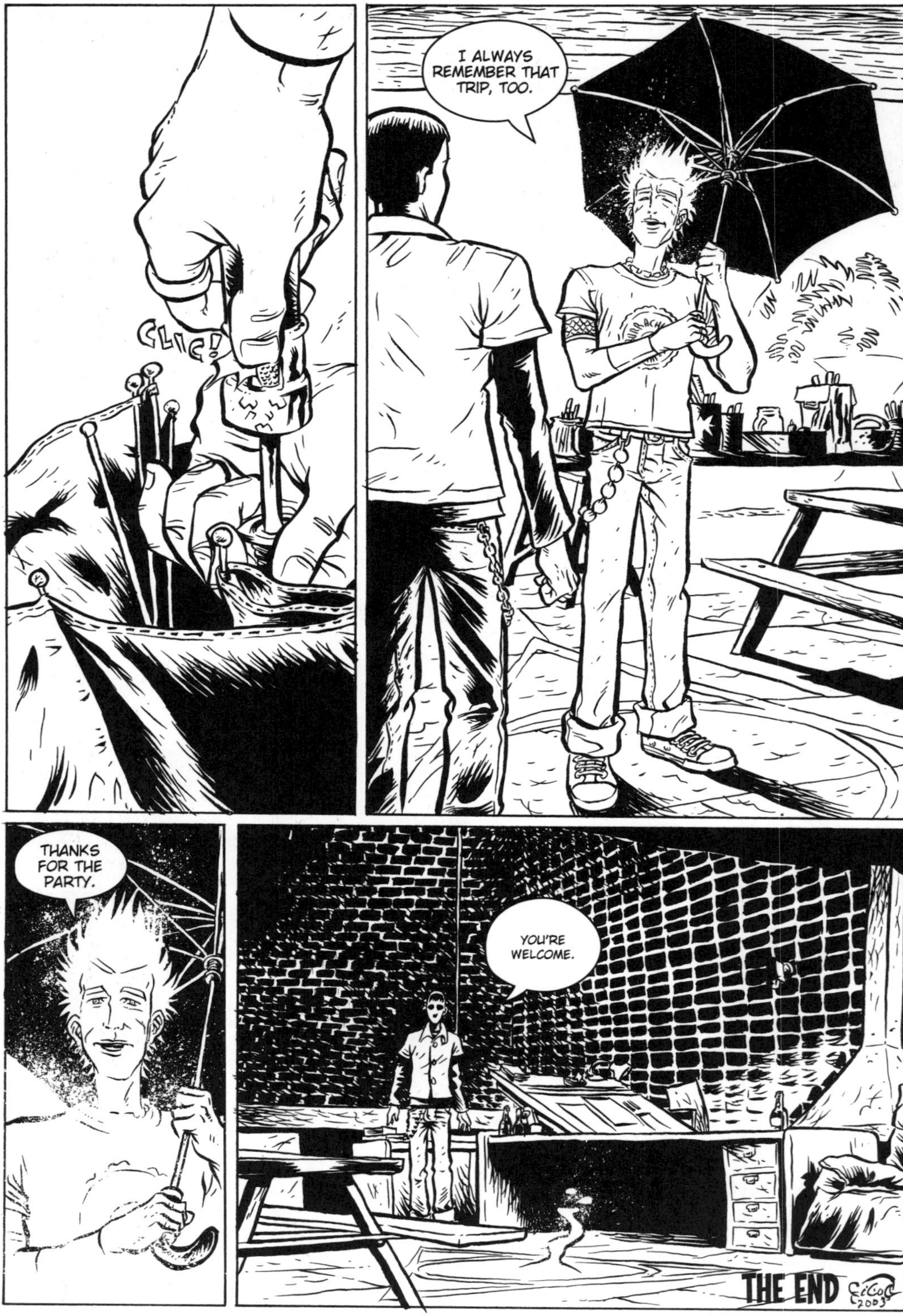
CLIC!
I ALWAYS REMEMBER THAT TRIP, TOO.
THANKS FOR THE PARTY.
YOU'RE WELCOME.
THE END

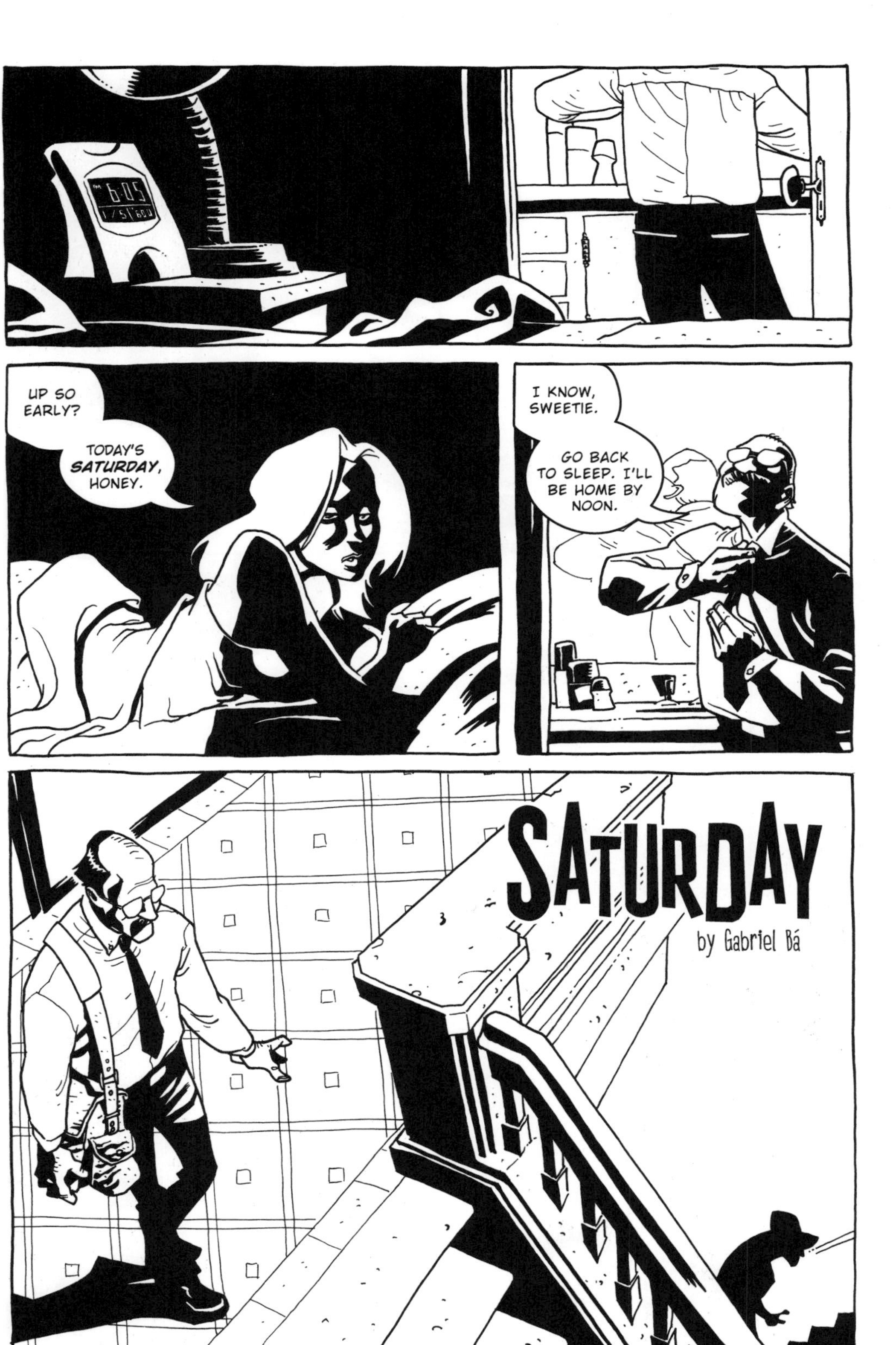
6:05
UP SO EARLY?
TODAY'S **SATURDAY**, HONEY.
I KNOW, SWEETIE.
GO BACK TO SLEEP. I'LL BE HOME BY NOON.
SATURDAY
by Gabriel Bá

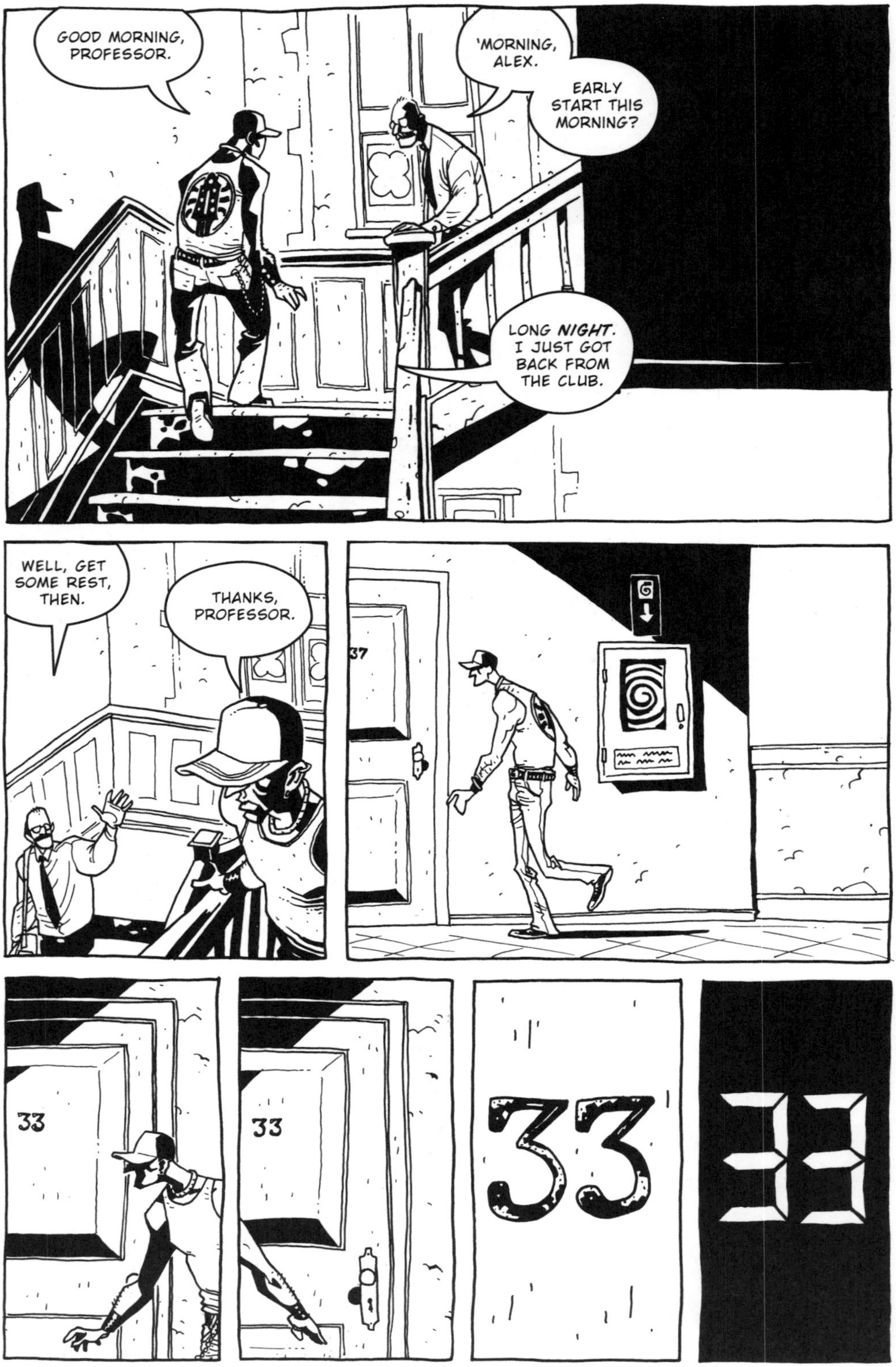
GOOD MORNING, PROFESSOR.
'MORNING, ALEX.
EARLY START THIS MORNING?
LONG **NIGHT**. I JUST GOT BACK FROM THE CLUB.
WELL, GET SOME REST, THEN.
THANKS, PROFESSOR.
37
33
33
33
33

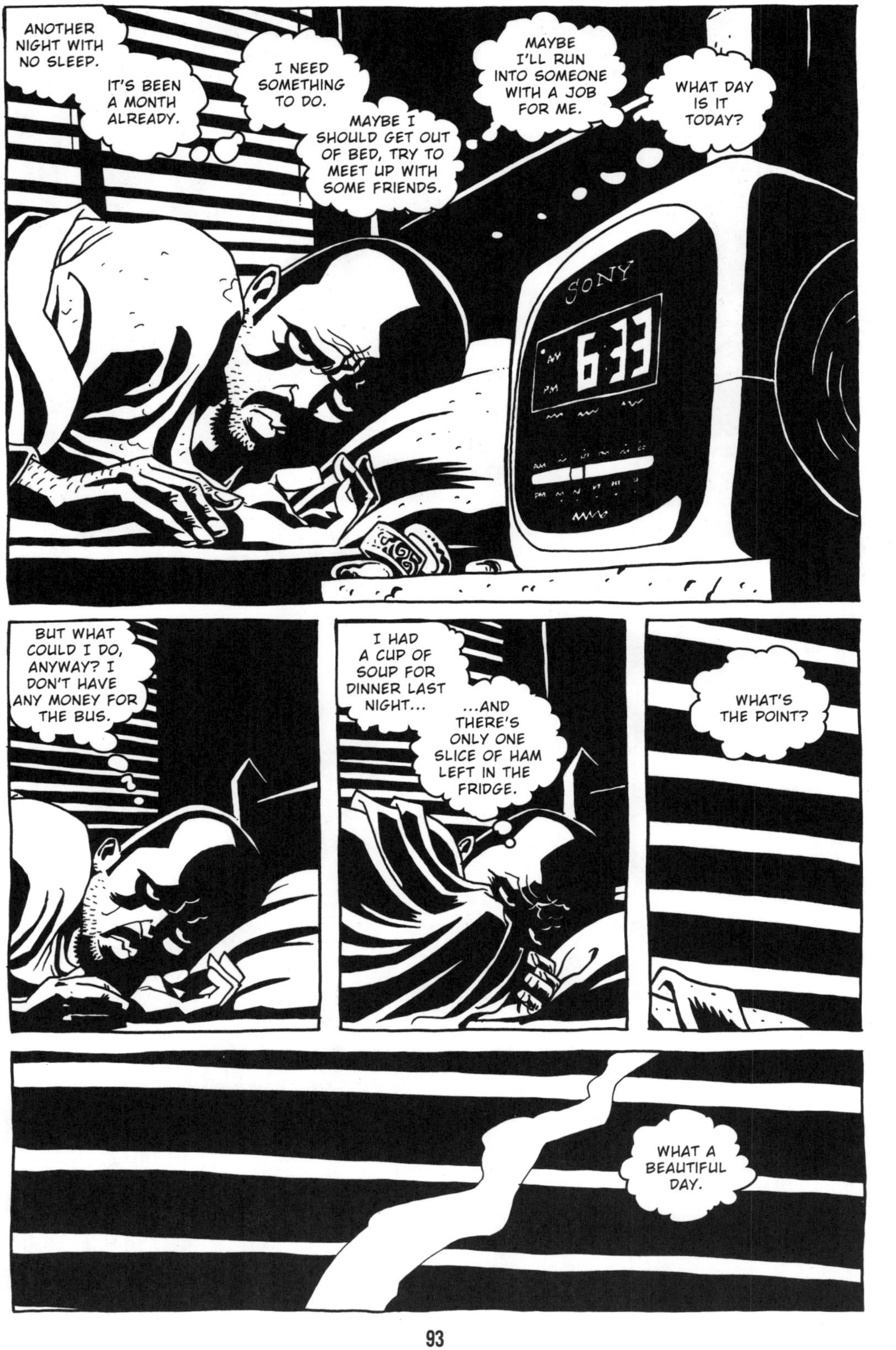
ANOTHER NIGHT WITH NO SLEEP.
IT'S BEEN A MONTH ALREADY.
I NEED SOMETHING TO DO.
MAYBE I SHOULD GET OUT OF BED, TRY TO MEET UP WITH SOME FRIENDS.
MAYBE I'LL RUN INTO SOMEONE WITH A JOB FOR ME.
WHAT DAY IS IT TODAY?
SONY
6:33
AM
PM
BUT WHAT COULD I DO, ANYWAY? I DON'T HAVE ANY MONEY FOR THE BUS.
I HAD A CUP OF SOUP FOR DINNER LAST NIGHT...
...AND THERE'S ONLY ONE SLICE OF HAM LEFT IN THE FRIDGE.
WHAT'S THE POINT?
WHAT A BEAUTIFUL DAY.

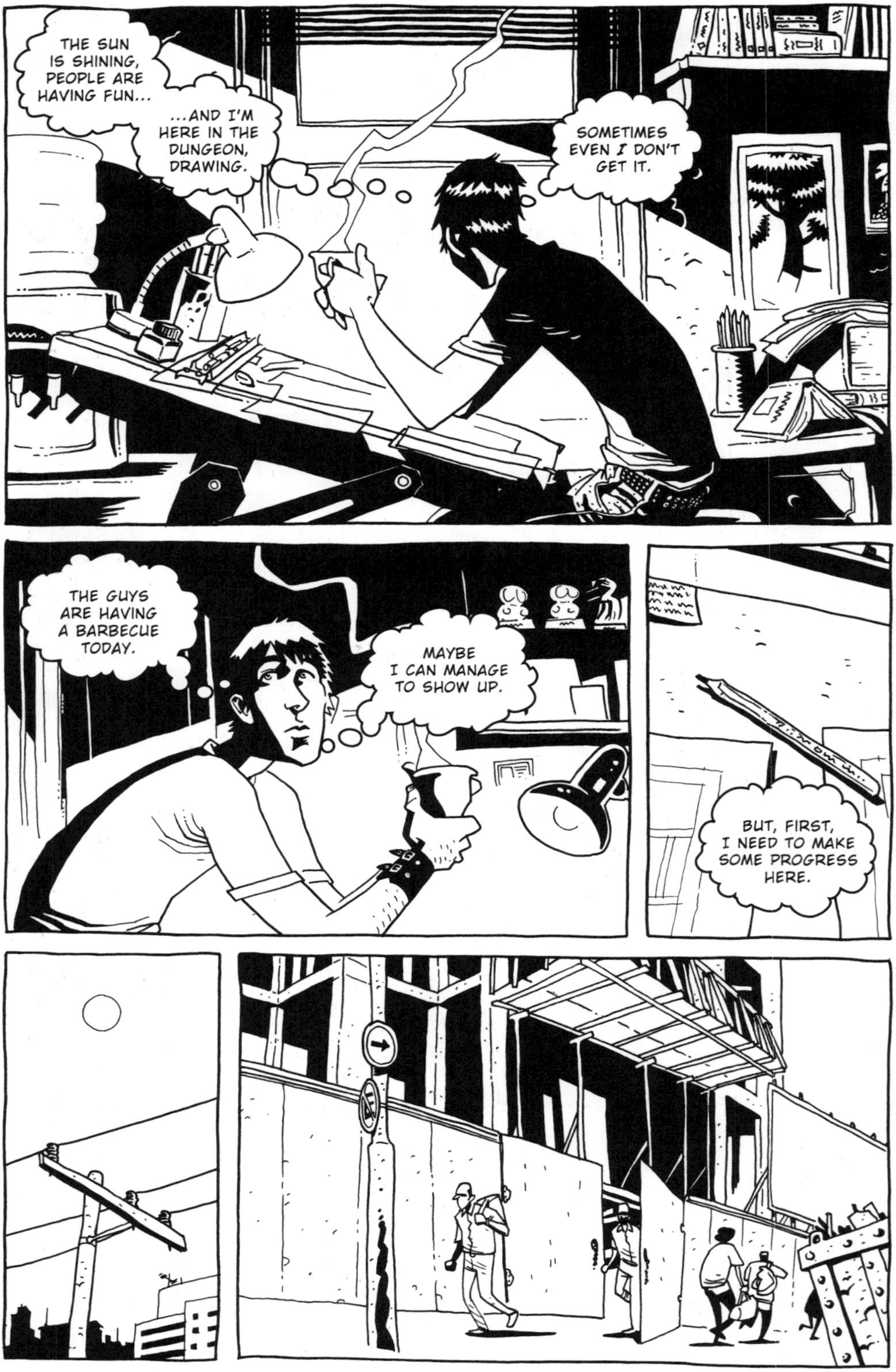
THE SUN IS SHINING, PEOPLE ARE HAVING FUN...
...AND I'M HERE IN THE DUNGEON, DRAWING.
SOMETIMES EVEN I DON'T GET IT.
THE GUYS ARE HAVING A BARBECUE TODAY.
MAYBE I CAN MANAGE TO SHOW UP.
BUT, FIRST, I NEED TO MAKE SOME PROGRESS HERE.

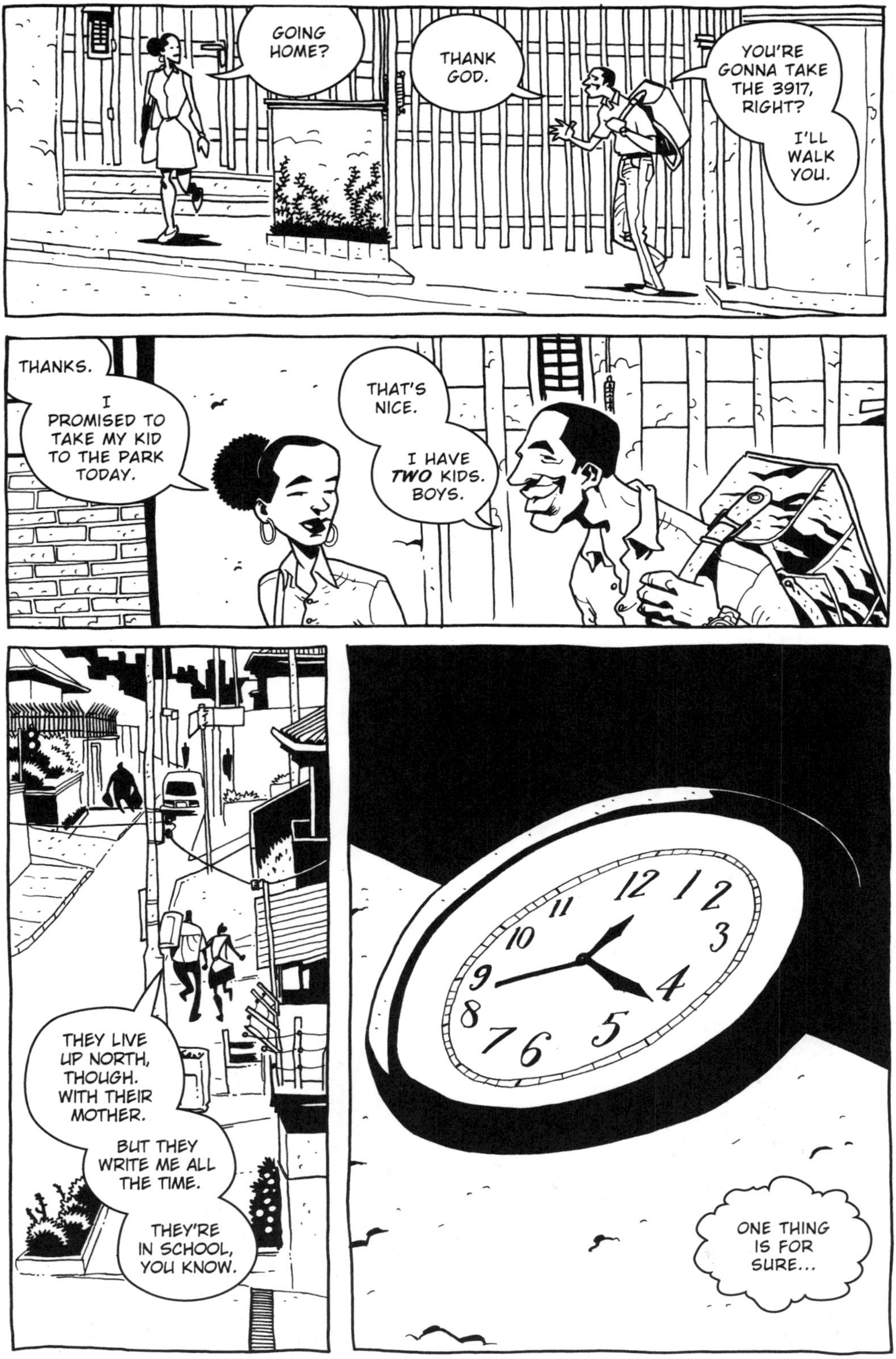
GOING HOME?
THANK GOD.
YOU'RE GONNA TAKE THE 3917, RIGHT?
I'LL WALK YOU.
THANKS.
I PROMISED TO TAKE MY KID TO THE PARK TODAY.
THAT'S NICE.
I HAVE *TWO* KIDS. BOYS.
THEY LIVE UP NORTH, THOUGH. WITH THEIR MOTHER.
BUT THEY WRITE ME ALL THE TIME.
THEY'RE IN SCHOOL, YOU KNOW.
ONE THING IS FOR SURE...

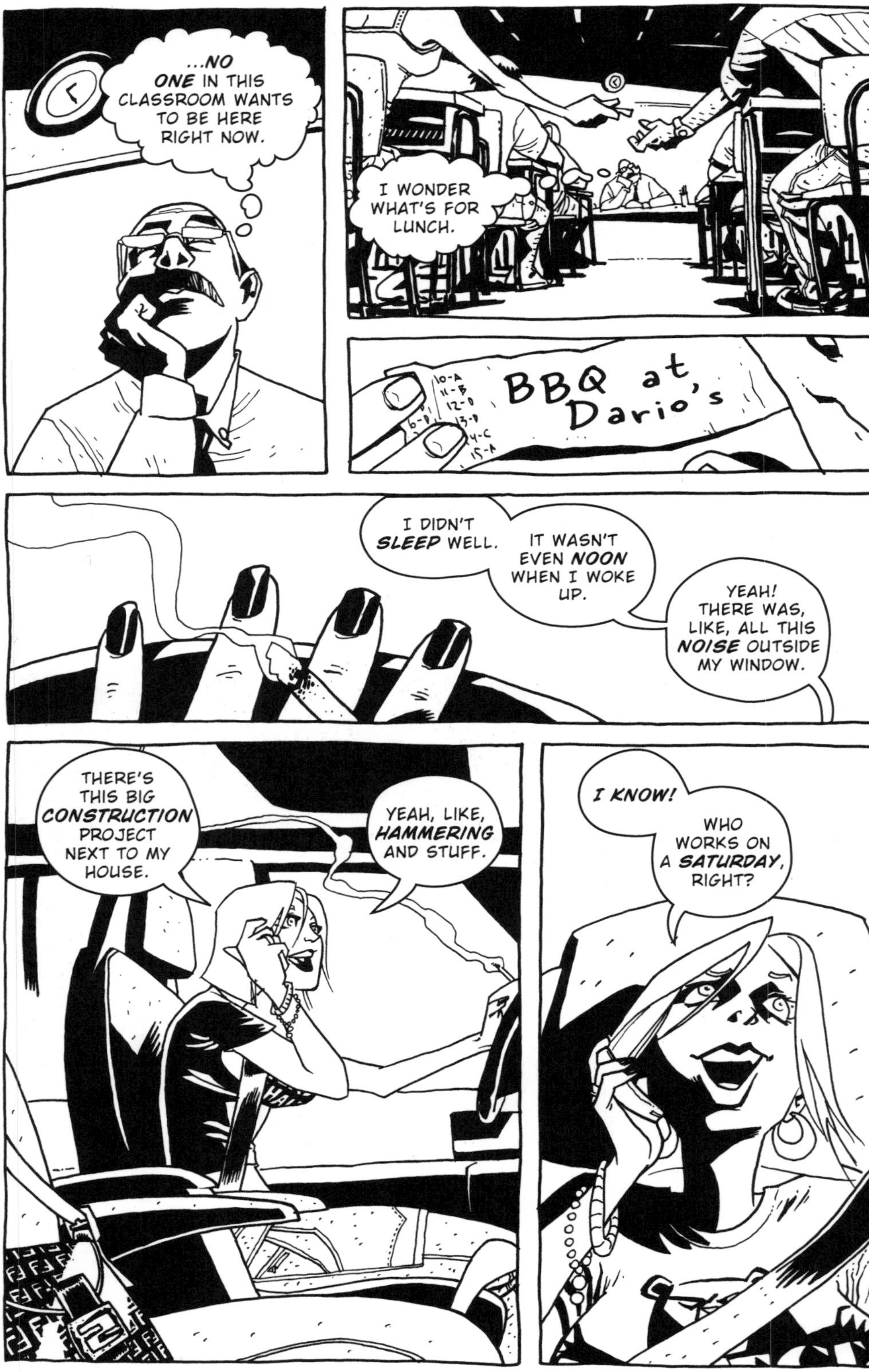
...NO ONE IN THIS CLASSROOM WANTS TO BE HERE RIGHT NOW.
I WONDER WHAT'S FOR LUNCH.
BBQ at Dario's
I DIDN'T SLEEP WELL.
IT WASN'T EVEN NOON WHEN I WOKE UP.
YEAH! THERE WAS, LIKE, ALL THIS NOISE OUTSIDE MY WINDOW.
THERE'S THIS BIG CONSTRUCTION PROJECT NEXT TO MY HOUSE.
YEAH, LIKE, HAMMERING AND STUFF.
I KNOW!
WHO WORKS ON A SATURDAY, RIGHT?

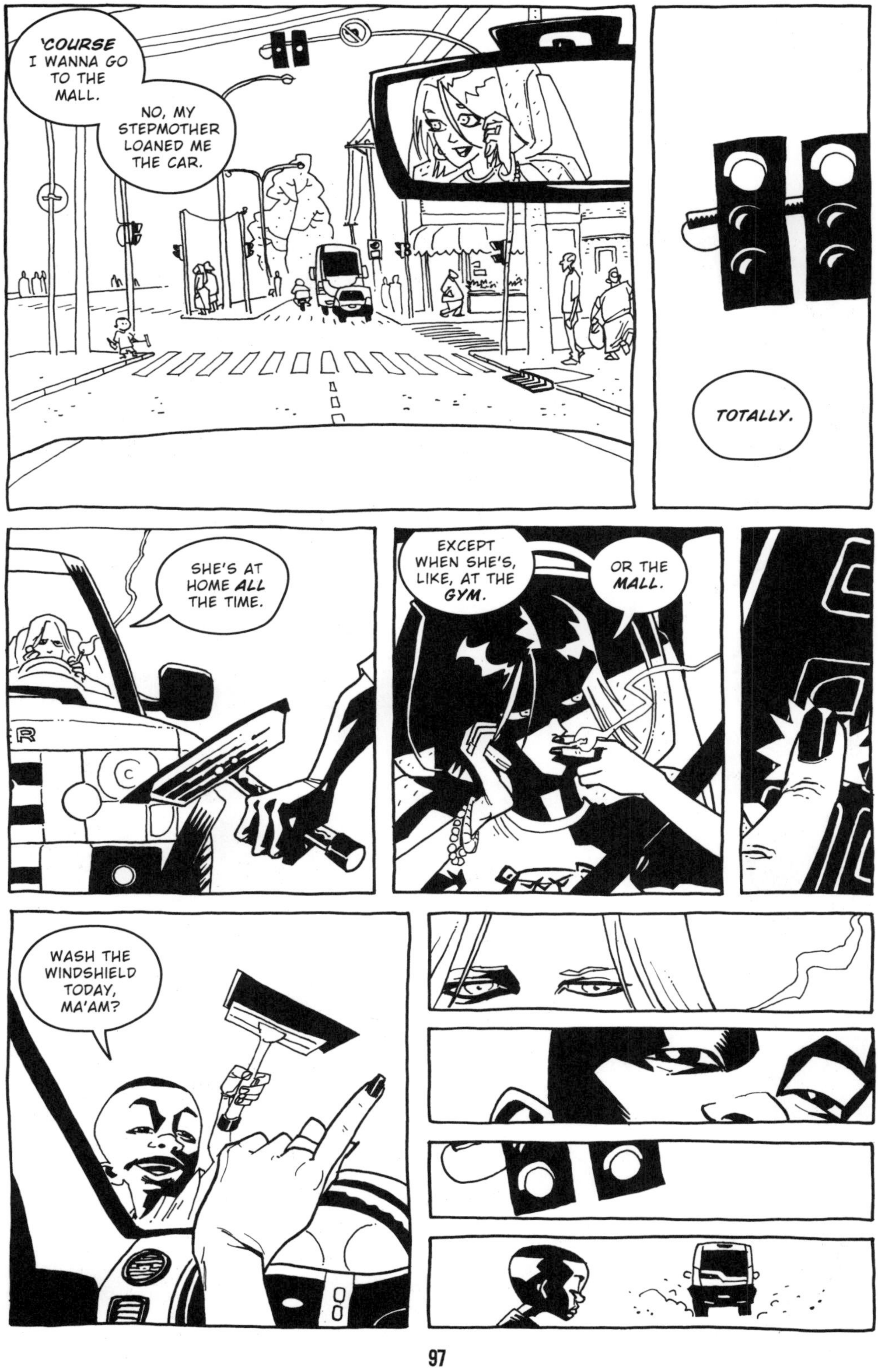
'COURSE I WANNA GO TO THE MALL.
NO, MY STEPMOTHER LOANED ME THE CAR.
TOTALLY.
SHE'S AT HOME ALL THE TIME.
EXCEPT WHEN SHE'S, LIKE, AT THE GYM.
OR THE MALL.
WASH THE WINDSHIELD TODAY, MA'AM?

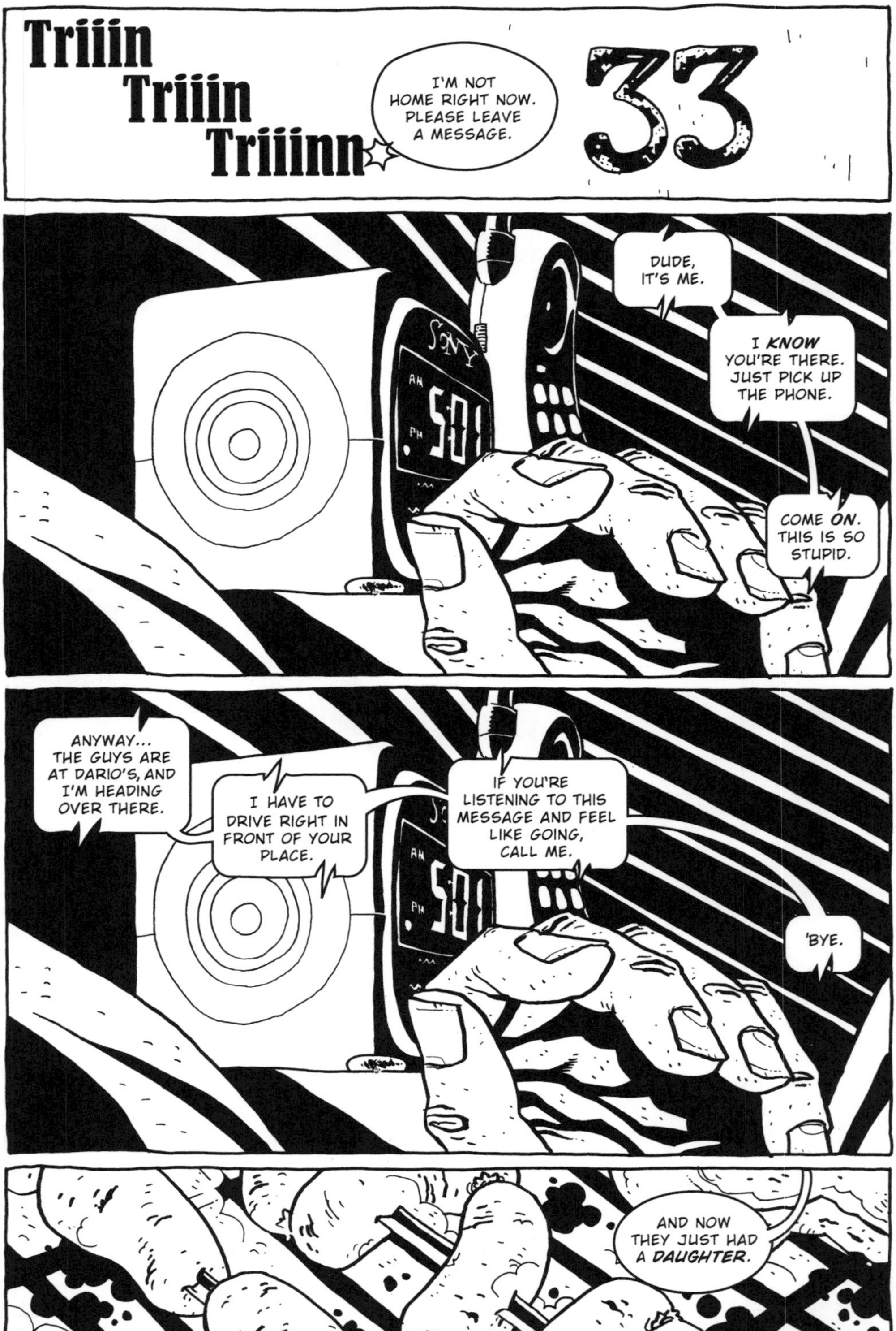
Triiin
Triiin
Triiinn
33
I'M NOT HOME RIGHT NOW. PLEASE LEAVE A MESSAGE.
DUDE, IT'S ME.
I KNOW YOU'RE THERE. JUST PICK UP THE PHONE.
COME ON. THIS IS SO STUPID.
ANYWAY... THE GUYS ARE AT DARIO'S, AND I'M HEADING OVER THERE.
I HAVE TO DRIVE RIGHT IN FRONT OF YOUR PLACE.
IF YOU'RE LISTENING TO THIS MESSAGE AND FEEL LIKE GOING, CALL ME.
'BYE.
AND NOW THEY JUST HAD A DAUGHTER.

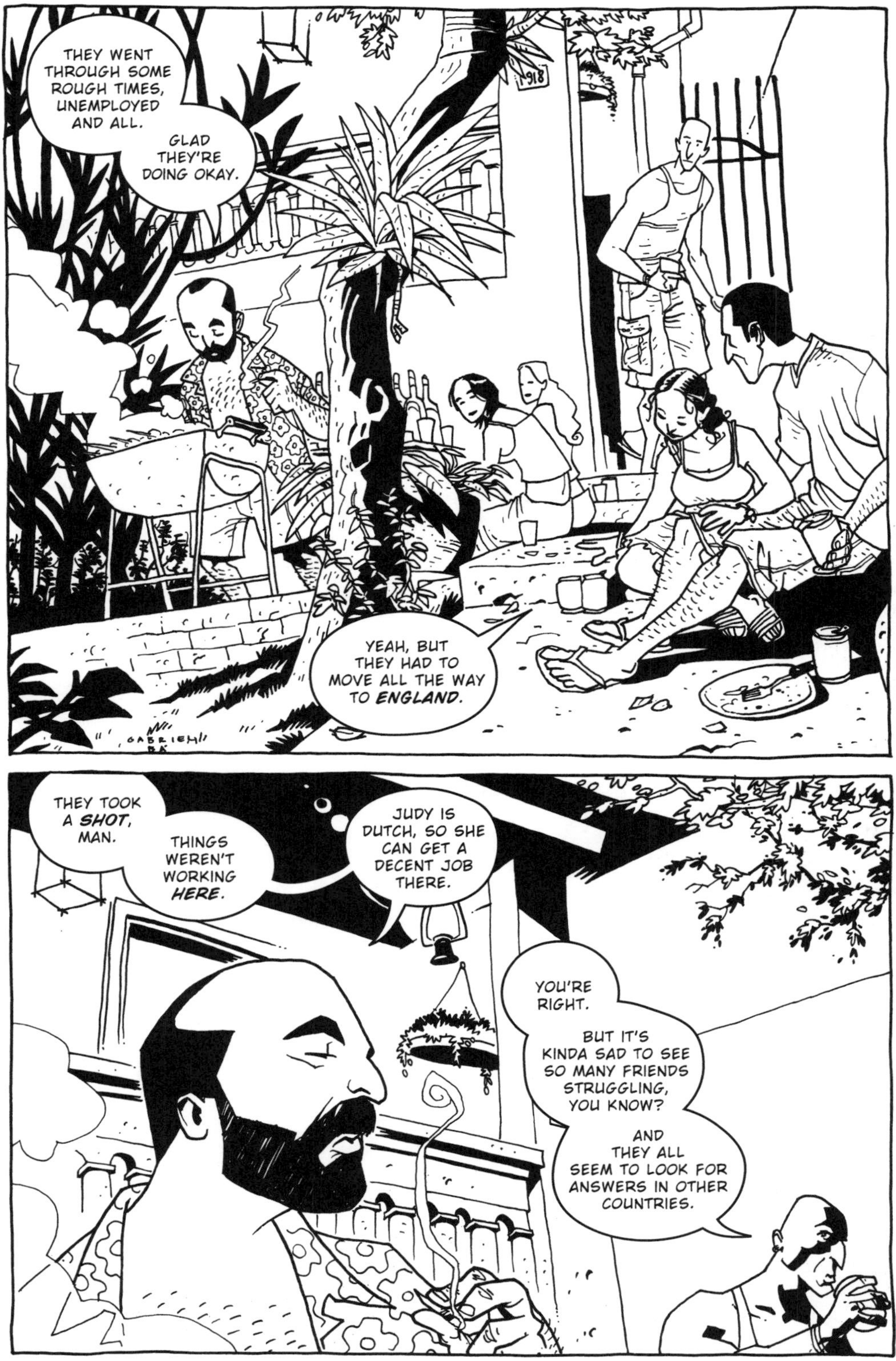
THEY WENT THROUGH SOME ROUGH TIMES, UNEMPLOYED AND ALL.
GLAD THEY'RE DOING OKAY.
YEAH, BUT THEY HAD TO MOVE ALL THE WAY TO **ENGLAND**.
GABRIEL BÁ
THEY TOOK A **SHOT**, MAN.
THINGS WEREN'T WORKING **HERE**.
JUDY IS DUTCH, SO SHE CAN GET A DECENT JOB THERE.
YOU'RE RIGHT.
BUT IT'S KINDA SAD TO SEE SO MANY FRIENDS STRUGGLING, YOU KNOW?
AND THEY ALL SEEM TO LOOK FOR ANSWERS IN OTHER COUNTRIES.

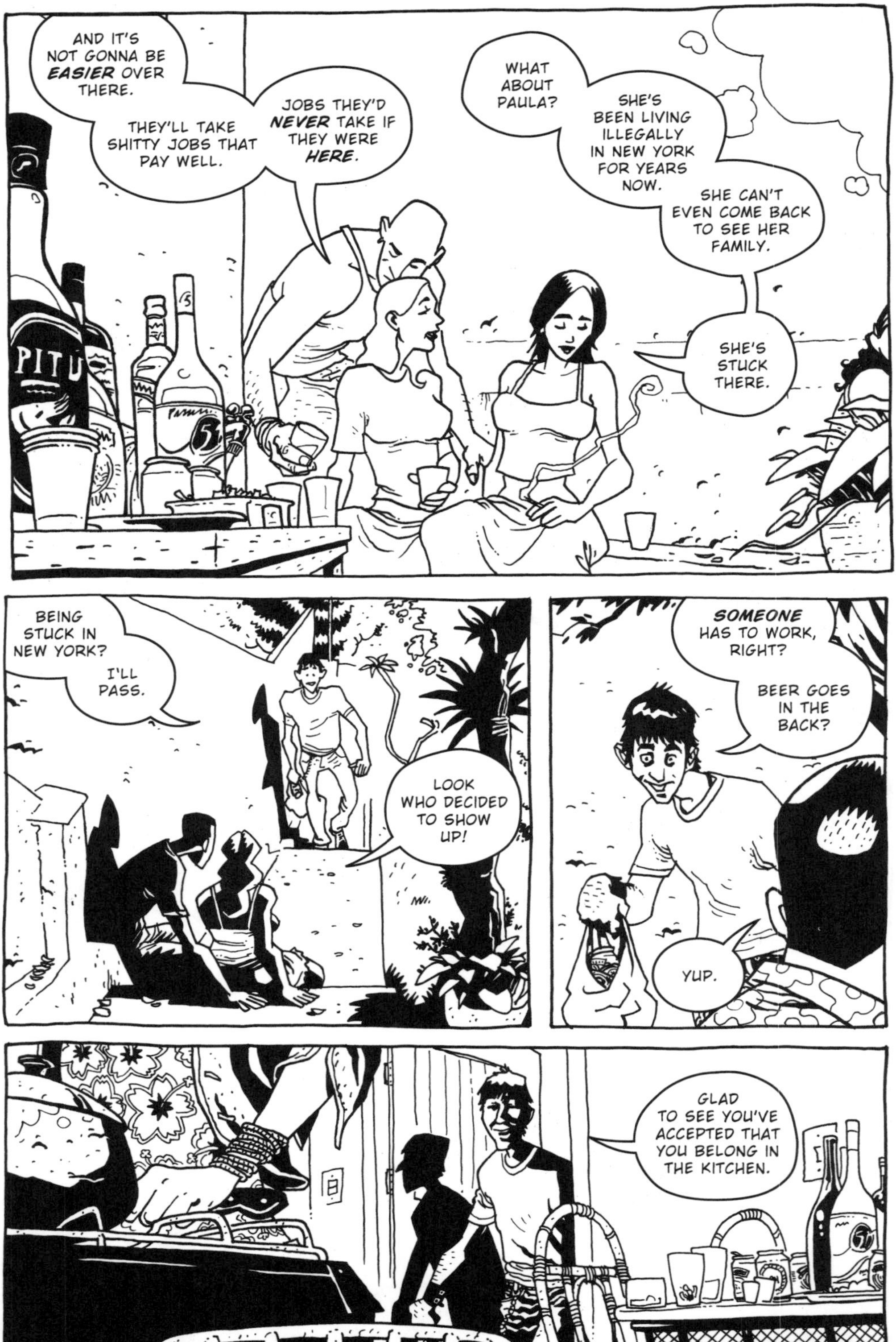
AND IT'S NOT GONNA BE EASIER OVER THERE.
THEY'LL TAKE SHITTY JOBS THAT PAY WELL.
JOBS THEY'D NEVER TAKE IF THEY WERE HERE.
WHAT ABOUT PAULA?
SHE'S BEEN LIVING ILLEGALLY IN NEW YORK FOR YEARS NOW.
SHE CAN'T EVEN COME BACK TO SEE HER FAMILY.
SHE'S STUCK THERE.
PITU
BEING STUCK IN NEW YORK?
I'LL PASS.
LOOK WHO DECIDED TO SHOW UP!
SOMEONE HAS TO WORK, RIGHT?
BEER GOES IN THE BACK?
YUP.
GLAD TO SEE YOU'VE ACCEPTED THAT YOU BELONG IN THE KITCHEN.

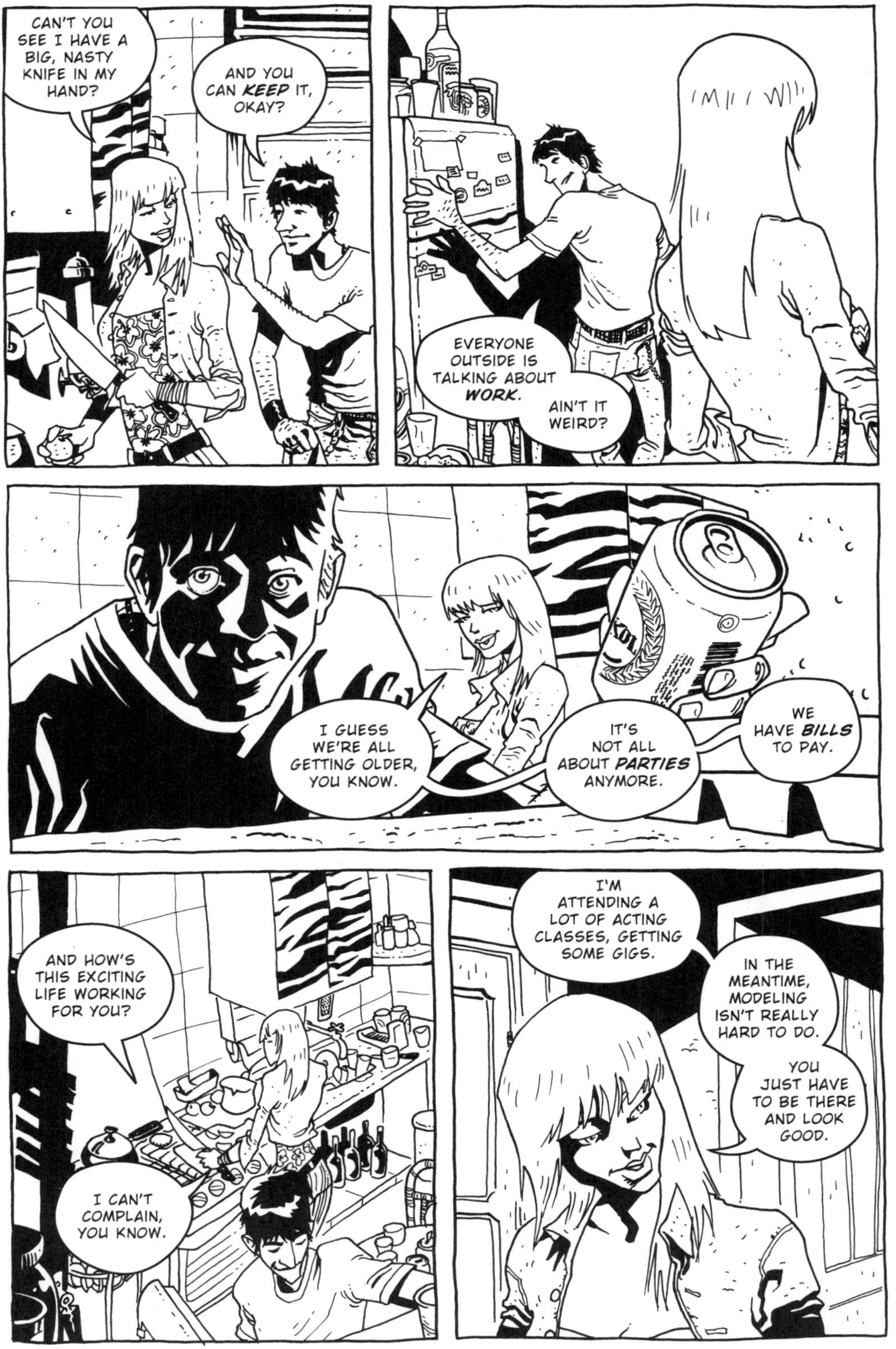
CAN'T YOU SEE I HAVE A BIG, NASTY KNIFE IN MY HAND?
AND YOU CAN **KEEP** IT, OKAY?
EVERYONE OUTSIDE IS TALKING ABOUT **WORK**.
AIN'T IT WEIRD?
I GUESS WE'RE ALL GETTING OLDER, YOU KNOW.
IT'S NOT ALL ABOUT **PARTIES** ANYMORE.
WE HAVE **BILLS** TO PAY.
AND HOW'S THIS EXCITING LIFE WORKING FOR YOU?
I CAN'T COMPLAIN, YOU KNOW.
I'M ATTENDING A LOT OF ACTING CLASSES, GETTING SOME GIGS.
IN THE MEANTIME, MODELING ISN'T REALLY HARD TO DO.
YOU JUST HAVE TO BE THERE AND LOOK GOOD.

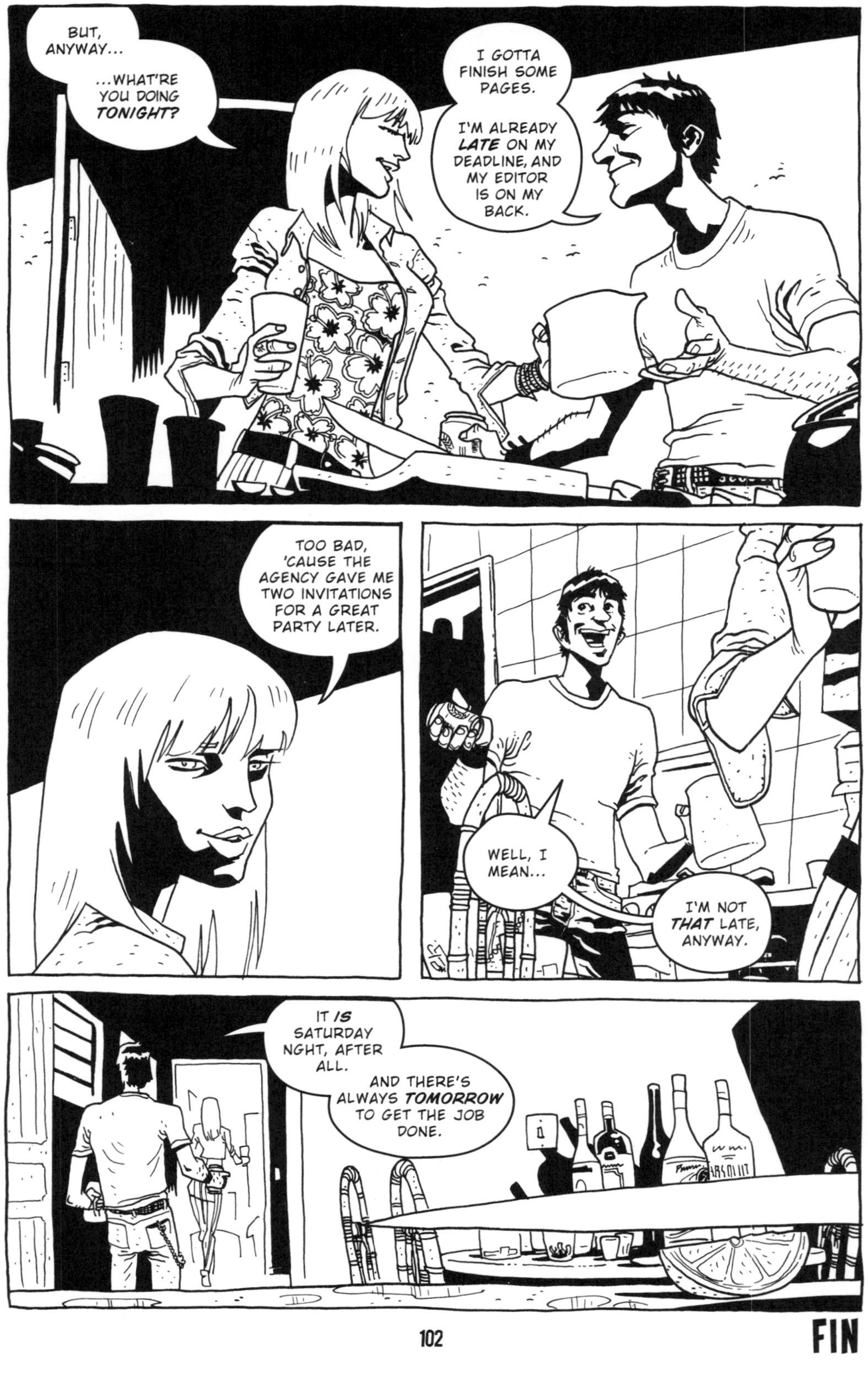
BUT, ANYWAY...
...WHAT'RE YOU DOING *TONIGHT?*
I GOTTA FINISH SOME PAGES.
I'M ALREADY *LATE* ON MY DEADLINE, AND MY EDITOR IS ON MY BACK.
TOO BAD, 'CAUSE THE AGENCY GAVE ME TWO INVITATIONS FOR A GREAT PARTY LATER.
WELL, I MEAN...
I'M NOT *THAT* LATE, ANYWAY.
IT *IS* SATURDAY NGHT, AFTER ALL.
AND THERE'S ALWAYS *TOMORROW* TO GET THE JOB DONE.

FIN

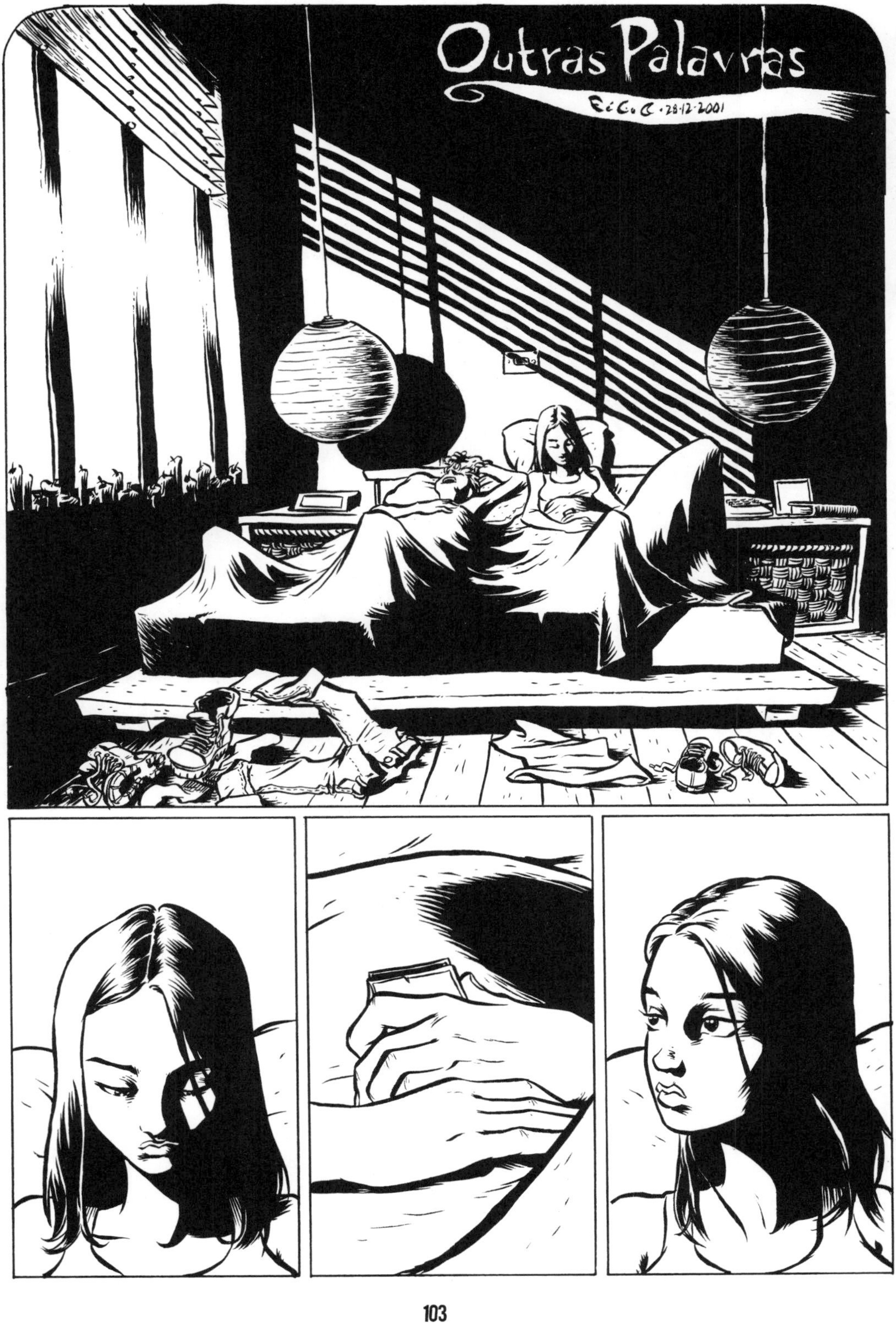
Outras Palavras
28-12-2001

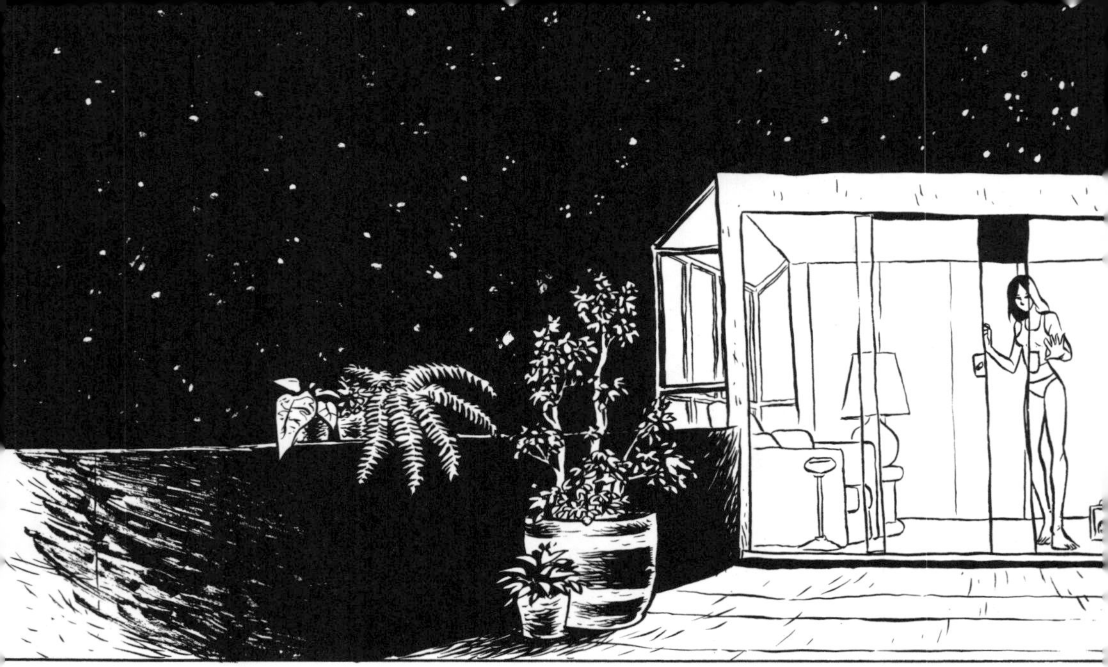

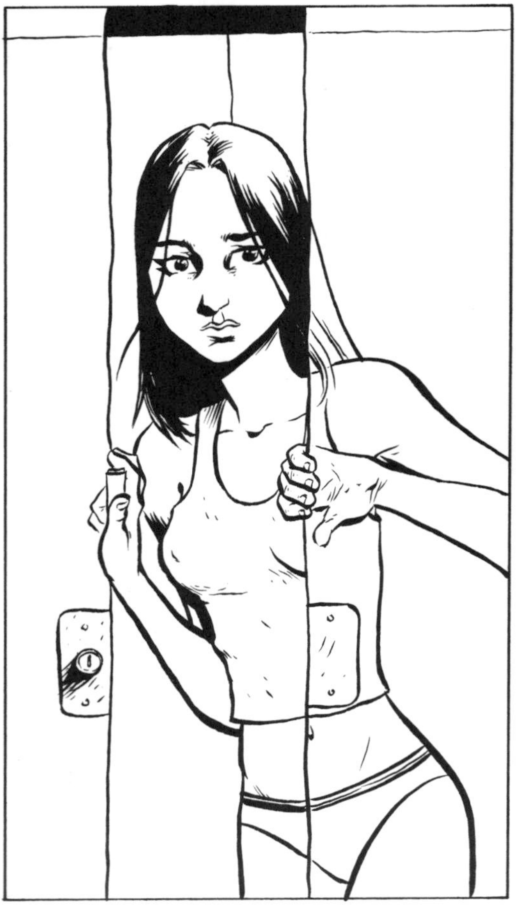

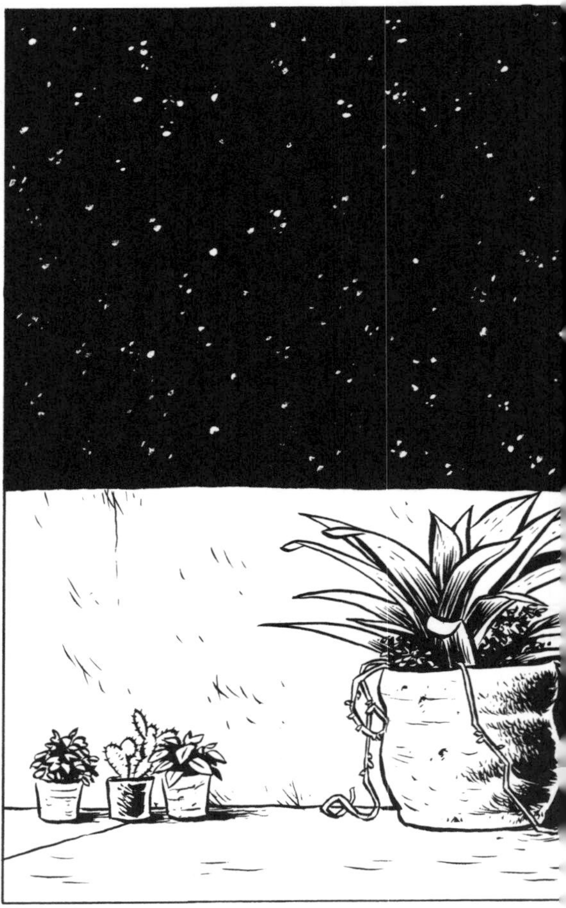

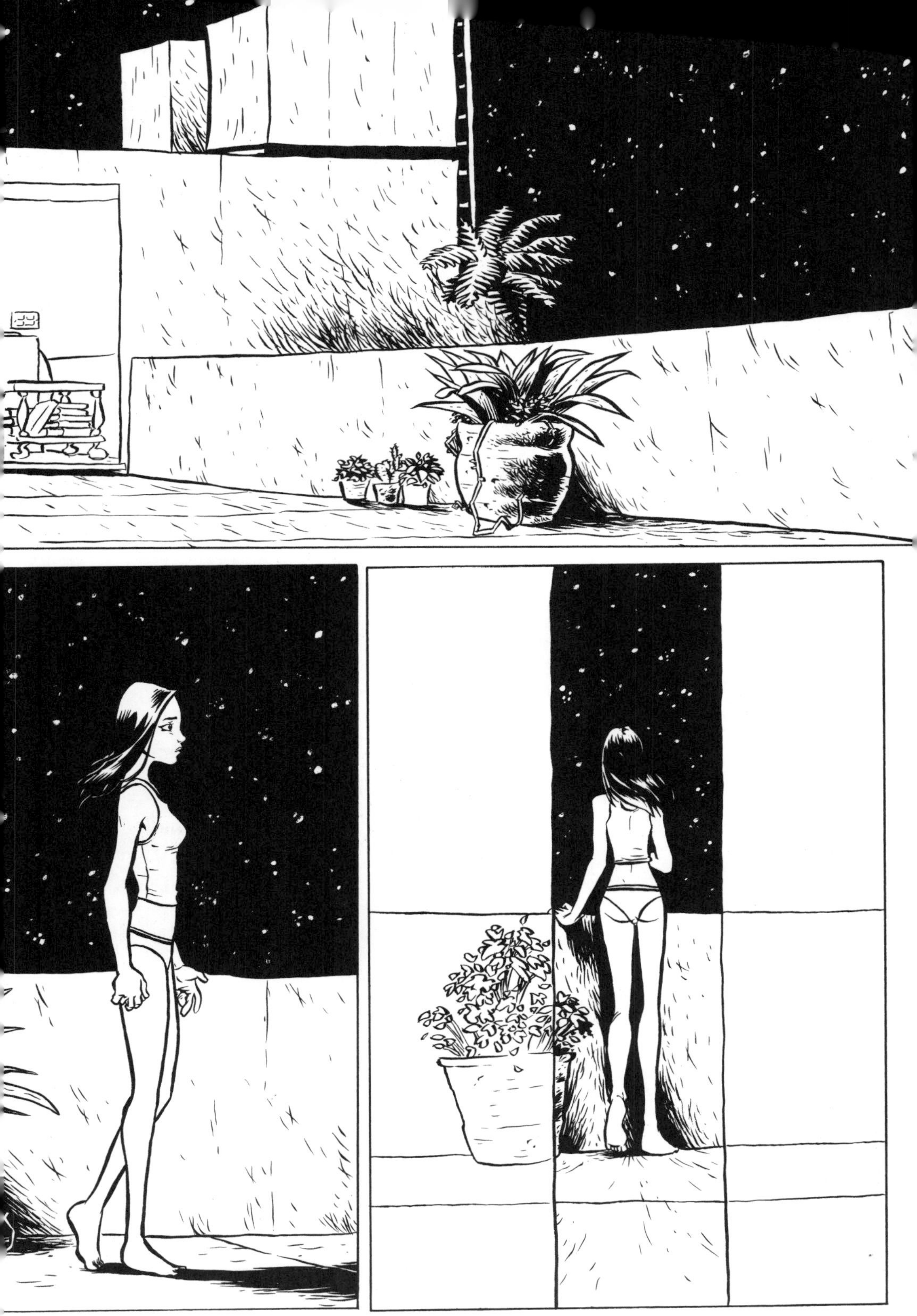

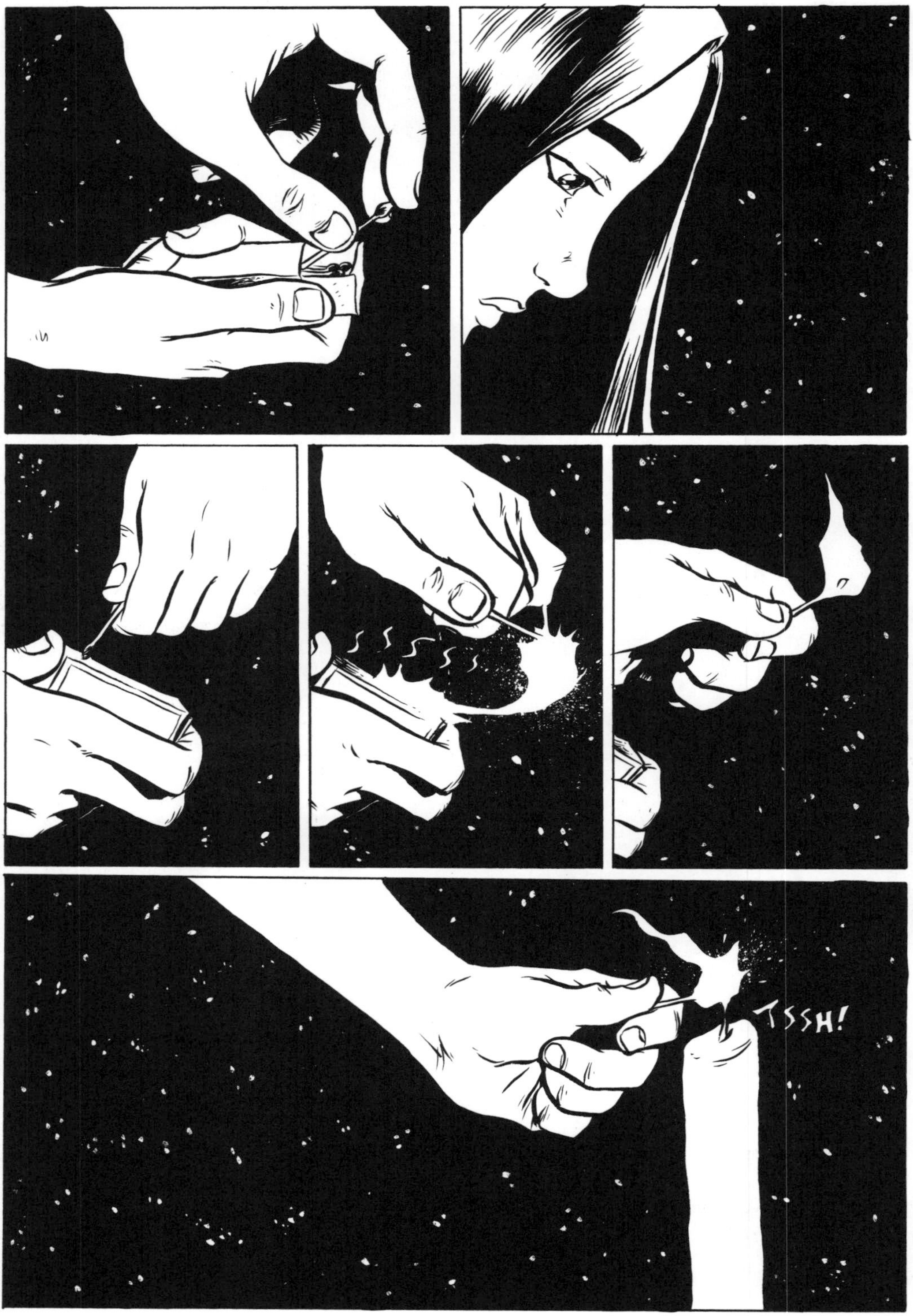
TSSH!

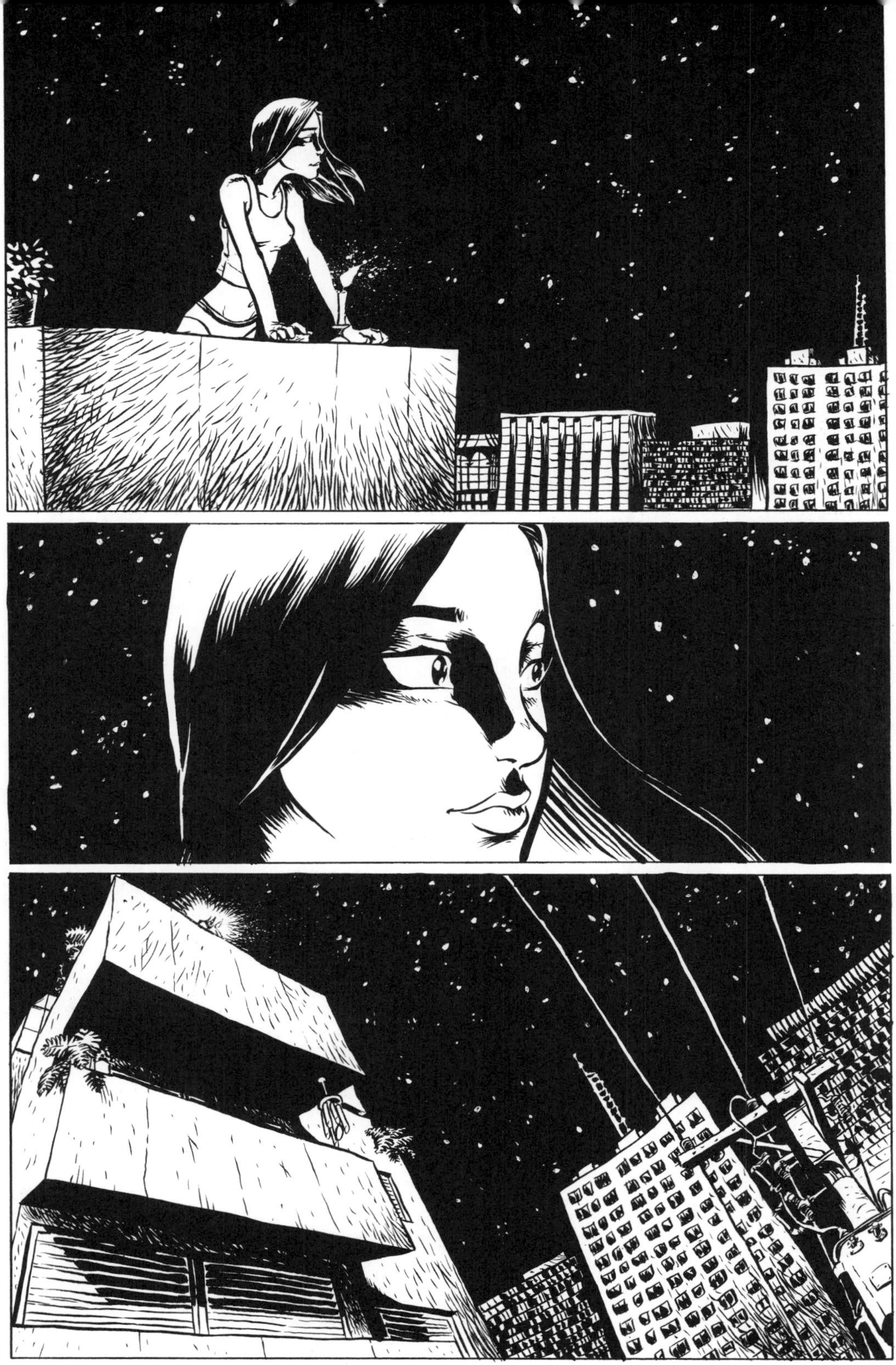

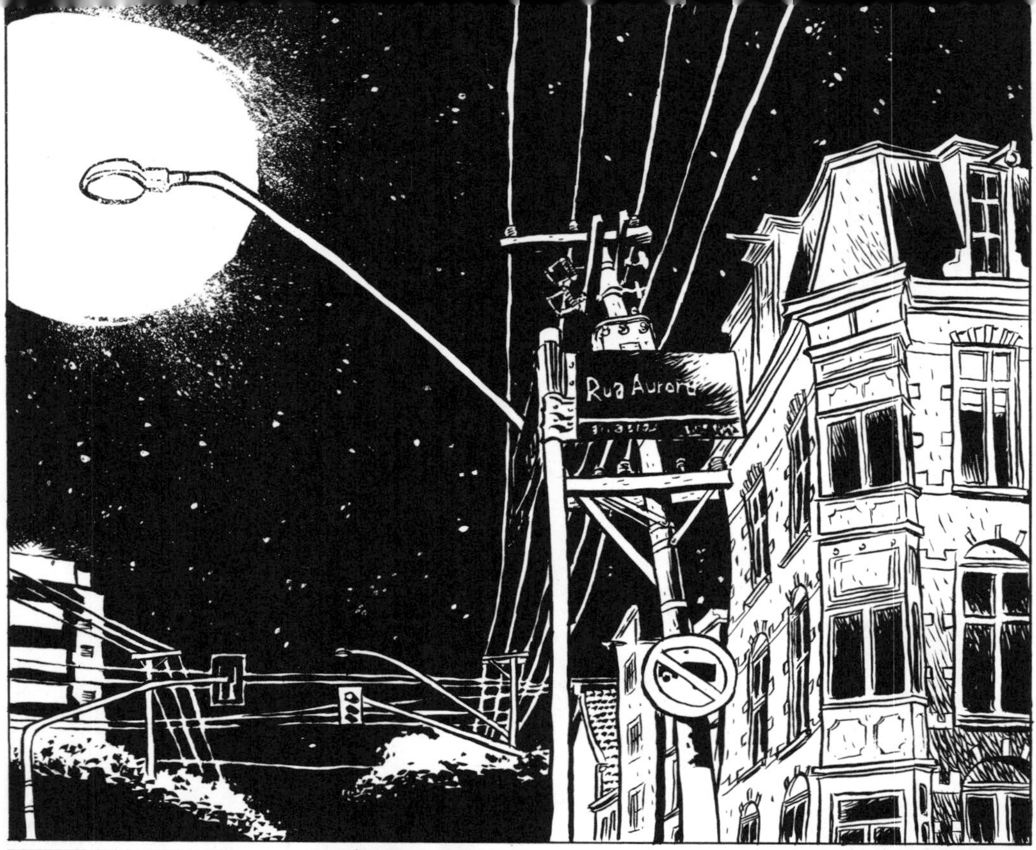
Rua Aurora

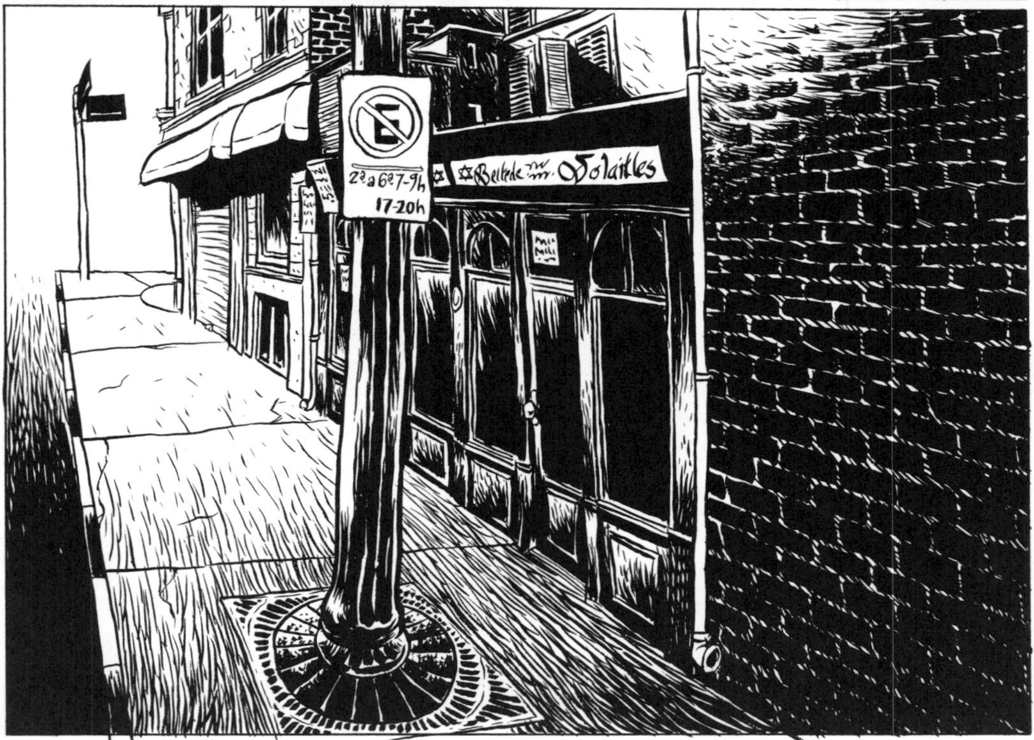
2ª a 6ª 7-9h
17-20h

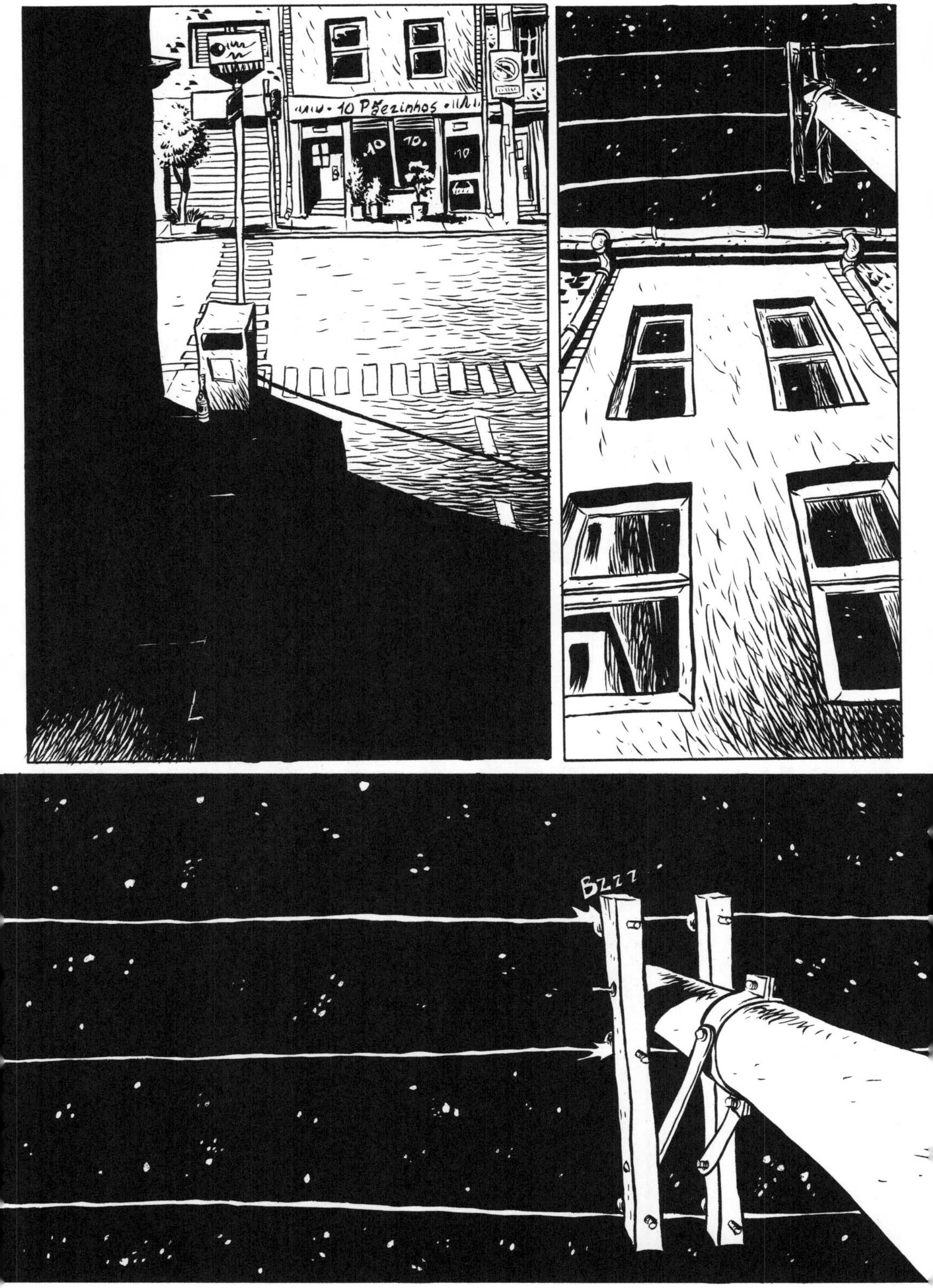
10 Pãezinhos
Bzzz

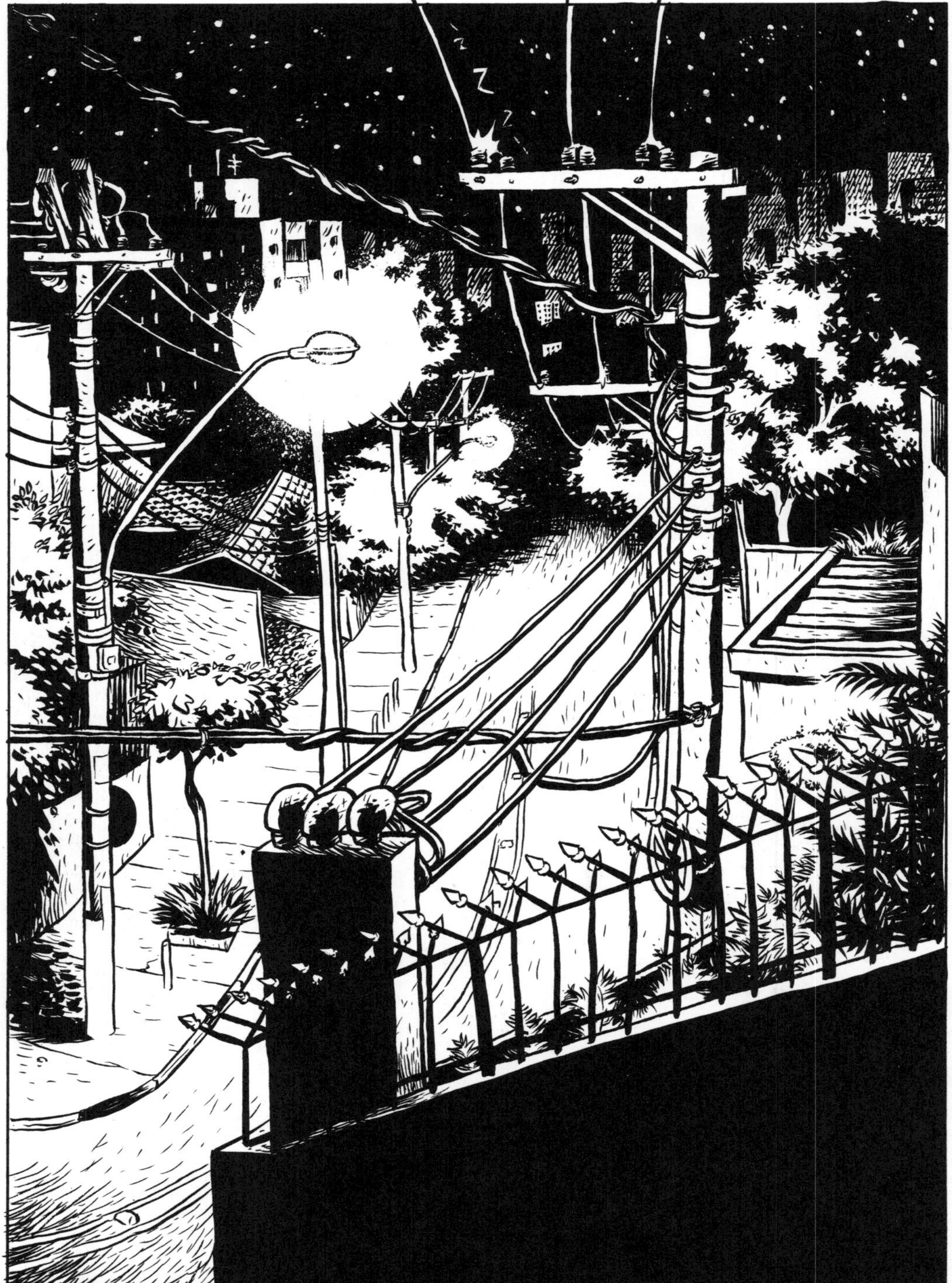

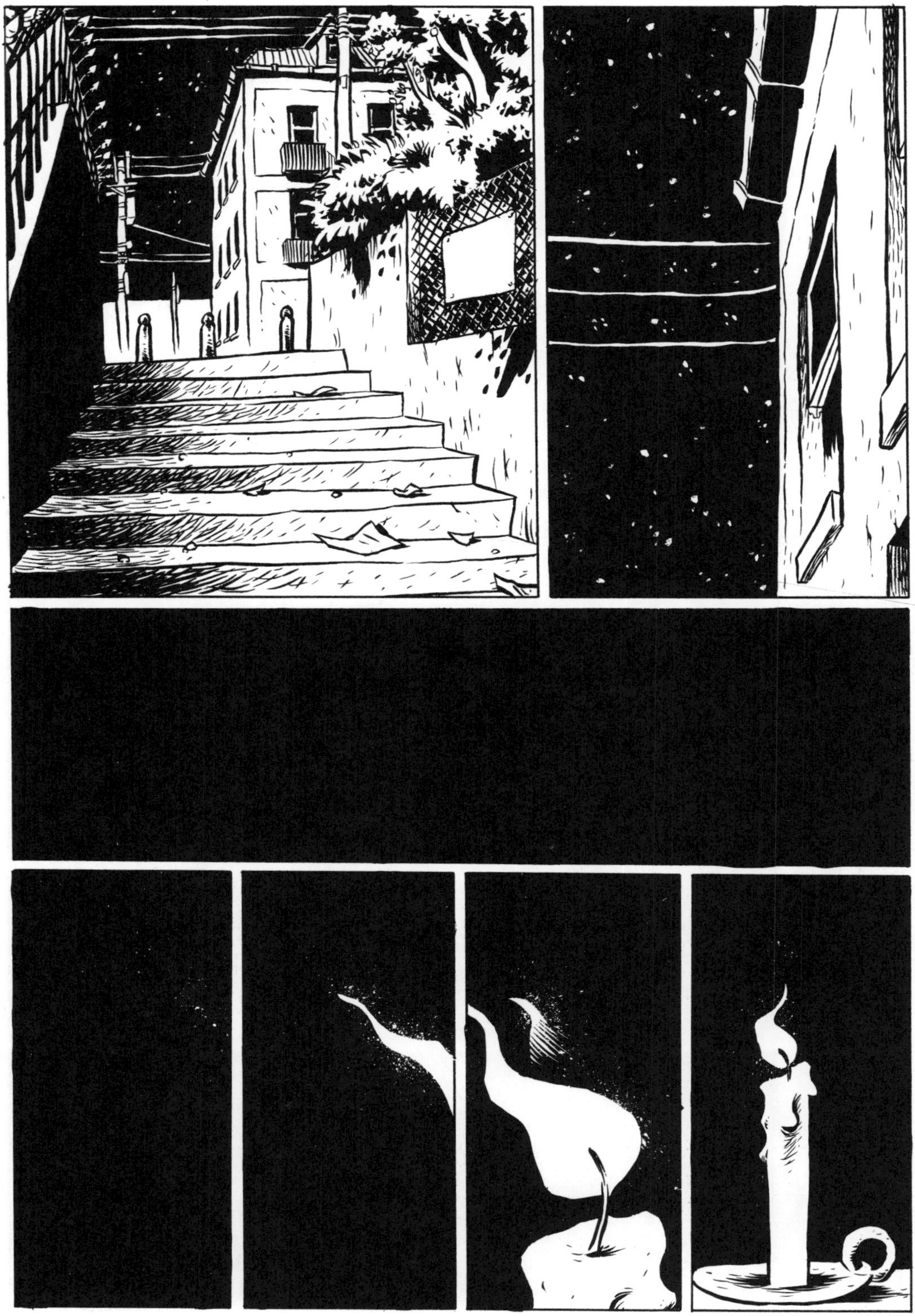

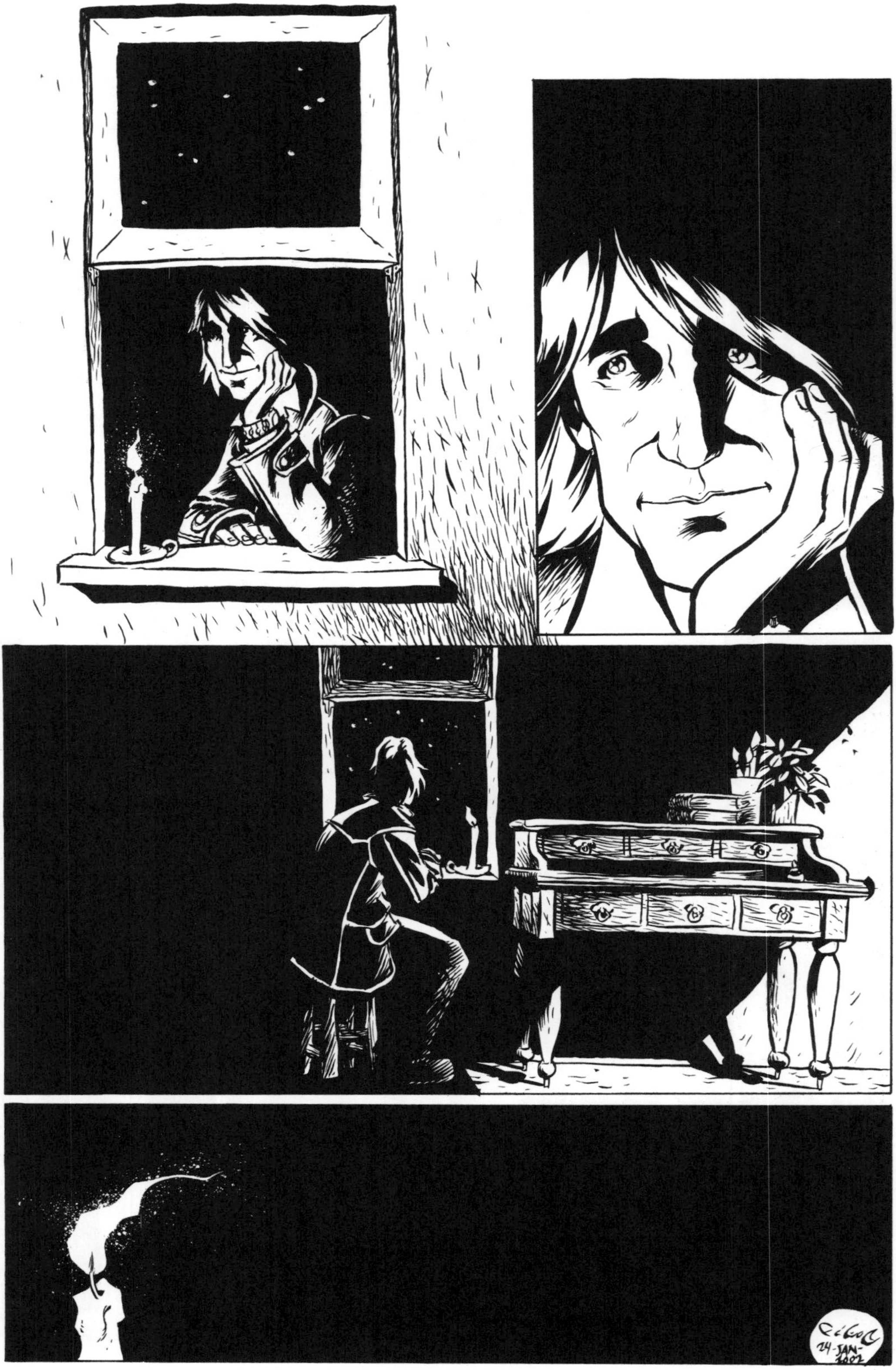